UNITED NATIONS CONFERENCE ON TRADE AND DEVELOPMENT

INFORMATION ECONOMY REPORT 2009

Trends and Outlook in Turbulent Times

UNITED NATIONS

New York and Geneva, 2009

NOTE

Within the UNCTAD Division on Technology and Logistics, the ICT Analysis Section carries out policy-oriented analytical work on the development implications of information and communication technologies (ICTs). It is responsible for the preparation of the *Information Economy Report*. The ICT Analysis Section promotes international dialogue on issues related to ICTs for development and contributes to building developing countries' capacities to measure the information economy, as well as to design and implement relevant policies and legal frameworks.

In this report, the terms country/economy refer, as appropriate, to territories or areas. The designations employed and the presentation of the material do not imply the expression of any opinion whatsoever on the part of the Secretariat of the United Nations concerning the legal status of any country, territory, city or area or of its authorities, or concerning the delimitation of its frontiers or boundaries. In addition, the designations of country groups are intended solely for statistical or analytical convenience and do not necessarily express a judgement about the stage of development reached by a particular country or area in the development process. The major country groupings used in this report follow the classification of the United Nations Statistical Office. These are:

Developed countries: the member countries of the Organization for Economic Cooperation and Development (OECD) (other than Mexico, the Republic of Korea and Turkey), plus the new European Union member countries that are not OECD members (Bulgaria, Cyprus, Estonia, Latvia, Lithuania, Malta, Romania and Slovenia), plus Andorra, Israel, Liechtenstein, Monaco and San Marino. Transition economies: South-East Europe and the Commonwealth of Independent States. Developing economies: in general all economies not specified above. For statistical purposes, the data for China do not include those for Hong Kong Special Administrative Region (Hong Kong (China)), Macao Special Administrative Region (Macao (China)) and Taiwan Province of China.

Reference to companies and their activities should not be construed as an endorsement by UNCTAD of those companies or their activities.

The following symbols have been used in the tables:

Two dots (..) indicate that data are not available or are not separately reported. Rows in tables have been omitted in those cases where no data are available for any of the elements in the row;

A dash (–) indicates that the item is equal to zero or its value is negligible;

A blank in a table indicates that the item is not applicable, unless otherwise indicated;

A slash (/) between dates representing years, e.g. 1994/95 indicates a financial year;

Use of an en dash (–) between dates representing years, e.g. 1994–1995 signifies the full period involved, including the beginning and end years;

Reference to "dollars" ($) means United States dollars, unless otherwise indicated;

Annual rates of growth or change, unless otherwise stated, refer to annual compound rates;

Details and percentages in tables do not necessarily add to totals because of rounding.

The material contained in this study may be freely quoted with appropriate acknowledgement.

UNITED NATIONS PUBLICATION

UNCTAD/IER/2009

Sales No. E.09.II.D.18

ISSN 2075-4396

ISBN 978-92-1-112778-2

PREFACE

The speed at which information and communication technologies (ICTs) have diffused around the world has vastly exceeded the expectations voiced at the World Summit on the Information Society gatherings in 2003 and 2005. More than half the world's people now have access to such technologies, and especially to mobile telephones. Moreover, mobile applications have become more than just tools for talking. Some least developed countries are pioneering new forms of mobile usage, for example to access information and to facilitate banking transactions and trade.

As documented in the *Information Economy Report 2009: Trends and Outlook in Turbulent Times,* however, there is still a long way to go before we can claim to have significantly narrowed the "digital divide" to achieve an information society for all. Wide gaps in ICT infrastructure remain, not least in the case of broadband networks. As also demonstrated by the United Nations E-government Survey, human capacities to manage the information economy are also uneven across countries.

This report focuses on the implications of the global economic crisis on ICT. The picture that emerges is one of great contrasts. Some parts of the industry have been seriously affected, with dramatic declines in trade and employment. At the same time, investments in telecommunications and trade in ICT-enabled services appear to be among the most resilient areas of the global economy; only one major telecommunications firm has gone bankrupt in this downturn. I encourage Governments and companies to do more in exploring how ICTs can support the path to recovery, promote effective governance and advance sustainable development.

This *Information Economy Report 2009* looks at the progress that has been made and discusses different options for countries hoping to seize the opportunities created by new technologies. Its information and analysis should prove valuable to policymakers and all others engaged in navigating our societies and economies in this turbulent global economic environment.

BAN Ki-moon
Secretary-General
United Nations

ACKNOWLEDGEMENTS

The *Information Economy Report 2009* was prepared by a team comprising Torbjörn Fredriksson (team leader), Cécile Barayre, Scarlett Fondeur Gil, Rémi Lang, Irina Stanyukova and Marie Triboulet (intern) under the overall guidance of Mongi Hamdi.

Considerable statistical support for chapter III was provided by Henri Laurencin, Sonia Blachier, Sanja Blazevic, David Cristallo and Ildephonse Mbabazizimana. Monica Morrica and Therese Sjögren extended administrative and secretarial assistance.

The *Information Economy Report 2009* benefited from significant inputs provided by Michael Minges, Raja Mitra and Fahad Rahman. Additional inputs were contributed by Nagwa El-Shenawi, Guoyong Liang, Youlia Lozanova, Taylor Reynolds, Marcia Tavares and Marcel Vaillant.

Useful comments on various parts of the text were given by Jimit Arora, Mariana Balboni, Frédéric Bourassa, Mario Cimoli, Charles Geiger, Angel Gonzalez Sanz, Alan Greenberg, Aminisha Gupta, Pierre Montagnier, Marta Pérez Cusó and Graeme Walker.

The cover and other graphics were done by Sophie Combette and Laurence Duchemin. Desktop publishing was done by Rafe Dent and the report was edited by Eleanor Loukass.

Financial support from the Government of Finland is gratefully acknowledged.

CONTENTS

Boxes		

Box figures

Box tables

Figures

Tables

LIST OF ABBREVIATIONS

3G	third generation
ACE	Africa Coast to Europe
ADSL	asymmetric digital subscriber line
ALADI	Asociación Latinoamericana de Integración
BPO	business process outsourcing
CDMA	code division multiple access
CIO	chief information officer
CIS	Commonwealth of Independent States
CPC	Central Product Classification
DESA	United Nations Department of Economic and Social Affairs
DFZ	duty free zone
DSL	digital subscriber line
EASSy	Eastern Africa Submarine Cable System
ECA	United Nations Economic Commission for Africa
ECLAC	United Nations Economic Commission for Latin America and the Caribbean
EIT	economies in transition
ESCAP	United Nations Economic and Social Commission on Asia and the Pacific
EU	European Union
EU27	The 27 member States of the European Union as at May 2009
EVDO	evolution, data optimized
EVDV	evolution data voice
FDI	foreign direct investment
GDP	gross domestic product
GSM	global system for mobile communication
HIPC	highly indebted poor countries
HS	Harmonized system
HSDPA	high speed downlink packet access
HSPA	High speed packet access
HSUPA	high speed uplink packet access
ICTPR	ICT Policy Review
ICTs	information and communication technologies
IMF	International Monetary Fund
IP	Internet protocol
IPTV	Internet protocol television
ISIC	International Standard Industrial Classification
ISP	Internet service provider
IT	information technology
ITC	International Trade Centre
ITU	International Telecommunication Union
KPO	knowledge process offshoring
LAN	local area network
LDC	least developed country
LLDC	landlocked developing country
LMDS	local multipoint distribution service
LTE	long term evolution
Mbps	megabit per second
MCIT	Ministry of Communications and Information Technology

MDG	Millennium Development Goal
MMDS	multichannel multipoint distribution service
MMS	multimedia messaging service
MTIC	missing trader intra-community
NGN	next generation network
NSO	national statistical office
OECD	Organization for Economic Cooperation and Development
PC	personal computer
PPP	purchasing power parity
PRSP	Poverty Reduction Strategy Paper
SIDS	small island developing states
SIM	subscriber identity module
SME	small and medium sized enterprise
SMS	short message service
TD-SCDMA	time division synchronous code division multiple access
TEAMS	East African Marine System
TNC	transnational corporation
UASF	universal access and service fund
USB	universal serial bus
UIS	UNESCO Institute for Statistics
UMTS	Universal Mobile Telecommunications System
UNCITRAL	United Nations Commission on International Trade Law
UNCTAD	United Nations Conference on Trade and Development
UNDP	United Nations Development Programme
UNESCO	United Nations Educational, Scientific and Cultural Organization
UN-ESCWA	United Nations Economic and Social Commission on Western Asia
VAT	value added tax
VoB	voice over Broadband
VoIP	voice over Internet Protocol
WACS	West Africa Cable System
WCDMA	wideband CDMA
WiMAX	worldwide interoperability for microwave access
WLL	wireless local loop
WPIIS	Working Party on Indicators for the Information Society
WSIS	World Summit on the Information Society
WTO	World Trade Organization

EXECUTIVE SUMMARY

Over the past few decades, information and communication technologies (ICTs) have proven to be a tremendous accelerator of economic and social progress. They have opened up a previously unimaginable array of possibilities in both developed and developing countries. The speed at which ICTs are diffusing has taken many observers by surprise. This is in no small part thanks to the mobile revolution. With more than 4 billion mobile subscriptions worldwide, one of the targets set by world leaders at the World Summit on the Information Society – that more than half of the world's population should have ready access to ICTs – may have been reached seven years ahead of schedule. But as emphasized in the *Information Economy Report 2009*, there is no room for complacency. Despite positive developments towards narrowing the digital divide, there is a long unfinished agenda to address in order to create a truly inclusive information society for all.

In the context of analyzing ICTs for development, this report takes stock of recent trends with regard to extending connectivity worldwide (chapter I). Special attention is given to the challenge of providing broadband access to the Internet. Chapter II monitors developments in enhancing the use of ICTs among enterprises and chapter III looks at how international trade in ICT goods and in IT (information technology) and ICT-enabled services is evolving. As the report was prepared in the midst of the most turbulent economic times since the Great Depression, potential implications of the economic crisis are discussed in all chapters. While uncertainties concerning the nature and outcome of the crisis complicate the analysis, tentative conclusions are drawn based on preliminary data and anecdotal evidence.

Chapter I. Monitoring Connectivity for Development

Monitoring the extent to which various parts of the world are becoming connected to such ICTs as fixed and mobile telephony, Internet and broadband is important as enhanced access is required to reduce the "digital divide". The dynamism of these different ICTs varies a great deal. While fixed telephone subscriptions are now in slight decline, mobile and (to a lesser extent) Internet usage continues to expand rapidly in most countries and regions. At the same time, there is a widening gap between high-income and low-income countries in the area of broadband connectivity.

The number of fixed telecommunications subscriptions in the world has been flat at around 1.2 billion since 2006, and even declining somewhat in the most recent years. In 2008, there were on average 18 subscriptions per 100 inhabitants in the world. In developed countries, teledensity was 47 while in developing countries it was 12. Slow or negative growth in fixed line subscriptions reflects significant developments in both voice over Internet Protocol (VoIP) and mobile telephony. In developed countries, existing fixed telecommunications infrastructure is increasingly leveraged for the introduction of "triple play" services (telephone, Internet and television) over an Internet Protocol-based platform. By contrast, the low diffusion of fixed telecommunications infrastructure in many developing countries will seriously delay the transition to these next generation networks (NGNs). Related concerns may lead some developing countries to expand their investments into fixed networks.

At the end of 2008, the number of mobile subscriptions reached 4 billion. Although growth was somewhat lower than in the previous year, it still remained close to 20 per cent in 2008. On average, there are now 60 subscriptions per 100 people, and in many developed, developing and transition economies penetration exceeds 100. Reflecting explosive growth, the penetration level in developing countries is now eight times higher than what it was in 2000. Almost every second person in developing countries is thought to have a mobile phone and fewer than a dozen developing nations have a mobile penetration of less than ten. Between 2003 and 2008, the most dynamic economies in terms of increased mobile penetration were outside the developed world. A common feature among these economies is increased liberalization and in some cases catching up with neighbouring nations of similar economic circumstances. Montenegro saw the highest increase in penetration, followed by Qatar, Bahrain and Maldives, a least developed country (LDC).

There were an estimated 1.4 billion Internet users around the world at the end of 2008. Reflecting that the number of users grew five times faster in developing than in developed countries, the former now account for more than half of the world total. China hosted the largest number of users (298 million), followed by the United States (191 million) and Japan (88 million). A little over one fifth of the world's population used the Internet in 2008. However, wide gaps remain. While more than half the population in the developed world is now online, the corresponding share is on average only 15–17 per cent in developing and transition economies. During the period 2003–2008, Andorra achieved the largest gains in Internet penetration, followed by Argentina, Latvia and Colombia.

There were an estimated 400 million fixed broadband subscribers around the world at the end of 2008. Developing countries accounted for almost 40 per cent of these subscriptions, making broadband one of the few ICTs where developed countries still represent the majority of users. The digital divide is particularly pronounced in the case of broadband. Average penetration was more than eight times higher in developed than in developing countries. There is furthermore a huge gap in terms of broadband speed. While high-income economies keep pushing the limits, low-income countries' broadband connections generally remain relatively slow. To make things worse, there is also a "broadband price divide": the cost of using fixed broadband tends to be the highest in low-income countries. However, the fastest growing broadband markets are found in large emerging economies. China has already emerged as the world's single largest broadband market, followed by the United States. Brazil has also moved into the top 10 broadband markets.

During the period 2003–2008, the Nordic countries were the world's most dynamic economies in terms of expanding the fixed broadband penetration. Meanwhile, no developing or transition economy reached the top 20 list – a vivid illustration of the widening gap that exists in broadband.

Countries are increasingly considering wireless technologies to overcome the broadband access gap. In 2008, there were an estimated 361 million 3G (third generation) mobile subscribers, the majority of which resides in developed countries. The digital divide in this area is even wider than in fixed broadband. While the average penetration in developed economies was about 29.8, it was only 1.1 in developing countries. The roll-out of mobile broadband in developing econ-

omies is set to accelerate in the near future. For example, China awarded 3G licenses in early 2009 and India was expected to follow suit.

Policies and regulations to facilitate broadband roll-out range from taxation and fiscal incentives to market liberalization, and may also include universal access and market stimulation. In adapting the policy and regulatory environment, operators should be encouraged to share state-of-the-art backbone infrastructure to avoid duplicative and fragmented low bandwidth networks. At the same time, a critical ingredient for ensuring sufficient broadband supply at reasonable prices is to expose operators to competition. Responding to the particular challenge of achieving more widespread deployment of broadband backbones and access networks in remote and less densely populated areas, governments can make use of universal access service funds (UASFs). Another way to enhance broadband access is through the promotion of public Internet access points or telecentres. In the case of international broadband connections, countries have to connect with undersea cable projects and, for landlocked countries, build out fibre links to connect with submarine cable landing stations in other countries.

Comparing the spread of the different ICTs with the distribution of income in the world shows that mobile access has become the most equitably distributed ICT. This is not surprising in view of the rapid diffusion of mobile subscriptions and given that the price of mobile use is generally lower than that of the Internet. Mobiles are also often available under easier conditions than fixed lines. Furthermore, mobile telephony does not require the basic literacy skills that are necessary for Internet access. While the distribution of fixed lines has not become much more equitable since 2005, reflecting stagnant growth, Internet access has.

There are concerns that the current financial and economic crisis the worst in 60 years – will impact negatively on the positive trends in ICT diffusion and the investment needed in order to ensure universal access to ICTs. As of June 2009, there was still great uncertainty about the degree to which it would affect different countries and economic sectors. The crisis is expected to influence developed and developing countries and various regions within developing countries differently.

Compared with most other industries, the mobile telephony sector in developing countries should have a good chance of weathering the storm. At the time this report was prepared, mobile growth continued in many developing countries. For example, well into 2009, subscriber growth remained strong in the two largest developing country mobile markets, China and India. Moreover, mobiles are increasingly replacing fixed lines for voice communications in developing nations. They are also used for new purposes – such as by small entrepreneurs – making them even more desirable. The demand for mobile telephony in many developing countries is thus likely to support further expansion, despite the crisis. Manufacturers and strategic investors are expected to continue investing in markets with strong potential. Where profit opportunities exist, the necessary finance can normally be found.

Beyond infrastructure, the production of various ICT goods and services has been seriously affected by the economic crisis. Various analysts have revised their growth expectations downwards as more information about the depth of the economic recession has become available. The volatile semiconductor industry has been among the worst hit. Revenue growth also turned sharply downwards into negative territory in the case of the largest makers of IT equipment such as computers and consumer electronic devices. The same applied to top manufacturers of communication equipment. By contrast, producers of IT and ICT-enabled services appear to have been more resilient to the crisis (see also chapter III).

Amidst these turbulent times, a priority in the ICT area for many developing countries will be to build on the gains already made. Governments can help by enhancing competition, reducing taxes and other fees on operators and speeding up the allocation of wireless spectrum. Another approach is to encourage infrastructure sharing, for example through the issuing of licenses for providers of turnkey mobile masts that can be shared by multiple operators. Moreover, governments could place increased emphasis on universal service obligations to secure continued roll-out in rural areas of different types of ICT infrastructure.

Chapter II. Making Use of ICTs in the Business Sector

The extent to which improvements in ICT infrastructure and access translate into economic growth and development is greatly affected by the way such technologies are used in the productive sector. Indeed, only when ICTs are effectively applied can there be a significant positive effect on corporate turnover and productivity. Countries are increasingly interested in measuring how ICTs are used as well as the related impacts. The need for such information has been accentuated by the economic crisis, as it can help policymakers understand how ICTs may contribute to economic recovery. In many countries, however, impact assessments are constrained by a lack of reliable and useful data.

For governments to be able to design and implement appropriate policies, access to reliable and internationally comparable information is essential. Developing ICT use indicators is a particular challenge for developing countries, many of which are at a nascent stage in terms of measuring ICT. There is generally more data from those developed and developing economies (particularly in Asia) that are relatively advanced in terms of ICT adoption by businesses. Unequal availability of ICT data can therefore be seen as yet another illustration of the digital divide. Patchy data from developing countries limit the scope for international comparisons. There has been slow but steady progress in data availability and quality, however, with more countries reporting data on ICT use by businesses. In addition, countries are increasing the number of ICT indicators collected through national surveys. Nonetheless, more efforts are needed to improve the data situation.

Through the Partnership on Measuring ICT for Development, the international community has defined internationally comparable ICT indicators. UNCTAD recommends that countries adhere as much as possible to the definitions and methodological recommendations of the core ICT indicators established by the partnership, and that the core indicators are reflected in the design of statistical surveys. Countries should also try to make ICT surveys, or ICT modules in existing business surveys, part of their mainstream statistical programmes. There is a clear relationship between data availability and requirements in the national statistical systems to conduct surveys.

Most empirical studies on the impact of ICTs have found a positive correlation between the use of ICTs and corporate performance measured by labour productivity. This also applies to ICT use by small and medium sized enterprises (SMEs) in developing countries. However, varying circumstances in developed and developing countries must be taken into account when assessing the impact of such use. The extent to which companies can benefit from enhanced access to ICT depends on their size, their industrial sector, the skills of the workforce, the availability of relevant content and whether or not their suppliers and customers are frequent users of ICTs.

Different types of ICT applications influence the performance of companies in different ways, but the use of computers, the Internet and broadband all point to beneficial effects. Mobile phones have emerged as the most widespread ICT in the developing world. In many developing countries, particularly in Africa, Asia and the Pacific, they are used extensively for voice communication and SMS (short message service), and increasingly also for other data applications such as m-commerce and m-banking. They enable users to access information, especially that relating to news, education, health, jobs and family. In a number of African countries, notably Kenya, South Africa, the United Republic of Tanzania and Zambia, mobile telephones enable individuals to gain access to banking. They provide the possibility to make person-to-person payments, transfers and pre-paid purchases without a bank account.

In the near future, Internet-enabled phones may help deliver locally relevant information and services to entrepreneurs in developing countries, the way SMS and voice technology are already doing. Microenterprises and SMEs, many of which are in the informal sector in developing countries, appear to be the most affected by the adoption of mobile telephony. In the agriculture and fisheries sectors in Asia and Africa, for example, mobile phones are used to conduct sales and purchases and to negotiate prices.

Data collected through the UNCTAD global survey of national statistical offices (NSOs) on ICT usage by businesses allow for a unique opportunity to compare the extent and nature of ICT use by businesses. While there are insufficient data from developing and transition economies to make regional comparisons with developed economies, in general companies in the latter tend to display higher levels of ICT use. The digital gap between companies in developing and developed countries is particularly pronounced in the case of Internet use, web presence and broadband access.

There are also wide variations within countries. First, in both developed and developing countries, large enterprises use ICTs (such as computers and the Internet as well as broadband) more than SMEs. This may partly be a result of their greater financial and human resources and partly of their greater need for such technologies.

There is also a rural/urban divide, which is more accentuated the more sophisticated the technology is. While the use of computers is relatively similar across middle-income economies, the gap is much wider in the areas of both Internet and broadband use. Data limitations make it difficult to draw any firm conclusions with regard to the use of ICTs in urban and rural areas of low-income countries, but the divide there is likely to be even more pronounced. This may constitute a particular challenge given that these are typically the economies with the greatest dependence on rurally based economic activities.

From the perspective of reaping maximum benefits from ICTs, it is important to consider how companies use them. Even in countries where the adoption of the Internet by enterprises is relatively high, the way it is used suggests a large unexplored potential. In many developing countries, the main purpose of Internet access is to send and receive e-mails; few companies use it as a marketing tool or to make banking transactions. To leverage the Internet more effectively, enterprises need to rethink some business and productive processes around new ICT tools and invest in ICT skills development.

In view of its potential positive contributions to growth and development, there are good reasons for governments to take active steps to promote greater use of ICTs in the business sector. Although it is up to each company to decide if and in what way ICTs could enhance its business performance, governments fill a critical function in terms of creating an environment that is conducive to the greater use of ICTs, especially in developing countries. Governments' role in stimulating ICT use is especially important in times of economic crisis.

There are various ways in which governments, with support from their development partners, can promote greater use of ICT by companies. Special attention should be given to SMEs, as they are lagging behind larger firms in terms of ICT uptake. In addition, SMEs typically represent the backbone of developing economies and employ a large majority of the workforce. Despite recent progress in infrastructure and connectivity, many bottlenecks still prevent entrepreneurs and small firms from using ICTs efficiently. Even if companies have access to basic ICT infrastructure, its use is often limited by low levels of ICT literacy, slow speed of connection, a lack of local content and high costs of use. Moreover, in rural areas of many developing countries, even basic connectivity remains a challenge.

Countries in which the business sector has been keen to adopt ICTs have typically shown a strong policy commitment towards such technologies, emphasized the development of a competitive ICT infrastructure at least in urban areas, taken steps to build a workforce with the necessary skills and technological capabilities and sought to create an enabling regulatory environment. Important areas of government intervention to encourage greater adoption and use of ICT in the business sector include making it a core element in a national ICT strategy, improving ICT infrastructure in underserved areas, building relevant skills, promoting the development of local content and strengthening the legal and regulatory framework.

Faced with the current economic crisis, many governments have identified enhanced ICT use as a strategy to quicken recovery. Several developed countries have made ICTs an integral part of their economic stimulus packages, both by stimulating the demand for ICT goods and by continuing to enhance the supply side (from infrastructure to spectrum). Measures aimed at supporting demand and shoring up the financial sector should help boost ICT use in that area. Measures targeting the rolling out of broadband to areas with low connectivity may help alleviate some infrastructure bottlenecks. Innovation through ICTs is also being encouraged, including in education, energy (for example, "smart power grids"), government, health care and transportation. While the effects of these measures remain to be seen, economic policies are increasingly looking at the cost and efficiency benefits of ICT to support the path to recovery.

Chapter III. Evolving Patterns in ICT Trade

During the past decade, the geographical composition of trade in ICT goods and services has experienced dramatic shifts. A growing share of such exports is accounted for by developing economies, especially in Asia. Trade patterns have already been affected by the current economic crisis, but the impact differs considerably between goods and services. While ICT goods are among those that have been the most negatively affected by the recession, IT and ICT-related services appear to be among the most resilient. Many companies see the "offshoring" of services as a way to reduce costs and improve their competitiveness.

While ICT goods belonged to the most dynamic areas of world trade until 2000, they have subsequently expanded less rapidly than global trade as a whole. Between 1998 and 2007, the value of exports of ICT goods rose from $813 billion to $1.73 trillion, representing 13.2 per cent of all merchandise trade. The share has diminished in recent years – from its peak of 17.7 per cent in 2000 – and the decline was accentuated in 2007, partly due to the rise in commodity prices. Despite the relative decline, ICT goods still account for a significant part of world trade.

There has been a sizeable shift in the geographical composition of exports of ICT goods. Between 1998 and 2007, the share of developing countries surged from 38 to 57 per cent. This was almost entirely attributable to economies in developing Asia, which in 2007 accounted for more than half of all exports of such products. Other developing regions as well as economies in transition remain marginal exporters of ICT goods. A result of the geographical shifts has been an expansion of South–South trade, which increased between 1998 and 2007 from 15 to 32 per cent of world exports of ICT goods. Most of this trade involves economies in Asia.

ICT goods exports are highly concentrated. The top five exporters – China, the United States, Hong Kong (China), Japan and Singapore – accounted for over half the world's exports of such goods in 2007. The degree of concentration has increased since 2003, when the cumulative share of the top five exporters was about 46 per cent. China is today by far the largest exporter, responsible for more than one fifth of all exports of ICT goods, more than twice the share of the second largest exporter, the United States. The growth of China's exports has been dramatic: its market share shot up from 3 per cent in 1998 to 20 per cent in 2007. Hong Kong (China) and the Republic of Korea saw the second and third largest increases in market share. At the other end of the spectrum, the United States and Japan saw the greatest declines, by 7 and 5 percentage points respectively.

For a number of economies, ICT goods constitute a significant share of total exports and thus account for important contributions to employment and production. In about 20 economies, this share is higher than the world average. It is especially high in some smaller economies, such as Costa Rica, Hong Kong (China), Malaysia, Malta and Singapore.

There have also been notable shifts in the product composition of trade. Among the main categories of ICT goods, telecommunications equipment has been the most dynamic. Between 1998 and 2007, its share of world trade in ICT goods exports rose from 14 to 18 per cent. By contrast, the category of computers and related equipment lost ground, its share falling from 34 to 25 per cent. Overall, electronic components were the largest subcategory of ICT goods in 2007.

Time will tell how the economic recession will influence global trade in ICT goods. However, early indications suggest that there could be significant repercussions. Although official trade statistics for 2008 and early 2009 were not yet available when this report was prepared, preliminary data show a dramatic decline in ICT goods exports in all of the top exporters of such products.

The downturn has hit many segments. For example, in the first quarter of 2009, worldwide sales of servers were down 25 per cent compared with one year earlier. Despite an upturn in April 2009, semiconductor sales were also 25 per cent down. Even the demand for netbooks, a new class of low-end laptops, dropped by 25 per cent in the first quarter. Sales of mobile phones were down about 9 per cent in the first quarter, while storage software and TV sales were down a more modest 5–6 per cent. The main bright spots among the ICT goods have been the sales of smart phones (such as iPhones and BlackBerries), which were 13 per cent higher than in the first quarter of 2008.

At the end of May 2009, there was still considerable uncertainty with regard to the development of world trade during the rest of 2009 and in 2010, with predictions of declines ranging from 2 to 8 per cent in 2009. Various surveys suggest that it may take a while before spending on ICT picks up. Most IT departments of large companies lowered their budgets in the first quarter of 2009 and only a few signalled increases. Expectations suggest that spending on IT products could start bouncing back between the first and the third quarter of 2010. But even when the recovery begins, it is likely that ICT goods exports will remain well below their pre-crisis level for an extended period of time.

IT and ICT-enabled services are of growing importance in world trade and have been more resilient in the crisis. Increased broadband connectivity in a rising number of countries has facilitated the reorganization of the production of many services and led to the expansion of export-oriented production of services in places offering attractive locational conditions. The resulting offshoring of services has only just begun but is expected to continue to expand geographically and sectorally as well as across business functions.

The scope of activities that are affected by offshoring continues to broaden. There is no internationally agreed approach to categorize the kinds of services that can be offshored, but it is common to make a distinction between "IT services" and "ICT-enabled services". The latter group covers front office services, back office services and various knowledge process offshoring (KPO). As indicated by the category names, some activities relate to specific industries, while many others are generic and relevant for businesses in virtually all industries. Skill requirements range from relatively low to very high levels of qualification. Financial services companies have been the leaders in making use of offshoring, accounting for an estimated 40 to 45 per cent of the global offshoring market. Among the next most important industries are high technology/telecommunications, manufacturing and retail.

Comprehensive official data on the spread and magnitude of offshoring in different countries do not exist. The *Information Economy Report 2009* reviews balance-of-payments statistics, data related to foreign direct investment (FDI) projects, company information and market analyses. The international community should take steps to address deficiencies in the current data situation. The lack of reliable and credible information increases the risk that the offshoring phenomenon is either exaggerated or underestimated, leading to misinformed policy decisions. In order to encourage the development of better data, UNCTAD intends to initiate new work related to the measuring of offshoring.

According to balance-of-payments data, world trade in IT and ICT-enabled services – broadly defined – amounted to $1.6 trillion in 2007, or 48 per cent of total services trade. The United States was by far the largest exporter of such services, followed by the United Kingdom. However, the exporters that saw the greatest increases in their market shares between 2000 and 2007 were India and Ireland. Other dynamic developing and transition economy exporters included Argentina, China, Kuwait, the Russian Federation and Singapore. At the opposite end of the spectrum, the largest declines in market shares during the same period were observed for the United States, followed by Japan, France and Canada.

According to market analyses, the global market for the offshoring of IT and ICT-enabled services was estimated to be worth around $90 billion in 2008, of which IT services accounted for 60 per cent. A closer examination of these data confirms a trend towards geographical diversification, at least in the case of

ICT-enabled services. In 2004, five countries – Canada, China, India, Ireland and the Philippines – accounted for as much as 95 per cent of the total market for business process offshoring; by 2008, their combined share had shrunk to 80 per cent as new attractive locations emerged. Major new destinations include Malaysia and Singapore in Asia; Czech Republic, Hungary, Poland and Romania in Europe; and Latin American economies such as Argentina, Brazil and Mexico. FDI project data confirm the growing importance of Latin America in the area of business process offshoring. In the case of IT services, fewer new locations have been able to challenge the position of the more established countries. India remains the preferred choice for exports of such services, with a market share in 2008 of about 55 per cent.

As noted above, exporters of IT and ICT-enabled services appear to have weathered the global economic crisis much better than ICT goods exporters. One reason is that the offshoring of services is seen as an important way to reduce production costs and enhance competitiveness. In the short term, the volume of offshoring of services is influenced by two opposing forces. On the one hand, services exports may decline due to a general slowdown in economic activity. This applies especially to services offshored by the financial industry, in which some companies may disappear altogether. On the other hand, as the recession adds pressure on companies across industries to reduce production costs, some will choose to offshore more and new services to lower-cost locations. In the longer term, as the global economy recovers, both the volume and the scope of offshoring are likely to grow significantly.

Several market analysts forecast that the export revenue growth of IT and ICT-enabled services will rebound relatively quickly, perhaps as early as in the second half of 2009 or early 2010. Many buyers who delayed contracts as an immediate reaction to the global economic crisis will find it increasingly difficult to postpone decisions any further, resulting in new contracts. Moreover, greater pressure to cut costs may imply that many firms will consider expanding the scale and scope of their offshoring activities. For companies in industries with limited experience with offshoring, the crisis may act as a trigger to explore opportunities from sourcing services from abroad. In the medium to long term, the greatest potential for more offshoring is expected to be in the health care, retail, retail banking, ICT and insurance industries. Existing users of offshoring as well as new ones are also likely

to show increased interest in sourcing a wider range of business functions. This would also translate into higher levels of offshoring. When the economic cycle eventually improves, a surge in IT and ICT-enabled services exports can be expected as more companies will have been exposed to offshoring.

Long-term growth prospects for the offshoring of IT and ICT-enabled services are promising for early starters (such as India) as well as for many other emerging locations. As the global offshoring business is poised to grow, there should be room for more countries to develop a sizeable export-oriented services industry if they can meet companies' needs for complementary assets in terms of skills and time zones. For African economies that will become connected to submarine fibre optic cables in the coming years, new possibilities will emerge to serve foreign locations with voice-based services, provided the right framework conditions are created.

Latecomer offshoring destinations in Africa, Asia and Latin America and the Caribbean will have to continue to improve their locational advantages and identify the niches in which they can compete most effectively. Key issues to address include the costs and quality of broadband connections, the availability of human resources in the areas targeted and the effective promotion of existing opportunities to potential investors. To the extent that countries choose to offer financial or fiscal incentives to lure investors into the production of ICT-enabled services, it is important to adapt the incentive schemes to the nature of such projects – with more emphasis on costs related to human resources than on capital investments. At the same time, countries should be cautious not to be too generous when offering incentives as it may fuel a race to the bottom among potential destinations. Those locations that have already emerged on the radar screen for services with low added value may aim to move gradually towards more sophisticated service production. The challenge then is to develop the kinds of human resources as well as the regulatory framework (protection of intellectual property and private data) necessary to be able to compete with other locations.

Supachai Panitchpakdi
Secretary-General, UNCTAD

CHAPTER I

MONITORING CONNECTIVITY FOR DEVELOPMENT

1

In many regards, the diffusion of information and communication technologies (ICTs) has gone faster than expected. Indeed, one target set by world leaders at the World Summit on the Information Society (WSIS) to ensure "that more than half the world's inhabitants have access to ICTs within their reach"[1] by 2015 has already been met – largely thanks to the mobile revolution. Nonetheless, there is no room for complacency. While mobile telephony has contributed to narrowing one aspect of the "digital divide", it cannot respond to all ICT needs. Many development challenges still remain and new ones are emerging.

This chapter reviews recent developments in worldwide connectivity with regard to fixed telephony, mobile communications, Internet and broadband. The first section takes stock of the current situation, highlighting differences in ICT penetration in countries at varying levels of development, and identifies the most dynamic economies in recent years. Section B presents recent developments in the digital divide, paying particular attention to the situation of specific country groupings. Section C focuses on the critical area of broadband connectivity, including its relevance for developing nations. The final section discusses the implications of the current financial crisis for the further roll-out of ICTs, notably in developing economies.

A. RECENT TRENDS IN THE DIFFUSION OF ICTs

Improved access to ICTs is necessary to narrow the digital divide. Monitoring the diffusion of different ICTs is therefore critical to assess the extent to which various parts of the world are becoming connected. In this section, recent trends across fixed and mobile telephony, Internet and broadband are described. While fixed telephone subscriptions are in slight decline, mobile and (to a lesser extent) Internet usage continues to expand rapidly in most parts of the world. At the same time, there is a widening gap between high income and low income countries in the area of broadband connectivity. The analysis draws on available information from the International Telecommunication Union (ITU) as well as national sources (box I.1).

1. Fixed telephony penetration in decline

The number of fixed lines in the world has essentially been frozen at around 1.2 billion since 2006 and even saw a slight decline in 2008 (figure I.1, top). Since 2004, developing countries have accounted for just over half of all fixed telephone lines. Global fixed line teledensity (fixed telephone subscriptions divided by population and multiplied by 100) stood at 18 in 2008 (figure I.1, bottom). In developed countries, teledensity was 47 while in developing countries it was 12. While the difference in penetration between developed and developing countries shrank from 44 in 2003 to 35 in 2008, it was mainly a result of significantly reduced

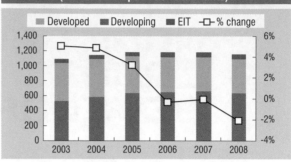

Figure I.1. Global fixed telephone subscriptions by main country groupings, 2003-2008 (millions and per 100 inhabitants)

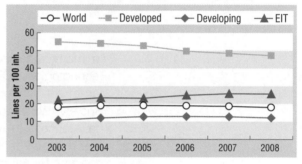

Source: UNCTAD, based on ITU and national data.
Note: EIT = economies in transition.

fixed line teledensity in developed economies (down from 55 in 2003) rather than an increased number of fixed lines in developing economies.

The slow or negative growth in fixed line subscriptions reflects, to a large extent, significant developments in both voice over Internet Protocol (VoIP) and mobile telephony. There is a growing move, primarily in developed economies, to replace traditional voice services delivered over the public switched telephone network with VoIP or, more appropriately, voice over broad-

---

Box I.1. A cautionary note on the data used in the *Information Economy Report 2009*

The data used in this chapter come primarily from ITU and national sources, such as ICT ministries and regulators, national statistical offices, operators and industry associations. A number of caveats should be made. In the case of fixed telephone lines, data are not always fully comparable due to the inclusion or omission of fixed wireless subscriptions with limited mobility (which are sometimes classified as mobile subscriptions). In addition, there is no standard definition for how voice over broadband (VoB) subscriptions should be classified. For mobile subscriptions, some countries include fixed wireless subscribers with limited mobility. There are also differences in the definition of an active user (i.e. when the subscription was last used). Regarding Internet users, many developing countries do not carry out surveys and the number of users is typically based on the number of subscribers or the amount of international Internet bandwidth. Among countries that do conduct surveys, the ages covered by the survey as well as frequency of use often vary. For those countries with survey data, the penetration figures generally refer to the number of users in the survey age range divided by the total population. In the case of broadband subscriptions, differences can arise due to the speed (defined as subscriptions with speeds of 256 kbps (kilobits per second) or higher) since some countries refer to "always on" connections without mentioning the speed. There may also be issues regarding the classification of broadband subscriptions over mobile networks.
Source: UNCTAD.

band (VoB).[2] In 2007, there were over 50 million VoB subscribers in the top ten economies (by the number of subscribers) serving 17 per cent of all households (table I.1).

Table I.1. Top 10 economies by number of VoB subscribers, 2007			
Economy	**VoB subscribers**		
	Total (thousands)	Share of households (per cent)	Share of broadband subscribers (per cent)
Japan	16,766	34	59
United States	12,404	10	18
France	10,838	41	70
Germany	3,900	10	20
Italy	2,405	10	24
Netherlands	2,172	30	38
United Kingdom	2,000	8	13
Canada	1,871	15	22
Sweden	623	14	19
Norway	459	22	32
Top 10	53,438	17	30

Source: UNCTAD, based on national data from government agencies and operators.

The VoB services are driven by so-called "triple play" bundles – telephone, Internet and television – that are becoming increasingly popular in developed economies. A prime example is France, where new broadband operators are effectively competing with incumbent France Telecom in the triple play market. This has driven broadband growth. The relatively small cable television market has made France ripe for television over Internet Protocol (IPTV). As a result, France had the world's biggest IPTV market in 2007, with over two million subscribers. Rapid take-up of triple play led the share of conventional fixed telephone subscriptions to shrink from 88 per cent in the first quarter of 2006 to 64 per cent in the second quarter of 2008, and the percentage of Internet Protocol in total telephone traffic to rise from 23 per cent to 42 per cent.[3]

The spread of triple play services is a manifestation of the transformation to Next Generation Networks (NGNs) where all services are provided over an Internet Protocol-based platform. This phenomenon has made the greatest progress in developed country markets in which fixed telecommunications infrastructure is well developed and broadband penetration high. Developing countries with low diffusion of fixed infrastructure may risk becoming marginalized from

the benefits of NGNs. This might lead some developing countries to invest more in fixed telecommunications infrastructure.

The second reason for the slow growth in fixed telephony is the rise of mobile telephony. In many developing countries, mobile phones are essentially replacing fixed telephone lines as the primary medium for voice communications. Given the high cost of fixed infrastructure compared to wireless solutions and limited access to electricity, especially in rural areas, the expansion of fixed telephony remains largely limited to urban areas, and particularly for business users. Recent studies suggest that even in developed countries, younger adults see mobile phones as more important than access to fixed telephone lines (see e.g. Pew Research Center, 2009).

In countries where there has been some growth in main lines, this has often been the result of so-called "limited mobility" telephone subscriptions using Wireless Local Loop (WLL) technology. The WLL operation is an alternative configuration of full mobility technology that is in compliance with the regulatory requirements of the country in which it is deployed.[4] The service is "limited" because users are restricted from moving beyond their cell range with their handset due to regulatory restrictions. These restrictions arise because the service provider does not have a full mobility license. Fixed wireless systems are less costly to install than traditional copper-based fixed lines.

As mobile telephony is becoming widely available in most places throughout the world, the lack of fixed lines no longer represents a barrier to basic voice telephony in developing economies. However, there may be other implications of a lack of fixed lines. First, it may limit the availability of ADSL (Asymmetric Digital Subscriber Line), with potentially less competitive pressure in the broadband market as a result. This is true even though wireless broadband is likely to grow in importance (section I.C.3). Secondly, as noted above, the lack of fixed line infrastructure in an economy means that households are unable to have next generation integrated triple play services. This is likely to slow down the move to NGNs and convergence and prevent citizens from benefiting from the applications, services, functionality and lower costs of triple play delivered over broadband networks. Whether these concerns will be important enough for developing countries to expand their investments in fixed networks on a large scale remains an open question.

2. The mobile revolution continues

a. Rapid growth in all parts of the world

At the end of 2008, the number of mobile subscriptions reached four billion.[5] Although growth was down somewhat from the previous year, it still remained close to 20 per cent in 2008 (figure I.2, top). On average, there are now 60 subscriptions per 100 people, and in a number of developed, developing and transition economies penetration exceeds 100 (figure I.2, bottom). Developing countries account for two thirds of all subscriptions, corresponding to a mobile penetration rate just short of fifty (48). This is more than eight times the level of penetration in 2000 and an increase of over 17 points in just the past two years.

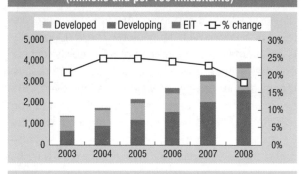

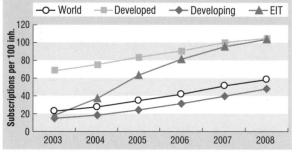

Figure I.2. Global mobile telephone subscriptions by main country groupings, 2003–2008 (millions and per 100 inhabitants)

Source: UNCTAD, based on ITU and national data.

Penetration close to or exceeding 100 is becoming the reality in a growing number of developing economies. In fact, two dozen of them have already surpassed that figure, and over thirty have achieved a mobile penetration rate of between 75 and 99. In Africa, Gabon, Seychelles and South Africa were close to 100 per cent mobile penetration at the end of 2008. In North Africa, average penetration stood at almost two thirds of the population and for Africa as a whole, it was over one third. Growth is expected to remain robust. The pan-regional mobile operator MTN, for ex-

ample, forecasts an average mobile penetration of 80 by 2012 in the fifteen African markets in which it provides services.[6] Only five African countries – Burundi, Djibouti, Eritrea, Ethiopia and Somalia – had a mobile penetration of less than ten at the end of 2008. They were characterized by either monopoly service provision or the absence of established strategic mobile investors.

In developing Asia, five economies had achieved mobile penetration of more than 100 in 2008 and another four reported penetration levels between 90 and 100. Overall, the average regional penetration was 45 subscriptions per 100 inhabitants. Excluding China and India, however, it was as high as 58. In both China and India, mobile penetration is likely to increase from the current levels of 48 and 29, respectively, as a result of industry restructuring, mergers and acquisitions and the award of third generation (3G) licenses.

In Latin America and the Caribbean, mobile penetration varies from among the highest to among the lowest levels in the world. America Móvil, Latin America's largest wireless telecom group, has predicted mobile penetration to reach 94 on average in its operating area by 2012.[7] At the end of 2008, three Latin American countries had a mobile penetration exceeding 100 and the regional average was 80. In the Caribbean, practically all of the anglophone island states have already achieved a penetration rate of over 100, with regional penetration reaching 70. In the case of mobile telephony penetration, the digital divide in the Americas has been inverted; many Latin American and Caribbean economies now boast higher penetration than Canada and the United States (figure I.3). However, Cuba, which has only one mobile operator, and Haiti – the only least developed country (LDC) in the region – are lagging behind in terms of penetration.

The share of the population covered by a mobile signal stood at 76 per cent in developing countries in 2006, including 61 per cent in rural areas.[8] Mobile coverage was close to or above 90 per cent in East Asia and the Pacific, Europe, the Commonwealth of Independent States (CIS), Latin America and the Caribbean, and around 80 per cent in the Middle East and North Africa; it looks set to approach practically full coverage in those regions in the near future. In sub-Saharan Africa, over half the population was covered, including 42 per cent in rural areas. The income barrier to mobile ownership has continuously been reduced thanks to more efficient network equipment and more affordable handsets.[9]

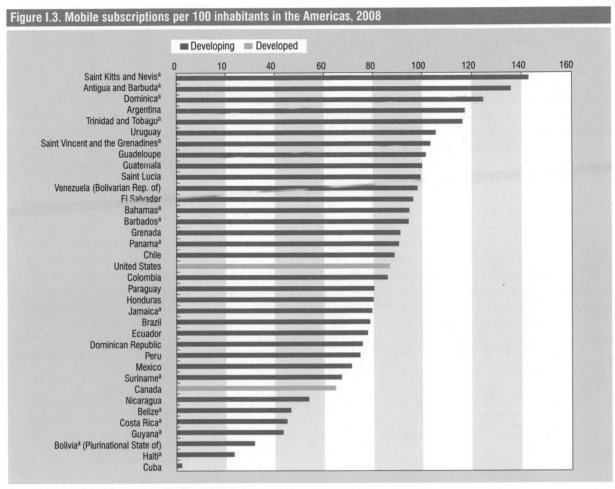

Figure I.3. Mobile subscriptions per 100 inhabitants in the Americas, 2008

Source: UNCTAD, based on ITU and regulator and operator data. See annex table I.1
Note: a = 2007.

The penetration of mobile phones has dramatically increased, even in the poorest countries. At the end of 2007, there were eight times as many mobile phones as fixed lines in the LDCs.[10] Towards the end of 2008, almost one out of every two persons in developing countries already had a mobile phone. Fewer than a dozen developing nations have a mobile penetration of less than ten (compared to some two dozen where penetration is already over 100).

Policymakers influence the speed at which mobile telephony is taken up in an economy. In fact, the main barriers to increased mobile phone penetration are related to the regulatory frameworks. A glance at countries with the lowest mobile penetration reveals supply constraints caused by market restrictions. Countries with similar economic circumstances but with a liberalized market generally show higher penetration rates. Taxes can also act as a barrier, particularly import duties on handsets or special mobile communications surcharges. The mobile industry has been seen as a cash cow in some countries. Though it already generates significant revenue for governments through traditional sales and income taxes and license fees, additional "mobile only" taxes risk slowing down further expansion, particularly among poorer segments of the population (see e.g. Uganda Communications Commission, 2007).

In order to expand coverage into rural and remote areas, government support may be required. Rural areas in some countries are often economically unattractive for operators to invest in. This is usually not due to a lack of demand but rather to economies of scale. As mobile telephony represents the most attractive option to expand telecommunications to rural areas, it may be appropriate to include mobile infrastructure in universal service subsidies. When issuing new mobile phone licenses, governments may also include specific obligations to participate in universal

Box I.2. Development gains from mobile telephony in two LDCs

Maldives is the only LDC with more mobile phone subscriptions than people. This South Asian nation consists of hundreds of small islands in the Indian Ocean. Mobile communications took off following the licensing of Wataniya Telecom as the second mobile operator in 2005. Wataniya launched its network in 2006 to compete with the incumbent Dhiraagu. Today, mobile services are available on all inhabited islands. Given the practical universality of mobile phones, the World Bank and the Consultative Group to Assist the Poor, a microfinance industry association, are working with the Maldives Monetary Authority to create a nationwide mobile banking network.[a] This is particularly relevant for Maldives, whose geographically dispersed population often does not have access to conventional banking services. Another important application of mobile phones in Maldives is disaster management. The country was hit hard by the 2004 tsunami. A disaster management plan has been drawn up with an important future role for mobile phones, especially text messaging to alert the public about emergency procedures.[b]

Uganda has a population of around 32 million, of which more than 85 per cent live in rural areas. The mobile market has progressively grown more competitive. Service began in 1995 when a private operator was licensed. This was followed by the entry of a second national operator in 1998 and the incumbent fixed line operator in 2001. A fourth operator launched operations in 2008 and was followed by France Telecom. The results of these changes have been dramatic. Uganda was the first African country to have more mobile than fixed telephones. Its mobile phone density increased between 1995 and 2008 from 2 to 234 per 1,000 people.[c] Given their low incomes, only about a quarter of the population has a mobile subscription. However, thousands of street vendors offer mobile access on a per call basis for Ugandans who do not have a subscription. Operators have made significant investments in infrastructure, particularly in rural areas with population coverage of over 90 per cent. Mobile communications have transformed the country socially and economically. Business and social contacts can be established and maintained more easily and over 100,000 people work in the mobile sector and related industries, including both direct employment by operators as well as indirect employment through the sale of air time or handsets.[d]

Source: UNCTAD.
[a] *See http://go.worldbank.org/I9I2VVSJP0.*
[b] *See http://www.itu.int/ITU-D/emergencytelecoms/events/ThailandWorkshop/final1/Session%202/SESSION%202%20%5BMaldives%5D%20Country%20Presentation.pdf.*
[c] *See http://www.ucc.co.ug/MarketReviewSept08.pdf.*
[d] *See http://www.gsmworld.com/our-work/public-policy/regulatory-affairs/policy-recommendations-for-developing-countries/taxation_and_growth_of_mobile_east_africa.htm#form.*

service funding schemes. In Uganda, for example, mobile operators are allowed to bid for universal service funds.[11] In South Africa, mobile operators agreed to distribute free SIM (subscriber identity module) cards in exchange for increased spectrum.[12]

Growth prospects remain favourable for developing countries, including LDCs (box I.2). A number of developing countries will be launching 3G networks in the coming years, enhancing the functionality of mobile services and driving the take-up of financial applications, Internet access and other data applications from portable handsets.

b. Mobile phone penetration rising most in developing and transition economies

The following charts and tables provide a snapshot of economies that have shown the greatest dynamism during the period 2003–2008 with regard to expanding the penetration of mobile phones.[13] Dynamism is measured by the change in penetration, which shows where growth has had the greatest absolute impact in terms of rapidly increasing the proportion of the population using mobile phones. For a complete listing of countries, see annex table I.1.

Between 2003 and 2008, the most dynamic economies in terms of increased mobile penetration (measured as number of mobile subscriptions per 100 inhabitants) were found outside the developed world (figure I.4). Only four developed economies appear in the top 20 list and these are all relatively new European Union (EU) members: Bulgaria, Latvia, Lithuania and Romania. One reason for the absence of other developed countries is that they had already reached high penetration levels in 2003.

A common feature among these top performers is liberalization and in some cases catching up with neighbouring nations of similar economic circumstances. Montenegro tops the list. Its rapid growth resulted in more than two mobile subscriptions for every inhabitant in 2008.[14] Like Serbia, also in the top 20 list, this country was part of the former Yugoslavia. The end of the war introduced greater stability and injected growth into the mobile sector with significant foreign investment. In both these countries, additional mobile operators entered the market during the period under consideration. For example, Montenegro attracted strategic investors from Germany and Norway to its mobile market and issued a new license to cross-border Serbian investors in 2007. In the case of the other dynamic European performers, relatively high incomes and continued steps towards market liberalization have driven growth with penetration converging to the level of other EU members.[15]

High incomes and market liberalization also help to explain the presence of the four Gulf states on the list. Bahrain, Oman and the United Arab Emirates all introduced second mobile operators during the studied period. In Qatar, a new mobile operator was licensed in 2007 and looming competition resulted in lower prices. Bahrain has since licensed a third operator. Greater competition has helped to reduce prices in all these countries, making mobile more affordable for lower-income segments, particularly the large immigrant workforce. The small island developing states (SIDS) on the list are representative of the mobile revolution taking place even in small economies.[16]

The belief that these economies would be too minor to sustain competition has been shattered as many of them have introduced additional mobile operators with spectacular results.[17] The five most dynamic economies by region are presented in table I.2.

In summary, the leading mobile performers over the past five years have certain regional and geographical similarities. Many of them can be characterized by policy changes resulting in the freeing of pent-up demand. In the economies that were formerly part of Yugoslavia, improved stability has facilitated an upsurge of investment in mobile networks. In the new EU members, regulatory alignment with the EU has liberalized markets (e.g. additional competition, mobile number portability and pressure on mobile termination rates) with penetration levels quickly converging with the rest of the EU. In the Gulf states and the SIDS, despite their relatively small markets, a mobile revolution has followed the introduction of competition. Many of the top performers are also middle- and high-income economies, in which additional market liberalization was all that was needed to bolster growth since purchasing power was already there. Given that most higher-in-

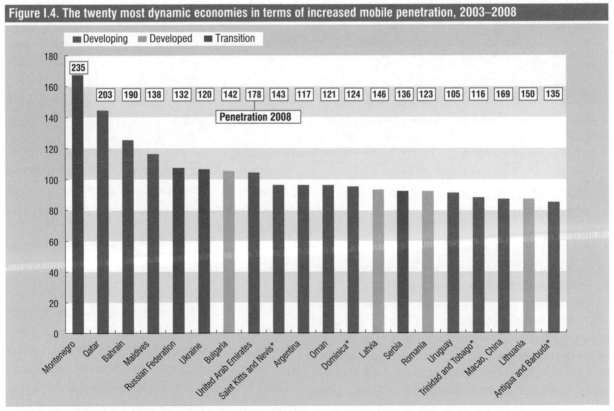

Figure I.4. The twenty most dynamic economies in terms of increased mobile penetration, 2003–2008

Source: UNCTAD, based on ITU and national data. See annex table I.1.
Note: * 2003–2007 change.

Table I.2. Top five most dynamic economies by region in terms of increased mobile penetration, 2003–2008					
	Economy 1	**Economy 2**	**Economy 3**	**Economy 4**	**Economy 5**
Developed economies	Bulgaria	Latvia	Romania	Lithuania	Poland
Developing economies	Qatar	Bahrain	Maldives	United Arab Emirates	Saint Kitts and Nevis
Africa	Gabon	Algeria	Libyan Arab Jamahiriya*	Tunisia	South Africa
Asia and Oceania	Qatar	Bahrain	Maldives	United Arab Emirates	Oman
West Asia	Qatar	Bahrain	United Arab Emirates	Oman	Saudi Arabia
East and South-East Asia	Macao (China)	Viet Nam	Thailand	Malaysia	Indonesia
South Asia	Maldives	Iran (Islamic Republic of)	Pakistan	Sri Lanka	Bhutan
Oceania	Fiji	Tonga*	Samoa*	French Polynesia*	New Caledonia*
Latin America and the Caribbean	Saint Kitts and Nevis	Argentina	Dominica*	Uruguay	Trinidad and Tobago*
Latin America	Argentina	Uruguay	Guatemala	El Salvador	Honduras
Caribbean	Saint Kitts and Nevis	Dominica	Trinidad and Tobago*	Antigua and Barbuda*	Dominican Republic
South-East Europe and the CIS	Montenegro	Russian Federation	Ukraine	Serbia	Armenia

Source: UNCTAD, based on ITU and national data. See annex table I.1.
*Note: * 2003–2007.*

come developing economies have reached close to market saturation, lower-income developing countries are likely to emerge as the most dynamic performers in this category in the future.

3. Most Internet users are now in the developing world

a. Fastest growth in the South

At the end of 2008, there were an estimated 1.4 billion Internet users around the world (figure I.5, top). The growth rate of 15 per cent was slightly lower than in 2007. In developing countries, the number of users grew by a quarter, or almost five times faster than in developed countries. As a result, developing countries now account for more than half the world's Internet users. China hosted the largest number of users (298 million), followed by the United States (191 million) and Japan (88 million) (annex table I.2). A little over

one fifth of the world's population used the Internet in 2008 (figure I.5, bottom).

Wide variations remain in the level of access. While more than half of the developed world population is now online, the corresponding share is only 15 per cent in developing economies and 17 per cent in transition economies.

Internet use is spreading rapidly in some developing countries, however. In Argentina, for example, penetration stood at around 15 per cent of the population five years ago; today, half of all citizens use the Internet. The Islamic Republic of Iran and Viet Nam have also experienced impressive growth, from less than 10 per cent half a decade ago to one third and one quarter of their respective populations in 2008. In Argentina, a high level of education coupled with growing competition between different Internet Service Providers

Figure I.5. Global Internet users by main country groupings, 2003–2008 (millions and per 100 inhabitants)

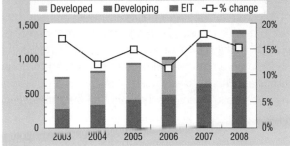
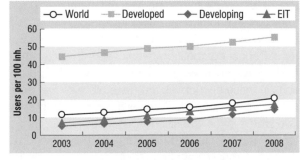

Source: UNCTAD, adapted from ITU and national data.

(ISPs) helped create the pre-conditions for growth. In the Islamic Republic of Iran and Viet Nam, government support to the ICT sector has been backed by resources and capacity-building to raise awareness and computer skills among the population.

Public Internet facilities such as Internet cafés, educational establishments and digital community centres are also important for boosting Internet usage in developing countries. This is particularly true for countries in which household connections are limited and many people work in the informal economy and therefore do not have Internet access from an office. Data from countries in South America illustrate this point (figure I.6). In Paraguay and Peru, over half of all Internet users log on from public facilities.

Despite positive Internet developments in many countries, its use is progressing only slowly in certain regions. Some developing countries are caught in a vicious circle, with insufficient demand due to high prices and inadequate infrastructure. The lack of demand in turn contributes to low levels of investment and high prices. One contributor to high prices is the cost of international connectivity (see section I.C). Another barrier to greater Internet take-up is low levels of education. Limited supply of web content in local languages and adapted to local needs is a further common impediment.

There is some uncertainty regarding the measurement, scope and analysis of Internet usage in developing nations. Since official surveys are seldom carried out, most available data are rough estimates generally based on the number of subscribers or

Figure I.6. Location of Internet access and share of Internet users in selected South American countries, 2007/08 (per cent)

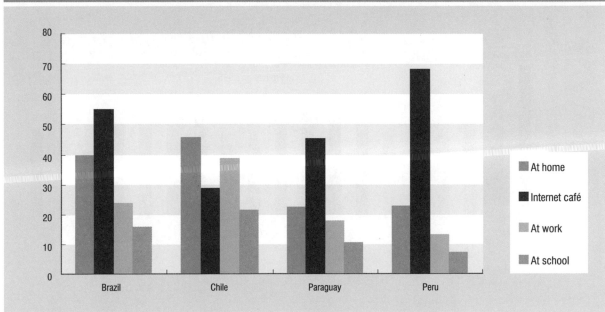

Source: UNCTAD adapted from national statistical offices data.
Note: Data for Brazil and Paraguay refer to 2007 and for Chile and Peru to 2008.

international bandwidth. Such estimates can be wide-ly off, especially given the large number of users that access the web from public facilities. The spread of mobile phones in the developing world could also be impacting the extent of Internet use as people use them to first send text messages, then move up to using them for e-mail and Internet access. While this development is still poorly documented, it suggests that there may be many more users in developing countries than suggested by current data.

b. Internet use has increased fast in many Latin American and Caribbean economies

During the period 2003–2008, Andorra achieved the world's largest gains in terms of Internet penetration (measured as number of internet users per 100 in-habitants), with an increase from 14 to 71 (figure I.7; annex table I.2). During the same period, Argentina was the second most dynamic economy, followed by Latvia and Colombia. In the case of Argentina, com-petition between incumbent telephone operators and cable television companies has dramatically reduced the cost of broadband access. Several small island

economies made it to the top 20 list, including An-tigua and Barbuda, Bahamas, Barbados, Bermuda and Saint Kitts and Nevis, attesting to the strong In-ternet demand in such economies. The liberalization of telecommunication markets in the Caribbean has led to reduced prices helping drive Internet demand. A relatively high level of migration – and therefore the need to communicate with relatives abroad through e-mail and instant messaging – as well as a burgeon-ing offshore ICT services industry has also stimulated Internet use in the Caribbean.

Developed economies account for six entries in the top 20 list, of which four are new EU members. Three transition economies are also included. Almost half of the most dynamic Internet performers are from Eu-rope. Deeper competition in their Internet markets has led to reduced prices and a boost in demand. Popula-tions in these economies are generally also well edu-cated, a prerequisite for successful Internet adoption. Two of the three transition economies are from the former Yugoslavia, with Internet growth explained by pent-up demand that had built up during the war and was released following massive investment in the tele-

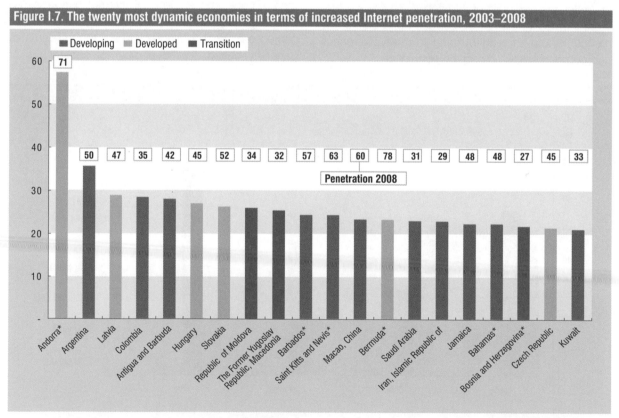

Figure I.7. The twenty most dynamic economies in terms of increased Internet penetration, 2003–2008

Source: UNCTAD, based on ITU and national data. See annex table I.2.
Note: * 2003–2007 change. For survey data, penetration figures refer to the number of Internet users in the survey age group divided by the entire population.

communications infrastructure. There is also strong demand in the Middle East reflected by the inclusion of the Islamic Republic of Iran, Kuwait and Saudi Arabia in the top 20. The growing availability of national language content in Arabic and Farsi has contributed to this growth, as have rising oil incomes. The most dynamic economies by region are presented in table I.3. Five economies featured on the top 20 lists for both mobile telephony and Internet use: Antigua and Barbuda, Argentina, Latvia, Macao (China) and Saint Kitts and Nevis.

4. Developing countries lag behind in terms of broadband connectivity

a. Growing use of both fixed and mobile broadband

Broadband is critical for the deployment of the most recent Internet-based services and can help advance various social and economic development objectives. Many applications do not run or do not operate effectively without sufficient bandwidth. This section looks at developments in both fixed and mobile broadband.[18] Distinguishing between fixed and mobile

broadband is not always straightforward. The Partnership on Measuring ICT for Development defines the two types as follows (UNCTAD, 2009a):

(a) Fixed broadband refers to technologies such as DSL (digital subscriber line) at speeds of at least 256kbit/s, cable modem, high speed leased lines, fibre-to-the-home, powerline, satellite, fixed wireless, Wireless Local Area Network and WiMAX (Worldwide Interoperability for Microwave Access);

(b) Mobile broadband access services include WCDMA (wideband code division multiple access), known as Universal Mobile Telecommunications System (UMTS) in Europe; high speed downlink packet access (HSDPA), complemented by high speed uplink packet access (HSUPA); CDMA2000 1x/EV-DO (evolution-data only) and 1xEVDV (evolution-data and voice). Access can be via any device (mobile cellular phone, laptop, smart phones, etc.)

Thus, the distinguishing feature is the type of communication technology used rather than the device through which access is achieved. With the growing use of smart phones, such as Blackberries or iPhones,

Table I.3. Top five most dynamic economies by region in terms of increased Internet penetration, 2003–2008					
	Economy 1	**Economy 2**	**Economy 3**	**Economy 4**	**Economy 5**
Developed economies	Andorra*	Latvia	Hungary	Slovakia	Bermuda*
Developing economies	Argentina	Colombia	Antigua and Barbuda*	Barbados*	Saint Kitts and Nevis*
Africa	Tunisia	Morocco	Seychelles*	Egypt	Gabon
Asia and Oceania	Macao (China)*	Saudi Arabia	Iran (Islamic Republic of)	Qatar*	Kuwait
West Asia	Saudi Arabia	Kuwait	United Arab Emirates*	Qatar*	Turkey
East and South-East Asia	Macao (China)*	Viet Nam	China	Thailand	Taiwan, Province of China
South Asia	Iran (Islamic Republic of)	Maldives	Pakistan	Sri Lanka	Bhutan
Oceania	New Caledonia*	Fiji*	French Polynesia*	Micronesia	Tonga*
Latin America and the Caribbean	Argentina	Saint Kitts and Nevis	Barbados*	Bahamas*	Colombia
Latin America	Argentina	Colombia	Venezuela (Bolivarian Republic of)	Guyana*	Peru
Caribbean	Antigua and Barbuda	Barbados*	Saint Kitts and Nevis	Jamaica	Bahamas*
South-East Europe and the CIS	Republic of Moldova	The former Yugoslav Republic of Macedonia	Bosnia and Herzegovina*	Montenegro	Serbia

Source: UNCTAD, based on ITU and national data. See annex table I.2.
*Note: * 2003–2007.*

it is becoming increasingly difficult to separate computers from mobile phones. Indeed, today there is more computing power in a smart phone than in the early PCs (personal computers).

The number of fixed broadband subscribers around the world was an estimated 398 million at the end of 2008. Developing countries accounted for almost 40 per cent of these, making broadband one of the few ICTs where developed countries still represent the majority of users (figure I.8, top). Global average broadband penetration stood at 5.9, with striking differences between developed and developing economies (figure I.8, bottom). Average penetration was more than eight times higher in the former (24) than in the latter (2.8). Moreover, this gap appears to be widening: broadband penetration in developed countries grew by 2.9 points in 2008, more than the overall average penetration rate in developing countries, which achieved an increase of only 0.7 points. Transition economies lag even further behind, with an average penetration of 2.6.

But this picture may start to change in the near future. The fastest growing broadband markets are already found in large emerging economies. China became the world's single largest broadband market in the

third quarter of 2008, and by the end of that year it had 83 million subscriptions compared with 79 million in the United States. Brazil has also moved into the top ten broadband markets. These emerging economies have the necessary economies of scale to achieve rapid broadband take-up. However, a large potential market is not sufficient in itself to trigger broadband growth; a threshold level of purchasing power and a regulatory environment that encourages competition are also needed.

A key reason for the slow adoption of fixed broadband in many low-income countries is the lack of fixed telecommunications infrastructure. More attention is therefore often paid to wireless technologies, such as 3G mobile, in the hopes that they will help overcome the abysmal broadband gap. In Pakistan, for example, the telecommunications regulator states that "it is believed that 3G mobile networks with a built-in feature of providing high speed data services will boost the broadband usage".[19] In Brazil, mobile broadband is already the fastest broadband alternative in some neighbourhoods.[20]

In 2008, there were an estimated 361 million 3G mobile subscribers, the majority of which resided in developed economies (figure I.9, top). Global average

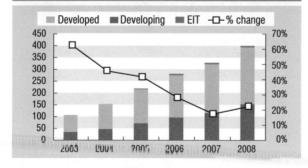

Figure I.8. Global fixed broadband subscribers by main country groupings, 2003–2008 (millions and per 100 inhabitants)

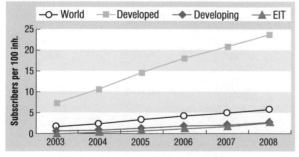

Source: UNCTAD, adapted from ITU and national data.

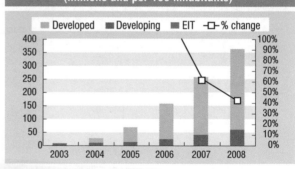

Figure I.9. Global mobile broadband subscribers by main country groupings, 2003–2008 (millions and per 100 inhabitants)

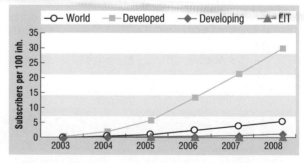

Source: UNCTAD, based on ITU and national data.

penetration stood at 5.4 with a huge gap between developed and developing countries: 29.8 versus 1.1 (figure I.9, bottom). While there were few subscribers in transition economies, this is expected to change with the launch of 3G networks in the Russian Federation and other economies in South-East Europe and the CIS. Meanwhile, the two largest developing economies, China and India, had not yet launched 3G networks at the end of 2008. China awarded 3G licenses in early 2009 (box I.3) and India was expected to follow suit. The roll-out of mobile broadband in developing and transition economies is therefore set to take off in the near future.

Box I.3. China's three 3G technologies

China will be one of the few countries in the world with three different kinds of mobile broadband networks. In early January 2009, the Ministry of Industry and Information Technology awarded three 3G licenses to three different operators in China for three different technologies. China Mobile received permission to use the home-grown TD-SCDMA (time division synchronous code division multiple access) technology, one of the ITU 3G IMT-2000 standards. This will be the world's first implementation of TD-SCDMA. China Unicom was approved to operate 3G using the WCDMA system, which has been widely deployed in many countries. Meanwhile, China Telecom was awarded a 3G license using CDMA2000 technology. It already operates a CDMA2000 network and the new license will allow it to upgrade to faster EV-DO speeds. Competition between these three different technologies could rapidly boost China's 3G take-up. Though the networks are incompatible for now, it is expected that they will evolve to the next generation mobile LTE (long-term evolution) standard (box figure I.3.1).

Source: UNCTAD.

Box figure I.3.1. A converged unified standard for mobile telephony in China

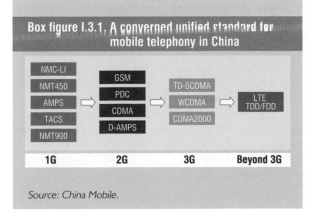

Source: China Mobile.

Mobile broadband statistics are not directly comparable to those of fixed broadband. While mobile subscribers may have a broadband subscription, they are often not aware of it (or they may find the pricing of data too high) and may therefore not make use of the data features. An analysis of EU data from mid-2008 found that just around a third of 3G subscribers actively used 3G-dedicated data services (European Commission, 2008). As a result, the number of active 3G users is likely to be far lower than the number of 3G subscriptions (box I.4). Finally, mobile broadband subscribers would predominantly be accessing the Internet through a handset and the experience of using the Internet on a mobile phone is not the same as access via a desktop or laptop computer.[21] Nonetheless, as the success of Apple's iPhone shows, many useful applications can be run from a portable handset.[22] This may be particularly beneficial to businesses in the developing world that need connectivity but have been hindered by the high cost of a computer and conventional fixed broadband connection. At the same time, handsets with 3G functionality are relatively expensive, which can be a barrier to their deployment in low-income countries.

The wide gap in broadband access represents a new challenge. As discussed later in this report (section I.C), broadband can help meet various development needs and allow countries to participate more effectively in the global digital economy. Limited broadband connectivity severely hampers the ability of companies and other users to exploit the benefits of ICTs. Meanwhile, the promise of wireless broadband for developing countries is still far from being realized. Though there are occasional success stories, there is still little evidence of wireless broadband having a significant impact on enhancing Internet access for developing countries on a wide scale. In terms of mobile broadband, many developing countries are stuck in the second generation and have yet to seize the opportunities offered by leapfrogging to 3G.

Some developing countries are showing signs of success with broadband implementation. Bahamas, for example, boasts the second highest broadband penetration among developing nations in the Americas region and some 80 per cent of its households access the Internet using broadband. This is the result of intense intermodal broadband competition between the incumbent telecommunications operator the Bahamas Telecommunications Corporation and newcomer Cable Bahamas (box I.5).[23] The former Yu-

Box I.4. OECD work on measuring mobile broadband

Increased use of mobile phones to access the Internet has created a need to adapt the way in which broadband connectivity is measured. Since 2000, the OECD has collected and reported broadband data to capture and record significant changes in the markets for Internet access. While some wireless broadband technologies (such as fixed wireless and satellite) were included from the outset, they have accounted for only a small percentage of total connections. In fact, even as of December 2008, less than 2 per cent of all reported broadband subscriptions were wireless. Due to speed limitations and difficulties determining actual use, however, Internet-enabled mobile phones were not included in the OECD broadband statistics.

In recent years, however, telecom operators have invested large amounts in the upgrading of mobile networks (such as HSDPA, CDMA2000 upgrades and WiMAX) to allow for higher speed connectivity. This has made it important to develop a methodology to better measure wireless broadband connectivity. Following contributions from member countries, in February 2009 the OECD presented a proposal for a new indicator made up of four major components: satellite, WiMAX, other/evolving and mobile broadband connections.[a] All components include connections with advertised data speeds at 256 kbit/s or higher.

The mobile category posed particular difficulties. Many mobile phones are "broadband capable" but never actually used to access the Internet. The challenge is therefore to find a way to integrate the mobile segment with other wireless technologies to create a meaningful and useful statistic. Following discussions at an expert meeting on 19–20 February 2009 in Lisbon, it was proposed that only subscriptions with actual Internet data usage during the previous three months should be included in the mobile broadband component. The mobile component also includes a subset counting the number of dedicated or "stand alone" data subscriptions. In the other categories, there is no actual use requirement for dedicated data subscriptions.

Local network services provided over Internet Protocol (IP) would not qualify as Internet usage under the proposed definition, nor would standard SMS (short message service) and MMS (multimedia messaging service) messaging. On the other hand, e-mail and instant messaging would qualify as Internet data access in terms of this data collection. If the mobile subscriber pays a monthly subscription fee for data access, the mobile device should also be considered "active".

Source: OECD.
[a] *The "other/evolving" category includes older fixed-wireless technologies such as LMDS (local multipoint distribution service) and MMDS (multichannel multipoint distribution service) as well as new, evolving wireless broadband technologies. Wi-Fi is not included in the definition, except when used as the transport technology for a fixed-wireless Internet service provider.*

goslav Republic of Macedonia has emerged as a Balkan broadband leader. This landlocked, mountainous nation recently achieved the second highest broadband penetration among the transition economies. Government licensing of alternative operators has spurred the incumbent to drop prices for its ADSL services. In addition, the country has possibly the world's first nationwide wireless broadband network installed through a public–private partnership involving the Ministry of Education, equipment vendor Motorola, a local ISP and United States foreign assistance (Hunsberger, 2006). One of the government's main goals for the network is to make Internet access available to schools and universities and some 500 are already connected. In addition, the network provides access in rural areas the ADSL network does not reach.

Box I.5. Broadband in Bahamas

The Cable Bahamas broadband network now covers 96 per cent of Bahamian homes. Subscriptions are available with speeds up to 9 Mbps; the entry level package with 1 Mbps is around $11 per month, one of the cheapest in the region. The incumbent has reacted by providing broadband using ADSL. It too has installed an island-wide fibre network and is upgrading its infrastructure to an NGN. It is planning to offer television over IP. Apart from the increase in television entertainment and high speed Internet access for consumers, they are also offering online banking and online interaction with the government. Broadband in the Bahamas has had an impact on the overall economy. Infrastructure construction has generated employment and created new businesses in disaster recovery and backup (particularly important given the number of hurricanes each year) as well as web hosting. The investment in broadband has also been important for the financial sector, one of the country's largest industries. Banks have benefitted from having state-of-the-art connectivity for promoting offshore business and providing clients with easy and rapid access to accounts wherever they are.

Source: UNCTAD, based on information from Bahamas Telecommunication Company and Cable Bahamas operating reports.

b. Broadband penetration has increased the most in the North

During the period 2003–2008, the Faroe Islands (with a population of only 48,000) was the world's most dynamic economy in terms of expanding broadband penetration (measured as the number of broadband subscribers per 100 inhabitants) (figure I.10; annex table I.3). The penetration ratio rose from 2 in 2003 to 29 in 2008. All Nordic economies feature among the most dynamic ones. Along with Canada and the Netherlands, they have achieved the highest household broadband penetration in the world with some three out of five homes connected at the end of 2008. These countries were already leading the world in household Internet penetration and their high broadband growth reflects the transformation from dial-up to virtually complete broadband access. They have emerged as broadband societies with virtually all Internet access being high speed. This group of countries has long been at the forefront of technological advance. They have highly educated populations with an affinity for adopting new technology.

Developed countries completely dominate the top 20 list. Furthermore, European economies occupy the first seven positions and eighteen in total. This may reflect the strong regulatory push towards local loop unbundling in Europe that has resulted in a number of new competitive broadband suppliers entering the market.[24] Although these new players initially operated a resale model, they have since climbed up the "ladder" and invested in their own fibre optic networks.[25] The dynamic competitive market in broadband access in many European countries is leading some regulators to relax regulatory requirements for local loop unbundling in an effort to encourage higher fibre optic build-out.

In Australia and New Zealand, which also made the top 20 list, broadband is growing rapidly, driven by a more competitive environment and strong government push to increase broadband connectivity.[26] Canada and the United States do not figure in the list, partly because they already had a relatively high level of fixed broadband penetration.[27] The fact that no developing or transition economy reached the top 20 is a vivid illustration of the widening gap that exists in the broadband area. The five most dynamic economies by region are presented in table I.4.

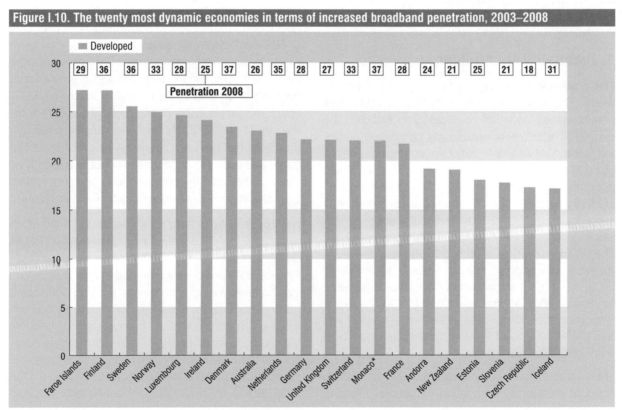

Figure I.10. The twenty most dynamic economies in terms of increased broadband penetration, 2003–2008

Source: UNCTAD, based on ITU and national data. See annex table I.3.

Table I.4. Five most dynamic economies by region in terms of increased broadband penetration, 2003–2008

	Economy 1	Economy 2	Economy 3	Economy 4	Economy 5
Developed economies	Faroe Islands	Finland	Sweden	Norway	Luxembourg
Developing economies	Singapore	Macao (China)	Saint Kitts and Nevis*	Barbados*	Hong Kong (China)
Africa	Seychelles*	Mauritius	South Africa	Tunisia	Morocco
Asia and Oceania	Singapore	Macao (China)	Hong Kong (China)	Republic of Korea	Bahrain
West Asia	Bahrain	Qatar*	Turkey	United Arab Emirates*	Saudi Arabia*
East and South-East Asia	Singapore	Macao (China)	Hong Kong (China)	Republic of Korea	Taiwan, Province of China
South Asia	Maldives	India	Sri Lanka*	Pakistan	Nepal*
Oceania	French Polynesia*	New Caledonia*	Fiji*	Tonga*	Vanuatu*
Latin America and the Caribbean	Saint Kitts and Nevis	Barbados*	Antigua and Barbuda *	Saint Lucia*	Uruguay
Latin America	Uruguay	Argentina	Chile	Mexico	Brazil
Caribbean	Saint Kitts and Nevis	Barbados*	Antigua and Barbuda *	Saint Lucia*	Saint Vincent and the Grenadines
South-East Europe and the CIS	Croatia	The former Yugoslav Republic of Macedonia	Russian Federation	Belarus	Montenegro*

Source: UNCTAD, based on ITU and national data. See annex table I.3.
*Note: * 2003–2007.*

B. MONITORING THE DIGITAL DIVIDE

1. Inequality is shrinking

There are various ways of measuring the digital divide.[28] The *Information Economy Report 2009* uses Lorenz curves and Gini coefficients to establish the degree to which ICTs are equally distributed across the world.[29] While this technique was originally developed to measure income inequality, it can be applied to compare cumulative shares of ICT facilities and utilization. A Lorenz curve for Internet users is illustrated in figure I.11. In 2000, 80 per cent of the world's population accounted for 14 per cent of all Internet users. The Lorenz curves for 2005 and 2008 are above those for 2000, indicating increasing equality with time. By 2005, 80 per cent of the world's population accounted for 35 per cent of Internet users and by 2008 they were responsible for 50 per cent. If the rate of Internet use was the same around the world, the curve would be a 45 degree diagonal line.

The Gini coefficient summarizes the Lorenz curve in a single number by calculating the ratio of the area between the Lorenz curve and the diagonal to the total area under the diagonal. Perfect equality would result in a Gini coefficient of zero and perfect inequality, a coefficient of 1. Figure I.12 shows the trend over time of Gini coefficients for several ICTs. Declining coefficients indicate decreasing inequality. Unsurprisingly, the biggest drop was in mobile access, as subscriptions are becoming spread more equitably. Mobile is now the most equitably distributed ICT, with a Gini coefficient of only 0.12. This is not surprising given that the price of mobile use is generally less than that of Internet and available under easier conditions than fixed lines. Furthermore, mobile telephony does not require the basic literacy skills necessary for Internet access.

Gini coefficients for fixed lines have not declined much since 2005, reflecting stagnant growth (section I.A). In developed nations, the number of fixed lines is dropping as consumers switch to mobile and VoB (negating the need for an extra dial-up line). In developing nations, consumers are opting for mobile as their primary and often only phone. Internet use has become more equally distributed and is in fact more equitably spread than fixed telephony. The biggest inequality is in broadband where the Gini coefficient was 0.47 in 2008. But even in this case, the inequality has narrowed since 2000.

Figure I.11. Lorenz curve for Internet users for the world, 2000, 2005 and 2008

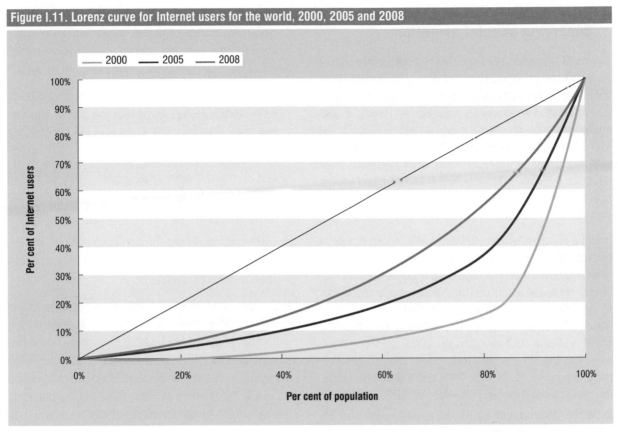

Source: UNCTAD calculations.

Figure I.12. Gini coefficients for the world, 2000, 2005 and 2008

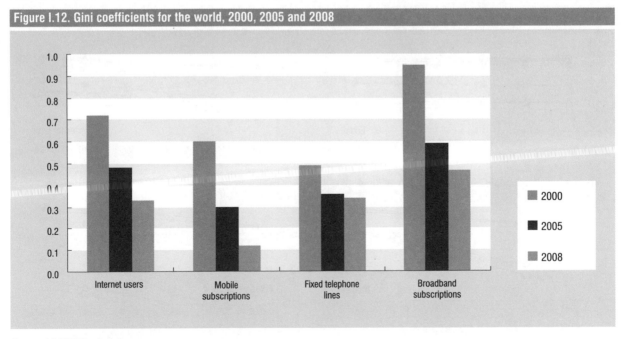

Source: UNCTAD calculations.

2. Developments in country groups deserving special attention

The WSIS Declaration of Principles highlighted the case of particular groups of countries as deserving special attention. This concerns those beset by particular geographic, development or financial characteristics and facing special challenges in overcoming the digital divide, notably small island developing states (SIDS),[30] LDCs,[31] landlocked developing countries (LLDCs)[32] and highly indebted poor countries (HIPCs).[33] This subsection takes a closer look at how ICT developments in these different groupings have evolved.

In terms of fixed telephony, there was little change in access between 2003 and 2008 (figure I.13, top). All the country groupings have fixed line teledensities below the world average. However, among SIDS, the average is above that for all developing countries. Even though they face completely different geographic circumstances, both the SIDS and the LLDCs do better than the LDCs or HIPCs. While there has been a marginal reduction in the gap between the averages for LDCs and HIPCs and the world average, the gap has not changed in the case of SIDS and LLDCs.

In mobile communications there has been significant improvement for most special country groupings (figure I.13, bottom).

(a) The SIDS mobile penetration was above the world average until 2005 but then fell below. Excluding Cuba, however, the average mobile penetration in SIDS would be 75, significantly above the world average;[34]

(b) LLDCs raised mobile penetration from 3 in 2003 to 33 by 2008. During this period, the gap in absolute penetration vis-à-vis the world average fell from 1:7 to 1:2;

(c) LDCs raised their mobile penetration from 2 in 2003 to 20 in 2008, reducing the gap vis-à-vis the world average from 1:13 to 1:3;

(d) In HIPCs, mobile penetration surged from 3 to 23. This implied a reduced gap to world average penetration from 1:9 to 1:2.5.

SIDS more than doubled their Internet penetration from 11 to 24 between 2003 and 2008 (figure I.14, top). It has remained above both the world and the developing country average. Geographic isolation, large diasporas, access to undersea fibre optic cables and offshore ICT industries in many SIDS help explain this elevated level of Internet access. LLDCs raised their Internet penetration from 1.3 to 5 during the same period, HIPCs from 0.7 to 2.7, and LDCs from 0.4 to 2.4.

Figure I.13. Fixed and mobile penetration by special country grouping, 2003–2008

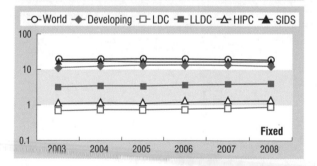

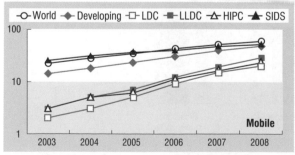

Source: UNCTAD, adapted from ITU and national data.
Note: Logarithmic scale.

Figure I.14. Internet and fixed broadband penetration by special country grouping, 2003–2008

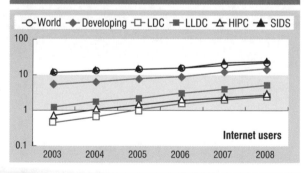

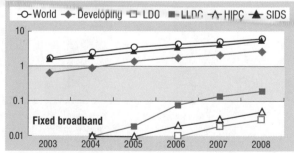

Source: UNCTAD, adapted from ITU and national data.
Note: Logarithmic scale.

Fixed broadband access is the one with the most glaring differences between the penetration rates of the special country groups (except SIDS) and the world and developing country average (figure I.14, bottom). SIDS display a broadband penetration slightly below the world average but above the developing country average. While the other three country groups have improved their penetration from a negligible level in 2003, they all had an average penetration in 2008 of less than 0.25 fixed broadband subscribers per 100 inhabitants. The absolute gap vis-à-vis the world average ranges from 30 in the LLDCs to over 200 in the LDCs. Mobile broadband reflects a similar situation. While several SIDS have launched 3G mobile networks, they are scarce in the other special country groups.

Thus, the difference between ICT penetration in the special country groupings and the world averages generally fell between 2003 and 2008. The SIDS are faring relatively better, with penetration for different ICTs often above the average levels in both world and developing countries. LLDCs are doing better than the HIPCs or LDCs but all these three groups are significantly below world and developing economy averages. The gap in broadband connectivity is particularly wide.

3. No room for complacency

Despite positive trends in ICT diffusion, much more needs to be done to achieve an information society for all. Important gaps remain within economies and societies (e.g. due to language of content; rural versus urban; gender; generation) that affect the demand for and the ability to use ICT. Improved access to ICTs (especially other than mobile phones) has mainly benefited the urban and young people speaking a dominant language.[35] An extra effort is therefore required to bring marginalized and disadvantaged groups into the information society through training and the creation of locally relevant content in appropriate languages (see also section II.0).

When assessing the impact of ICT diffusion, it is important to consider the use of different ICTs in various contexts. Developing countries have embraced mobile technology and the gap with developed countries for that technology is narrowing rapidly. The uses to which mobiles are put – voice communications, messaging, Internet access and broadband connections – can to some extent substitute for services delivered over fixed infrastructure using a computer. So while a wide gap in

fixed technology persists, roughly analogous services may be available using mobile phones.

However, the nature of services delivered over fixed versus mobile connections differs. On the one hand, an e-mail composed and read over a computer provides significantly more functionality and ease of use than a text message (or an e-mail) on a mobile phone. Similarly, Internet access using a full-fledged browser over a broadband computer connection is not comparable to accessing the Internet on a mobile handset with a small screen, cumbersome keyboard and customized Internet viewing software. On the other hand, an e-mail on a computer cannot be accessed on the move and might be read too late to have a real value to the user. Ultimately, the success of a technology is measured by how well it matches the context, affordability and environment in which it exists. As noted by one scholar (Heeks, 2008: 27-28):

> Back in the 1990s, the initial model serving the global North consisted of a PC via landline. But attempted rollouts faced major hurdles as the South's poor proved far harder to reach. The model was too costly to be sustainable or scalable. ... We can keep pushing down the PC-based route when less than 0.5 per cent of African villages so far have a link this way. Or we can jump ship to a technology that has already reached many poor communities. Mobile telephony, for example, already reaches out to more than half the African population.

Mobile phones are widely affordable and available and serve dozens of important uses in developing countries. They allow farmers to obtain product prices and help small and microenterprises stay in touch with clients (chapter II). The functionality of different ICT services and the device on which they are used merits more research, particularly in relation to the digital divide. In the area of broadband access, there is still a large gap between countries at different levels of development, regardless of fixed or mobile high speed connections. This is a concern since many economically and socially relevant applications in the areas of government, business, health and education require broadband access to reach their full level of functionality (section I.C).

Despite good progress, particularly in mobile communications, governments must not become complacent. Existing gains must be sustained, particularly in light of the current crisis (see section I.D). More policy intervention is required to expand broadband access in developing countries. Africa deserves special mentioning in this context. Its countries are lagging behind other developing regions particularly in Internet and broadband take-up (figure I.15). Other developing regions often boast a broadband penetration ten times higher than in Africa. These figures include northern African nations and South Africa, which account for most Internet users and broadband subscriptions in the region. Internet and broadband take-up in sub-Saharan Africa is thus far lower. Urgent attention is needed to address this situation and bring the continent more meaningfully online.

Furthermore, the goalposts are changing. Two decades ago, a common objective was to reach a certain teledensity and to promote telecentres in rural areas; today's information society is more person-oriented and ICTs have become more important, even in the poorest countries. The full right to communicate and participate in the information society requires having a tool to access, compose, send, receive and process information at any time and in any place. The mobile revolution suggests that this can be achieved in all countries by all adult citizens having a portable handset, as long as countries adopt the appropriate regulatory frameworks, including incorporating mobile communications into universal service policy. This might be a more appropriate policy objective than teledensity or general coverage targets.

C. ADDRESSING THE BROADBAND CHALLENGE

1. Reasons to promote broadband connectivity

As noted above, the digital divide between developed and developing economies is particularly wide in the case of broadband. For example, Australia, a country with 21 million inhabitants, has more broadband subscribers than the whole of Africa. There is furthermore a huge gap in terms of broadband speed. While high-income economies keep pushing the limits, low-income countries' broadband connections generally remain slow.[36] The situation in the Asia-Pacific region is illustrative; high-income economies such as Japan and the Republic of Korea boast minimum bandwidths for an entry level broadband package that are much higher than the maximum broadband speeds in, for example, Bangladesh, Cambodia and Tonga (figure I.16). To make things worse, there is also a "broadband price divide". In 2008, the average fixed broadband price at purchasing power parity was $27.6 for developed countries and $289 for developing countries (ITU, 2009a). The cost of using fixed broadband tends to be the highest in low-income countries. Out of

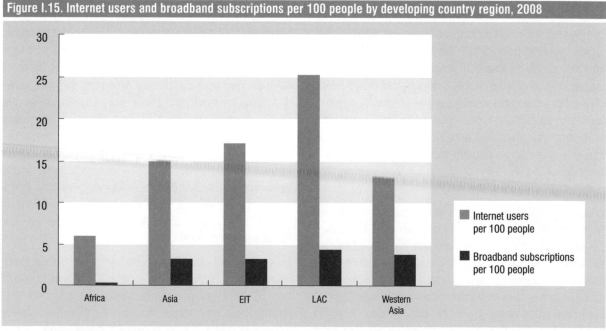

Figure I.15. Internet users and broadband subscriptions per 100 people by developing country region, 2008

Source: UNCTAD adapted from ITU and national data.
Note: LAC = Latin America and the Caribbean.

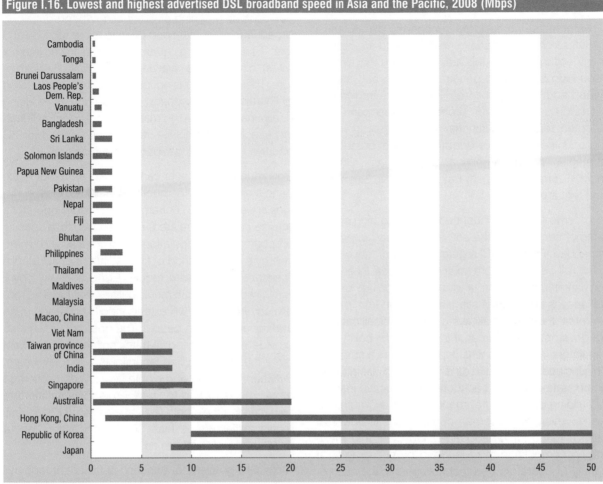

Figure I.16. Lowest and highest advertised DSL broadband speed in Asia and the Pacific, 2008 (Mbps)

Source: ITU.
Note: The range of speeds in the chart shows the advertised lowest and highest consumer broadband plans offered using DSL technology.

the 20 countries with the most expensive broadband access, 14 are from sub-Saharan Africa and another three are islands in Oceania (ibid.).

There are good reasons for developing countries to prioritize broadband connectivity in their development strategies. Although broadband may not be needed for every user, there are many applications that do not run or operate effectively without sufficient bandwidth. Improved broadband connectivity can help to achieve education and health targets set out in the Millennium Development Goals (MDGs). Its use has contributed to social and economic development, for example, in the context of distance education in the Solomon Islands and disaster management in China and Myanmar (ITU, 2008b). Health care costs can be lowered by using telehealth, which can reduce the number of tests, in-person visits and patient transfers (Alexander, 2008). Communities that are not connected via broadband are unable to benefit from such critical services.

Broadband is also crucial for e-government. It underpins public administration networks allowing processes to flow more smoothly. This can make a government more efficient and accountable, enabling it to tackle development challenges more effectively. E-government delivered through broadband facilitates citizen access to programmes and services and improves the flow and speed of government information to poor and isolated communities, helping to empower and improve their development prospects.[37] Furthermore, broadband is essential to support new industries such as ICT-enabled services (chapter III), and it can help stimulate domestic industry and employment growth in content development, infrastructure roll-out and e-commerce (chapter II).

2. Policy options

Governments increasingly recognize the potential benefits from broadband connectivity and are designing specific policies in this area. Countries that already have high broadband penetration, such as Canada, Japan and the Republic of Korea, have implemented tailored policies for promoting broadband and adopted related regulations. Examples of developing countries that have adopted national broadband strategies include Argentina, Chile,[38] Egypt, Ghana, India,[39] Jordan, Malaysia, Pakistan, Qatar, Singapore and Sri Lanka.

In order to promote enhanced access to high speed Internet services in different ways a broad approach is needed. Policies and regulations to facilitate broadband roll-out range from taxation and fiscal incentives to market liberalization, and may also include universal access and market stimulation. Apart from e-government, there is not always a need for significant extra government resources. Fine-tuning the policy and regulatory environment is typically more important. This includes steps such as encouraging operators to share state-of-the-art backbone infrastructure instead of building duplicate, fragmented, low bandwidth networks, leveraging operator contributions to universal service funds for broadband deployment and maximizing competition in broadband by encouraging a variety of operators and technologies. In the case of international broadband connections, this includes participating in undersea cable projects and, for land-locked countries, building out fibre links to connect with submarine cable landing stations in other countries (see section I.C.4).

Governments should be careful not to champion any specific broadband technologies. In many countries, broadband services are provided by private operators and technology choices form part of their financial and engineering plans. The complexity involved in predicting what technology will best suit the needs of the future suggests that government policy should be technologically neutral. Nevertheless, government decisions influence the direction of broadband technology both directly and indirectly, through standards and spectrum policy, import duties and taxes, and broadcasting and other laws. Governments also make technological choices for the implementation of their own administrative networks. The capabilities of various broadband technologies, particularly wireless – arguably the most relevant in the developing country context – are discussed in section I.C.3.

Pro-broadband taxation and fiscal incentives cover areas such as reducing or eliminating import duties on broadband equipment and offering tax reductions and loan assistance (e.g. guarantees and lower interest rates) to companies investing in broadband infrastructure. There are various options that can be considered to liberalize the broadband market, such as reducing or eliminating barriers to market entry and fully allocating spectrum, especially frequencies needed for 3G and fixed wireless broadband technologies.[40]

Coverage requirements can be used as a tool to expand the availability of mobile broadband. Most countries impose some requirement in a mobile operator's license conditions related, for example, to a specific proportion of the population being covered by the service by a certain period of time. Winners of 3G mobile licenses in Brazil were required to collectively cover within two years 1,836 municipalities that have no mobile coverage. This will extend mobile coverage to an additional 17 million people. The operators must also provide 3G coverage to all state capitals and cities with more than half a million inhabitants within two years. Between the fourth and eighth years, these coverage requirements extend to smaller municipalities so that by the end of the eighth year, at least 60 per cent of all municipalities with at least 30,000 inhabitants (about 3,800 municipalities) are covered.[41]

A critical ingredient for ensuring sufficient broadband supply at reasonable prices is to expose operators to competition – both intramodal and intermodal. Intramodal competition refers to competition within the same technology, such as ADSL, whereas intermodal refers to competition between competing technologies such as between ADSL, cable modem, fibre optic and wireless technologies. The healthiest broadband markets have a high degree of both intramodal and intermodal competition.[42]

Such an environment is not common in developing countries, partly due to the often limited number of fixed lines. A lack of intermodal competition may also reflect the absence of cable television networks or restrictions in telecommunications and broadcast laws.[43] Countries can do more to encourage convergence to generate broader intermodal competition. At the same time, there have been competitive constraints affecting the potential of new wireless technologies. For example, the needed spectrum has often been awarded to incumbent operators either by direct awards or through high license fees that only established companies can afford. Some countries have escaped the latter problem by reserving specific frequencies for new operators. Developing countries should make extra efforts to encourage broadband competition by facilitating the entry of new players in order to increase the diversity of supply and reduce prices.

In most developing countries, national backbones have typically comprised a collection of various transmission links (microwave, overhead cable and satellite). They have generally been low speed and often duplicated by each operator. More attention should be paid to ways in which complementary services or even competing services can share core infrastructure. For example, there is growing momentum towards consolidating national fibre backbones by encouraging infrastructure sharing[44] and extending fibre to more remote and rural areas outside urban areas where there are usually metropolitan fibre rings.

Achieving more widespread deployment of broadband backbones and access networks in remote and less densely populated areas is a particular challenge. Efforts need a degree of pragmatism. There will be situations where fibre is not practical at the moment, and where it may be more realistic to bridge the gap with various fixed wireless solutions or more traditional microwave. Increased deployment can be facilitated by the adoption of a universal access and service policy that complements a national broadband policy aimed at creating an enabling environment. Governments might require operators to make specific minimum speeds available to households or provide subsidies or other incentives using universal access and service funds to operators for rolling out broadband infrastructure. Such funds have been used, for example, in countries like the Dominican Republic, India and Peru to increase the reach of and access to broadband networks and services in rural areas. They can help stimulate market forces, launch innovative rural service pilot projects and create demand for advanced ICT connectivity and services.[45]

Another way to enhance broadband access is through the promotion of public Internet access points or telecentres. Public facilities can become a leading location of access for Internet users in developing countries. In Peru, around 70 per cent of Internet users access the Internet from public Internet centres ("cabina pública") compared to about 20 per cent or less from home and from work (figure I.6). Steps that facilitate public Internet locations include delicensing public Internet facilities, promoting inexpensive broadband

tariffs for public Internet centres and deregulating the Wi-Fi spectrum. Uganda's rural communications development fund has also been successful in rolling out infrastructure outside the main urban areas. It has contributed to the establishment of Internet Points of Presence in over 70 district capitals and 55 Internet cafés in district capitals as of December 2007.[46] In South Africa, extending Internet access through mobile broadband powered public facilities is critical given the lack of other options.[47] For example, MTN is using HSDPA to provide Internet connectivity in community access centres. Known as MTN@ccess, the operator has provided a 3G connection in a poor township in Johannesburg. Computers in the centre are connected at speeds of up to 1.4 Mbps, equivalent to fixed broadband technologies.[48]

Focus on universal broadband access through public Internet facilities is likely a prime concern of many developing countries, especially at low levels of income. As countries move up the development ladder, broadband access from home becomes more demanded, facilitating accessibility for users, particularly for households with children. Some countries view a major barrier to home broadband availability to be the lack of PCs and have launched programmes to facilitate home PC ownership. North African countries such as Egypt and Tunisia are seeking to extend PCs into homes hoping that broadband access will then follow.[49]

There is scope for greater involvement by national governments and development partners. The development impact that broadband can have is only slowly becoming reflected in poverty reduction strategy papers (PRSPs) (box I.6).[50] Some countries highlight the importance of ICTs for reducing poverty in terms of their impact on increasing efficiency, improving livelihoods, modernizing public administration and creating new jobs and services. Some desirable ICT impacts will be optimally achieved only through broadband networks. At the same time, for many poor countries, it will take time before broadband connectivity is adequately provided. In these cases, it is important to continue to explore what can be achieved for development through text messaging, financial applications and e-government using mobile phones (Heeks, 2008).

Box I.6. Some PRSPs emphasize the role of broadband

Ghana's PRSP refers to the establishment of "a national communications backbone facility to provide access throughout the country" and "the development of electronic commerce to enhance production, productivity and to facilitate business transactions. Government intends to establish Information Technology (IT) parks and incubator areas equipped with the necessary infrastructure for ICT-related businesses."[a] Broadband is indispensable for achieving the Ghanaian plans for a backbone, e-commerce and IT parks.

Sri Lanka makes specific mention of broadband in its PRSP, discussing the e-Sri Lanka initiative to apply the benefits of "modern technology to the workings of government and the private sector. … A broadband network will be developed and extended through the countryside to ensure that e-Sri Lanka is accessible to the poor."[b] It describes the use of a development fund for helping to finance a domestic broadband network with particular focus on rural areas and providing connections to small and medium-sized enterprises (SMEs) in small towns.

Source: UNCTAD.
[a] *Government of Ghana: Ghana Poverty Reduction Strategy 2003–2005: an agenda for growth and prosperity. http://go.worldbank.org/ BMEZ9ICHC0.*
[b] *Government of Sri Lanka: Regaining Sri Lanka: vision and strategy for accelerated development. http://www.imf.org/External/NP/prsp/2002/ lka/01/120502.pdf.*

3. Exploring the wireless broadband option

As noted above (section I.A), fixed broadband technologies are the most used worldwide.[51] A major factor holding back the diffusion of fixed broadband in developing countries is the shortage of fixed infrastructure – whether copper telephone lines for DSL, coaxial cable for cable modems or fibre optic networks. Cable television is not widely available in all developing regions and when it is, the technology deployed is often not suitable for broadband without significant upgrading and capital expenditure.[52] Meanwhile, fibre optic to the home is a limited and expensive proposition. In many developing countries, wireless solutions therefore appear to be more economically attractive in the short term for bridging the broadband divide.

Different technologies are emerging to facilitate the roll-out of wireless broadband. Wireless broadband options include fixed technologies such as Wi-Fi and WiMAX, and mobile 3G. Bandwidth available with wireless varies widely depending on the version and type of technology. Today, higher speed wireless technologies are competitive compared with most mass market DSL and cable modem offerings.[53] Fixed wireless has been used as an Internet access alternative for a number of years. Initial implementations were proprietary and fell short of true broadband speed. Wi-Fi is widely used and Wi-Fi chips are now implanted in most laptop computers. Wi-Fi operates over a limited range at broadband speed. It can be a useful access solution for certain situations, e.g. connecting users in airports, Internet cafés or geographically small localities. The experience of Maldives shows that Wi-Fi can be a suitable access technology in compact places and where there is connectivity to backhaul infrastructure (box I.7).

The other two main options are the IP-based WiMAX and the 3G mobile cellular technologies based on WCDMA and CDMA2000 1x / EV-DO.[54] WiMAX provides voice functionality using IP technology. Likewise, 3G mobile technologies can also be used for data traffic using USB (Universal Serial Bus) or data cards.

Box I.7. Wi-Fi in Maldives

Though Wi-Fi is most commonly used for hotspots, it can help to support broadband connectivity by providing access distribution from a broadband backbone, particularly in countries with suitable geographical characteristics for this technology. In Maldives, incumbent operator Dhiraagu has installed its so-called "Wireless Zone Service" on a majority of the country's inhabited islands – most of which are just several kilometres wide – with plans to extend the service to all inhabited islands. The service offers prepaid billing so users can access broadband at their convenience without monthly charges. The initial phase of providing the service to all atoll capitals in the country was completed in February 2007. The next phase involves the provision of service on all islands with a population exceeding 900 people.[a]

Source: UNCTAD.
[a] *Dhiraagu press release: Dhiraagu extends Wireless Zone Service to additional 27 islands. 2 August 2007. http://www.dhiraagu.com.mv/me dia_centre/press_releases.php?id=593&cat=pressreleases.*

According to the WiMAX Forum, an industry association, some 430 million people in 135 countries were covered by WiMAX technology in 2008, a figure projected to grow to 800 million by 2010.[55] Though coverage is expanding, the number of actual subscribers remains small; around two million subscribers worldwide as of June 2008.[56] Reasons for the much lower number of subscribers include small-scale deployments in many countries; that the technology is still being refined; limited competition; that operators deploying WiMAX networks are the same as those already providing fixed, mobile or broadband services; and delays in the allocation of spectrum for WiMAX.

One advantage of WiMAX is that it is relatively low cost to deploy compared to 3G or fixed broadband networks. This may make it an attractive technology in rural areas, for example. It may also be an option for new players who would be interested in entering the broadband market. In many countries, however, only existing operators have been awarded WiMAX licenses or they have been granted more favourable spectrum than new entrants. This has constrained competition and held back the potential of WiMAX. The world's largest deployment of WiMAX is run by Tata Communications in India (box I.8).

Third generation (3G) mobile technology is also touted as a competitor to fixed broadband. Mobile bandwidths are continually evolving upwards (box I.9) and are today competitive with mid-level DSL and cable modem offerings. The two main 3G technologies are WCDMA (and its upgrade technology HSDPA that supports higher bandwidth) with around three quarters of the 3G mobile broadband market and CDMA2000 1x / EV-DO with a quarter share.[57] As of April 2009, 92 countries had established WCDMA-based networks (including 47 in developing nations and eight in transition economies) and 66 countries had CDMA2000 1x / EV-DO networks (including 44 in developing countries and five in transition economies).[58]

Coupled with a data card, 3G can be a viable alternative to fixed line broadband. While such 3G use, which generally implies connecting computers rather than mobile handsets to the Internet, currently accounts for a small portion of mobile users, it represents a significant share of all broadband subscribers in some developed countries.[59] It is also emerging as an alternative to fixed broadband in developing countries that have launched 3G and where there are relatively few fixed broadband connections. In South Africa, for example, subscribers using 3G data cards now ac-

count for more than half the total number of broadband subscribers (figure I.17).[60] Other non-3G wireless technologies account for another 10 per cent of broadband subscribers. 3G broadband has been successful because the only other fixed alternative is ADSL. The HSDPA networks deliver download speeds of up to 3.6 Mbps with plans to upgrade to 7.2 Mbps.

Spectrum allocation is a key issue for wireless broadband. Broadband WCDMA networks have traditionally employed spectrum in the 2.1 GHz band. Many developing countries have been slow to allocate the needed frequency for WCDMA.[61] For example, China awarded 3G licenses only in early 2009, and India had yet to allocate WCDMA frequency at the time this report was drafted. In Latin America and the Caribbean, Brazil was the only country that had allocated WCDMA frequency in the 2.1 GHz band at the end of 2008. New frequency bands are being exploited for mobile broadband. For example, CDMA2000 EV-DO is available for the 450 MHz band, which allows wider coverage and is therefore attractive for rural areas (box I.10). WCDMA (as well as HSDPA) has been introduced in the 900 MHz band (Ovum, 2007). This is attractive for existing GSM operators, who do not have to wait for 2.1 GHz spectrum allocations and can instead leverage their existing frequency to introduce mobile broadband services.[62]

The development of mobile broadband in a country tends to be evolutionary. Data access using less than broadband speeds can be achieved with GPRS/EDGE derived from 2G GSM networks or CDMA 2000 1x. As demand grows, operators move up to higher speed technologies such as CDMA 2000 1x / EV-DO, WCDMA/HSDPA, mobile WiMAX and eventually LTE (box I.9). The timing and choice of technology is basically a function of what systems operators in the country are deploying and of the licensing and spectrum allocation framework.

4. Addressing the international connectivity challenge

International Internet connectivity is vital for countries. In some developing nations, limited domestic content means that many users will access overseas websites that require sufficient bandwidth to ensure adequate quality of service. Countries that aim to develop export-oriented ICT-enabled services require good international connectivity to transmit information quickly with minimal latency (chapter III). Both fibre optic cable systems and satellite networks can pro-

Box I.8: WiMAX expanding in India

In India, Tata Communications is deploying the world's largest commercial WiMAX network. It was launched in December 2007 and by the end of 2008, it had networks in Bangalore, Chandigarh, Delhi and Hyderabad with over 750 base stations and around 35,000 subscribers. Tata estimates that it will have over 10 million WiMAX subscribers by 2013. This strategy reflects an option where there is a lack of other wireless solutions, since 3G mobile broadband has yet to be licensed in India.

Source: UNCTAD, based on Tata Communications (2009).

Box I.9. From 2G to 4G

There has been a gradual improvement in speed over time, with technologies often competing with each other in bandwidth capability (box figure I.9.1). This has been particularly true in the GSM (Global System for Mobile Communication)/WCDMA/HSDPA versus CDMA 1x / EV-DO camps with one technology announcing a speed breakthrough and then the other technology following suit.

Many countries have GSM networks, where GPRS (general packet radio service) or EDGE (enhanced data rates for GSM evolution) can be deployed without a major upgrade by overlaying them over the GSM network. GPRS is not a broadband solution but is faster than plain GSM. The next step up is EDGE, which is often perceived as filling the gap between GPRS and 3G networks. The upgraded versions of EDGE (called Evolution) can today offer broadband speeds of up to 1 Mbps with average throughput of around 400 kbps (Ericsson, 2007). It should normally not incur major regulatory obstacles and does not necessarily require new spectrum allocation.

Although some developing countries have mobile CDMA2000 networks, this technology has often been introduced as a fixed wireless solution. CDMA2000 1x offers an option for Internet access equivalent to or faster than a dial-up fixed line. It can be upgraded to CDMA2000 EV-DO which comes in several versions, all operating at broadband speeds. Attractive features of CDMA2000 networks include their cost effectiveness compared to fixed lines and that they can typically be upgraded to broadband speeds without requiring new spectrum allocation.

WCDMA-based mobile systems have seen an increase in advertised bandwidth from an initial 384 kbit/s to over 40 Mbps today. Likewise, EV-DO theoretical speeds have increased from 2.5 Mbps to over 280 Mbps. Though announced speeds are usually far higher than the actual implementation bandwidth, mobile wireless technologies can today compete with non-fibre-based fixed broadband in terms of throughput. LTE mobile technology, or so-called fourth generation mobile, claims speeds of over 300 Mbps although it will be some time before LTE is widely deployed.[a]

Source: UNCTAD.
[a] In February 2009, Verizon Wireless announced plans to deploy the first LTE network in the Americas by 2010. LTE speeds achieved during Verizon trials have reached 50 to 60 Mbps. Verizon plans to use 700 MHz spectrum, which would achieve wide coverage at significantly lower cost than other frequencies. See Verizon press release: Verizon Wireless fosters global LTE ecosystem as Verizon CTO Dick Lynch announces deployment plans. 18 February 2009. http://news.vzw.com/news/2009/02/pr2009-02-18.html.

Box figure I.9.1. Evolution of mobile technologies

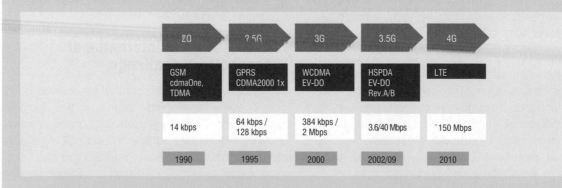

Source: UNCTAD, adapted from CDMA Development Group and Ericsson.

Box I.10. Mobile broadband at 450 MHz – the case of Czech Republic

Mobile technology using the 450 MHz frequency can cover a wider distance than most networks using higher frequencies. Fewer base stations are required, reducing investment costs and making it attractive for dispersed rural areas. The Czech mobile operator O2 has been using EV-DO operating at the 450 MHz frequency for several years. The latest release it implemented offers peak speeds of up to 3.1 Mbps. The network has over 100,000 subscribers and provides coverage in areas where there is no other broadband option. According to the network equipment supplier, the CDMA 450 MHz solution reduces capital investment and operating costs.[a] EV-DO operating at 450 MHz has proven a good fill-in technology in Czech Republic to reach areas to which the fixed line broadband network does not extend.

Source: UNCTAD.

[a] *See Nortel news release: Telefónica O2 Czech Republic drives faster mobile broadband with Nortel wireless technology. 6 February 2008.*
http://www2.nortel.com/go/news_detail.jsp?cat_id=-8055&oid=100235760.

Figure I.17. Use of 3G data cards in South Africa

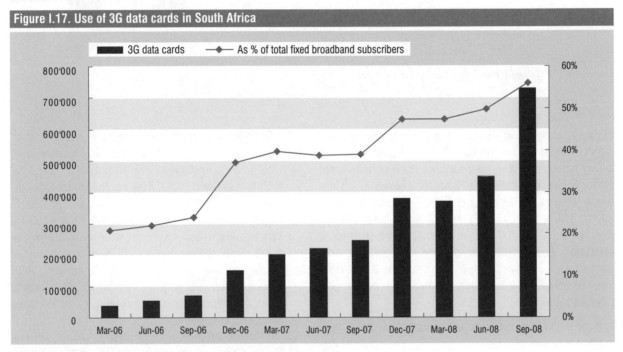

Source: UNCTAD, adapted from MTN, Telkom and Vodacom operating reports.

vide international connectivity. While satellite remains important,[63] particularly for landlocked countries and rural and remote areas and to ensure redundancy, fibre optic systems are critical since they support high speed at a more attractive cost. A 2007 study found that a leased circuit between Africa and Europe cost about $130,000 per month using satellite compared to $25,000 for submarine cable.[64] Furthermore, the option of fibre connectivity puts pressure on satellite operators to keep costs competitive.

Governments have encouraged investment by liberalizing the international connectivity market. Most nations that are fortunate to border the sea have been able to leverage this advantage by connecting to one of the dozens of fibre optic submarine cables ringing the earth. The rapid growth of undersea fibre optic has

given many countries the option of different cables, enhancing competition and helping to reduce prices. When there is only one system available with access to the international cable, this can be a point of friction, especially when the landing station is controlled by the incumbent operator. In an effort to ensure that international bandwidth prices are reasonable, some countries have regulated the tariff that can be charged.[65]

One region that has been largely excluded from the mesh of undersea fibre optic is sub-Saharan Africa. As of mid 2009, there was only one intracontinental undersea cable – SAT-3 – running up the African west coast. Even with this cable, not every West African coastal country is connected. Moreover, some countries on the SAT-3 have been unsuccessful at expand-

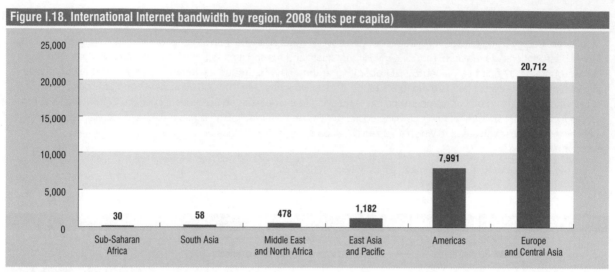

Figure I.18. International Internet bandwidth by region, 2008 (bits per capita)

Source: UNCTAD adapted from World Bank and national data.

ing international connectivity due to monopoly control over ownership.[66] In other parts of sub-Saharan Africa, a few countries have international fibre connections through landing stations of specific cables, such as Cape Verde (Atlantis), Djibouti (SEA-ME-WE2), Mauritius (SAT-3/WASC/SAFE) and Sudan (SAS). However, most of East Africa, a number of West African countries and landlocked nations are still disconnected. Unsurprisingly, then, sub-Saharan Africa has the world's lowest international Internet bandwidth per capita (figure I.18).

A number of initiatives are underway to improve this situation, however:

(a) After years of discussion, the Eastern Africa Submarine Cable System (EASSy) finally began construction in March 2008 and is slated for completion in the first half of 2010. It will connect Djibouti, Kenya, Madagascar, Mozambique, Somalia, South Africa, Sudan and the United Republic of Tanzania. In addition, there will be inland spurs to around a dozen adjoining countries.[67] The estimated cost of the cable is around $250 million and the project is receiving financing assistance from the International Finance Corporation and other development agencies;[68]

(b) Concerned about delays with EASSy, the Government of Kenya endorsed the East African Marine System (TEAMS) cable, which will link Kenya with the United Arab Emirates. The award to build the $82 million cable was made in October 2007 with TEAMS slated for completion in 2009;[69]

(c) SEACOM is another cable for the east coast of Africa. It links Kenya, Madagascar, Mozambique, South Africa and the United Republic of Tanzania, with Europe and India. The cable became operational in July 2009;[70]

(d) There are plans to supplement the existing SAT-3 West African cable with new ones. In November 2008, France Telecom signed a memorandum of understanding to create the 12,000 km-long ACE (Africa Coast to Europe). Extending from Gabon to France, it would provide connectivity for 20 West African countries;[71]

(e) The West Africa Cable System (WACS) will link South Africa to Europe via a dozen other countries. It was initially targeted for launch in the middle of 2010 but has been delayed.

D. FUTURE OUTLOOK AND IMPLICATIONS OF THE FINANCIAL CRISIS

The WSIS target that "more than half the world's inhabitants have access to ICTs within their reach" by 2015 was met in some respects already in 2008 as a result of the rapid spread of mobile telephony. Moreover, good progress has been made towards reducing the inequality in the distribution of ICTs (section I.B). There are concerns that the current financial and economic crisis – the worst in 60 years – will impact negatively on these positive trends and the investment needed in order to ensure universal access to ICTs. At the time of drafting, there was still great uncertainty about the degree to which it would affect different countries and economic sectors. The crisis is expected to influence developed and developing countries and various regions within developing countries differently (figure I.19). Although all groups will experience slower growth, developed economies and economies in transition are forecast by the International Monetary Fund to witness the deepest contraction in output in 2009.

Evidence from Asia and Latin America, which have recent experience with earlier economic crises, suggests that telecommunications services may be more resilient than other industries during this economic downturn. In Argentina, for example, telecommunications fared better during other economic downturns than the economy as whole (figure I.20). In Indonesia, mechanisms established in the aftermath to the Asian financial crisis have kicked in to temper the impact of the current one. Mechanisms include a share buy-back scheme to reduce the effect of the crisis on stock prices. Incumbent telecommunications operator PT Telkom has been buying its shares on the local stock market to preserve their value.[72]

Compared with most other industries, the mobile sector in developing countries should have a good chance of weathering the storm. At the time this report was prepared, the crisis had had a relatively mild impact on mobile growth in several of the largest developing country markets. According to the latest available data, growth continued in the two largest developing country mobile markets – China and India – also in 2009. The world's biggest mobile operator, China Mobile, added on average 6.5 million new mobile subscribers in January–April 2009, as compared with 7.6 million one year earlier.[73] In India, which surpassed the United States in 2008 to emerge as the world's second largest mobile market, some 10.4 million new wireless subscribers were added in November, another 10.8 million in December and a record level of 15.6 million new subscribers in March 2009. The total wireless

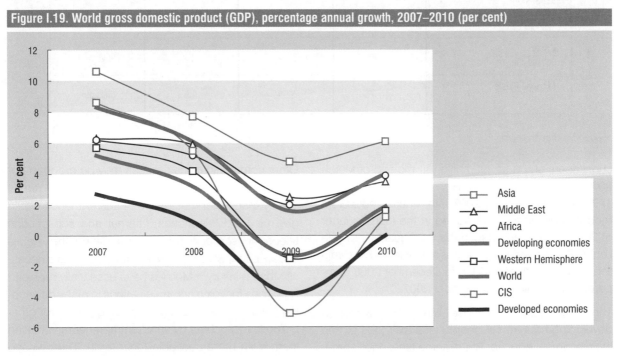

Figure I.19. World gross domestic product (GDP), percentage annual growth, 2007–2010 (per cent)

Source: International Monetary Fund (IMF) (2009).

Figure I.20. Telecoms and the economy in Argentina

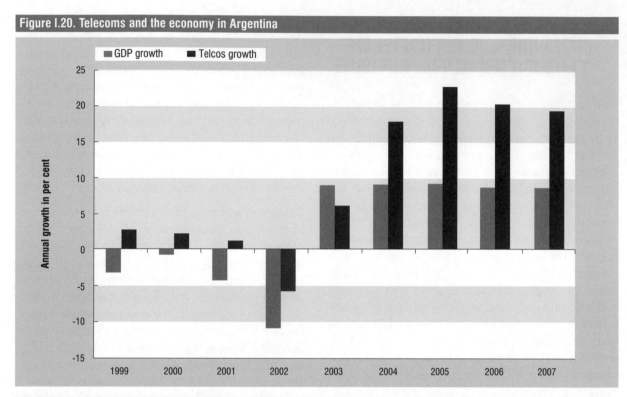

Variations of GDP and Telecom Industry, in Constant Prices of 1993 (1993-2007)

Economy's status	GDP	Telecom Sector	Elasticity	
	Annual Change - Average		(Telcos/GDP) - Average	
Expansion '94, '96, '97, '98, '03, '04, '05, '06, '07	7.5%	18.6%	2.5	Elastic
Crisis '95, '99, '00, '01	-2.9%	3.3%	-1.2	Inverse
Extreme Crisis '02	-10.9%	-5.9%	0.5	Inelastic

Source: Telecom Argentina.

cubscribers stood at 392 million at the end of March 2009 compared to 233.6 million in January 2008 and 149.6 million in January 2007.[74] In Nigeria, more GSM mobile subscribers were added in the fourth quarter of 2008 (5.2 million) than in the third quarter (2.1 million).[75] Brazil's market slowed somewhat with 3.6 million new subscribers added in December 2008 compared to 4.7 million in December 2007.[76]

The crisis could affect those with mobile phones in developing countries if people lose their jobs or see their incomes reduced. At the same time, once somebody gets a mobile phone, it is difficult to give it up.

Other communications services may be dropped before mobile in the midst of economic crisis. A recent survey found that most users in Latin America would give up fixed telephones, Internet and subscription telephone services before surrendering the mobile subscription, which is now regarded more as a necessity than a luxury.[77] Mobiles have essentially replaced fixed lines for voice communications in many developing nations. They are also increasingly used for other purposes – such as by small entrepreneurs – making them even more desirable (chapter II). The demand for mobile telephony in many developing countries is thus likely to continue to grow despite the crisis, as mobile networks are still in early stages of development (ITU, 2009b). As noted by one observer:

Pakistan is experiencing significant macroeconomic problems, yet the mobile market steams ahead. ... Many African countries have experienced strong mobile growth despite economic problems. For India, I do not see any noticeable slowdown in subscriber growth until 2012. The marginal subscriber in India today is going to be a pre-paid user and not overly concerned about a credit crunch or an economic slowdown [78]

To what extent will the crisis negatively affect the availability of capital for investments in telecommunications networks? Ericsson (Sweden), the world's largest supplier of telecom equipment in April 2009 remained relatively optimistic about the resilience of the wireless telecom market:[79]

The effects of the global economic recession on the global mobile network market are so far limited. We have seen operators, in a few markets where local currencies have depreciated dramatically, postpone investments. Some operators are also more cautious with longer-term investments in fixed networks, such as roll-out of fibre networks. Most operators, however, have healthy financial positions, there is a strong traffic growth and the networks are fairly loaded. It remains difficult to more precisely predict how operators will act in the current environment. However, investments in wireless networks largely continue, and roll-outs of new networks and new technologies accelerate in markets such as the US, China and India. Telecom plays a critical role for growth and development of societies, and fixed and mobile broadband roll-outs are now on political agendas in most countries.

It is likely that manufacturers and strategic investors will continue to invest in markets with strong potential. Where profit opportunities exist, the necessary financing can usually be found. Given the still large untapped demand, manufacturers may ease financing terms and global economic institutions may work to ensure a healthy flow of funds to developing countries. Growth is high and profit is strong so it would be illogical to siphon off investment.

There appears to be continued interest among investors based in both developed and developing countries in expanding and upgrading ICT networks in developing country markets, despite the crisis. With weaker demand prospects in developed countries, telecom investors based in the North may give more attention to projects in developing countries, including LDCs, as they offer interesting growth prospects.

The mobile investor Vodafone (United Kingdom) recently consolidated its African holdings by increasing its ownership in pan-African operator Vodacom. France Telecom has forecast higher growth in Africa and the Middle East than in other developing regions, partly due to their better resistance to the economic downturn.[80] In October 2008, it purchased a mobile operator in Uganda, increasing its presence in the region to over a dozen operations.[81] Citing the growth potential of emerging markets, TeliaSonera (Sweden) purchased stakes in telecom operators in Cambodia and Nepal in September 2008, the first LDCs to be added to the company's investment portfolio.[82]

South–South investment, already a major source of funding for developing country mobile networks, is also likely to continue despite the crisis. Large investors from developing countries announced that their fundamentals are strong, that demand remains robust and that they do not envision much negative impact from the crisis in their operating regions. For example, in early 2009 Sudan's incumbent telecommunication operator, Sudatel, which has embarked on an ambitious investment programme in Africa, expected the impact of the crisis to be minimal in the low-income countries in which it operates.[83] Mobile Telecommunications Company (with the Zain brand), MTN Group and Orascom, which are among the top foreign investors in African telecommunications, may be in a position to further strengthen their positions in the wireless market. Zain (Kuwait) recently raised $4.5 billion from its owners and is well placed to invest in smaller companies that are struggling as credit becomes tight. When releasing the company's annual results for 2008 in March 2009, the Chief Executive Officer made the following upbeat comment: "Zain views this crisis as an opportunity to make further acquisitions given valuations of many prime telecom assets are considerably lower than they were just six months ago and we are actively pursuing such prospects."[84]

Some local companies in developing countries could profit from the hesitancy of foreign investors. Those with strong balance sheets and cash may see opportunities for domestic telecommunications investments that they might otherwise have been shut out of by larger outside investors.

There is of course a risk that project financing and aid could become less accessible as global liquidity is "sucked away" when banks in developed nations are bolstered by huge government infusions of funds. Multilateral institutions such as the World Bank have announced initiatives to counteract this by, for example, encouraging countries to pledge a proportion of their stimulus funds to international assistance.[85] Bilateral assistance may also help: ZTE, the Chinese ICT equipment vendor, announced in March 2009 that the China Development Bank had pledged a credit line of $15 billion to help ZTE with overseas project financing.[86]

The crisis is likely to affect various segments of the ICT market in different ways. In terms of infrastructure, mobile telephony may be best equipped to weather the storm considering its high growth and established players operating the service in most countries. The visible trend towards fixed–mobile substitution is therefore likely to be further accentuated by the crisis (ITU, 2009b). Other parts of the industry may be more negatively affected. This includes large-scale infrastructure investments such as broadband and investments in newer technologies such as WiMAX.[87] Global sales of WiMAX equipment had already fallen in the third quarter of 2008 (ibid.). In those cases where financing has already been obtained in advance for projects with a lengthy implementation, the impact may be felt more strongly in future years as projects that should have been planned now for implementation later are

postponed. Although some ICT infrastructure projects could be cancelled, it is more likely they will be scaled down. More infrastructure sharing is another likely effect of the crisis as it can help reduce the cost of network roll-out (ibid.).

The picture will, however, vary greatly by country and company, as illustrated by the case of Egypt (box I.11). Telecom operators that are well endowed with cash may find interesting opportunities as a result of the crisis. Conversely, those that are riddled by high debt–equity ratios are in a more vulnerable situation. According to some analysts, most major operators have a relatively low refinancing risk, while many smaller players are more exposed due to high leverage (ibid.). Moreover, network upgrades scheduled for the next few years may be postponed due to a lack of credit. For example (ibid.):

(a) Thailand's largest provincial fixed line telecom operator, TT&T, has suspended a $1.5 billion investment plan due to the crisis;

(b) Vodafone has cut its capital expenditure plans by £200 million for 2009;

(c) Sprint, in the United States, reduced its capital

Box I.11. The international crisis and ICT in Egypt

Although it is still too early to assess the full impact of the global economic crisis on ICT developments in Egypt, a preliminary assessment suggests a mixed picture. On the one hand, many of the transnational corporations (TNCs) already present in the country see Egypt as a promising, emerging and relatively stable market in the crisis. ICT companies such as Microsoft, HP, Vodafone and Intel have all indicated expansion plans for Egypt as a potential market and a regional office for the Middle East in addition to other potential markets like South Africa and Turkey. Various European companies, such as Valeo, the French automotive components supplier, are further exploring Egypt as an option for the offshoring of services, to reduce production costs.

On the other hand, the economic crisis has led the government to postpone the auction for a second fixed line phone license for a year, in response to the changes taking place in international markets. Some TNCs operating in Egypt have also announced plans to manage the crisis by revaluating the expenditures and prioritizing them to serve more productive activities. These plans include cost reductions by adopting a conservative marketing strategy and freezing of non-revenue-generating employment, in addition to limiting non-essential travelling and telecommunication costs.

The Egyptian Ministry of Communications and Information Technology (MCIT) has adopted various policies and strategies to confront the crisis. It promotes ICT usage in different economic and social sectors through tailored initiatives and programmes; provides targeted support to software companies; and encourages banks and other financial institutions to offer credit facilities to local companies investing in the ICT area. MCIT is also advocating a higher degree of outsourcing by ministries and other government entities. It is actively promoting inward foreign investment into Egypt due to its comparative advantages compared to other markets, as way to promote ICT exports. It is expected that these efforts will help boost the domestic demand for ICTs, create new jobs in the sector and help ICT companies to better manage the crisis.

Source: UNCTAD, based on company interviews and information from MCIT.

spending on wireless infrastructure to $217 million in the third quarter of 2008, down from $813 million a year earlier.

Beyond infrastructure, the production of various ICT goods and services has been seriously affected by the economic crisis (see e.g. OECD, 2009a; ITU, 2009b). Market analysts have revised their growth expectations downwards as more information about the depth of the economic recession has become available. In early April 2009, Forrester Research lowered its forecast for IT spending by United States businesses and Government, suggesting that it would fall by 3.1 per cent in 2009 from last year, down from an earlier forecast of a 1.6 per cent increase in spending.[88] According to the IDC forecast in February 2009, worldwide IT spending will grow by just 0.5 per cent in 2009 in constant currency, down from a November 2008 forecast of 2.6 per cent growth.[89] The greatest impact was expected to be seen for hardware producers, with a decline in overall spending by 3.6 per cent in 2009, with particularly sharp falls in outlays for servers, PCs and printers. The volatile semiconductor industry has been among the worst hit; utilization rates for semiconductor facilities dropped from 87 per cent in the third quarter of 2008 to below 70 per cent in the fourth quarter (OECD, 2009a). Revenue growth turned sharply downwards into negative territory in the case of the largest makers of IT equipment such as computers and consumer electronic devices, and the same applied to top manufacturers of communication equipment (ibid.). By contrast, producers of IT- and ICT-enabled services appear to have been more resilient to the crisis (ibid.; see also chapter III). Worldwide spending on software and IT services was still expected to grow 3.4 per cent in 2009.[90]

Amidst these turbulent times, a priority in the ICT area for many developing countries will be to build on the gains already made in the most accessible of ICTs, mobile telephony. Governments can help by enhancing competition, minimizing taxes and other fees on operators and speeding up the allocation of wireless spectrum. Another approach could be to encourage infrastructure sharing, for example through the issuing of licenses for providers of turnkey mobile masts that can be shared by multiple operators (ITU, 2009b). Thirdly, governments could place increased emphasis on universal service obligations to secure continued roll-out in rural areas. Mobile telephony has proven that it can be a profitable business with benefits for both consumers and business.

NOTES

[1] See the Geneva Plan of Action, para. 6j, available at http://www.itu.int/wsis/docs/geneva/official/poa.html.

[2] VoB refers to subscription-based telephone services – where the subscriber has a telephone number – and not computer–computer or computer–telephone services.

[3] Data from l'Autorité de régulation des communications électroniques et des postes (ARCEP).

[4] Most WLL networks are based on CDMA2000 at 450 MHz or 850 MHz. WLL services can give a subscriber both toll-quality voice and data capabilities at the same time (see Qualcomm, 2004).

[5] The GSM-UMTS family dominates with 87 per cent of all active digital mobile subscriptions worldwide, followed by CDMA (12 per cent) and others (see http://www.wcisdata.com/newt/l/wcis/research/subscriptions_by_technology.html.)

[6] MTN Group Limited (2009).

[7] America Móvil (2008).

[8] Population coverage refers to the percentage of inhabitants that live within range of a mobile signal and not to the number of subscriptions per 100 inhabitants (ITU, 2008a).

[9] The use of solar powered handsets has lowered the barrier to mobile in rural areas with no electricity. See http://www.monitor.co.ug/artman/publish/sun_business/Sun-powered_cell_phone_here_Tatum_Anderson_81529.shtml.

[10] See e.g. http://www.unctad.org/en/docs/a63d72_en.pdf.

[11] In Uganda, any licensed operator is allowed to bid for projects funded by the universal service fund through a competitive process. See "Rural Communications" at: http://www.ucc.co.ug/rcdf/default.php.

[12] "The 1800 MHz frequency spectrum band obligations require Vodacom to provide a minimum of 2,500,000 SIM card packages with certain privileges to designated individuals within five years." Vodacom (2007).

[13] Data used are from the ITU, supplemented by statistics from national regulatory authorities, statistical offices and telecommunications operators.

[14] One reason for the high penetration – apart from the introduction of a third mobile operator in 2007 – is a large ratio of pre-paid, particularly impacted by the large number of tourists the country receives. See Agency for Telecommunications and Postal Services (2008).

[15] Another factor is that almost all of these countries have declining populations, which artificially inflates penetration each year.

[16] See http://www.authorstream.com/Presentation/Goldye-9398-w14-minges-Markets-Monopoly-Mobile-Morals-Small-Island-Developing-States-Case-Studies-ppt-powerpoint/.

[17] In the East Caribbean region, mobile penetration had reached 98 by March 2007 with competition in that market characterized as remaining "intense, as the providers remained focused on marketing strategies to expand their market shares and profitability in the market". See Eastern Caribbean Telecommunications Authority (2007).

[18] International definitions vary regarding the access speed for a transmission service to be considered broadband. The ITU has defined broadband as a connection providing at least 256 kbit/s in both directions, the Organization for Economic Cooperation and Development (OECD) defines broadband as a connection of at least 256 kbit/s in one direction and the EU defines it as a capacity of at least 144 kbit/s. UNCTAD follows the ITU definition of broadband.

[19] See http://www.pta.gov.pk/index.php?option=com_content&task=view&id=361&Itemid=590.

[20] See http://hspa.gsmworld.com/upload/papers/documents/29012009123139.pdf.

[21] Internet use on portable handsets requires specially configured browsers for small screens.

[22] There has been a noticeable surge in data traffic as result of the iPhone and its ease of accessing the Internet. See New York Times (2008).

[23] The latter started as a cable television provider that later upgraded its network using hybrid coaxial fibre technology. It also interconnected islands in the Bahamas with fibre optic cable and completed an undersea high speed link to the United States.

[24] A study on competition in the European broadband market found that "competition is positively correlated with penetration as countries with more competitive markets tend to have a higher broadband penetration as well as a faster growth". The study also found that "intermodal competition (mainly between DSL and cable networks) is a result of intramodal competition". See European Regulators Group (2005).

[25] See OPTA (2005).

[26] The Government of Australia has established a Department of Broadband, Communications and the Digital Economy. Projects and policies include guaranteeing that the price of broadband service in rural areas will be no higher than what is charged in urban areas and building a national broadband network providing bandwidth of at least 12 Mbps to 98 per cent of homes and businesses. See http://www.dbcde.gov.au/. In New Zealand, the government has announced the goal of rolling out ultra fast broadband to 75 per cent of New Zealanders. See http://www.med.govt.nz/templates/StandardSummary____38669.aspx.

[27] Their rankings in broadband penetration in the world in 2008 were twelfth and nineteenth respectively.

[28] See, for example, ITU (2009a), OECD (2001) and Orbicom (2002).

[29] This methodology has been applied in earlier UNCTAD publications (UNCTAD, 2005 and 2006a; ITU and UNCTAD, 2007).

[30] For a list of SIDS, see http://www.unctad.org/Templates/Page.asp?intItemID=3645&lang=1.

[31] For a list of LDCs, see http://www.unctad.org/Templates/Page.asp?intItemID=3641&lang=1.

32   For a list of LLDCs, see http://www.unctad.org/Templates/Page.asp?intItemID=3632&lang=1.

33   For a list of HIPCs, see http://www.imf.org/external/np/exr/facts/hipc.htm.

34   Cuba accounts for around one third of the SIDS population. In contrast to most other SIDS, it has not liberalized its mobile market and mobile penetration remains very low.

35   Numerous surveys on ICT confirm this. In Malaysia, 85 per cent of household Internet users were under the age of 45 and 85 per cent of households with Internet access were in urban areas (2008); in Mexico, 90 per cent of Internet users were under the age of 45. See Malaysia Communications and Multimedia Commission (2008). and INEGI (2007). For an example about the barriers facing Internet users unable to use the web in their native language see "Sociolingo's Africa – Uganda: language and the internet". http://sociolingo.wordpress.com/2008/02/18/uganda-language-and-the-internet/.

36   The concept of broadband in developed countries usually includes connections speeds higher than 256 kbps. For example, as of 2008 the United States Federal Communications Commission defined broadband as connections above 768 kbps. Moreover, the average advertised download speed for all OECD countries was 17.4 Mbps in September 2008 (http://www.oecd.org/sti/ict/broadband).

37   See World Bank: Case studies – empowerment through information. http://go.worldbank.org/N2XUIZGY40.

38   Chile's Digital Agenda calls for a doubling of broadband connections between 2007–2012 with broadband deployment in rural areas funded by the Universal Access and Service Fund. See http://www.estrategiadigital.gob.cl/node/122.

39   India announced its broadband policy in 2004 to accelerate the growth of broadband services. Government of India: Broadband Policy. http://www.dot.gov.in/broadbandpolicy2004.htm.

40   See http://www.gsmworld.com/newsroom/press-releases/2009/2437.htm .

41   Anatel press release: Última área licitada registra ágio médio de 36,41%. 20 December 2007. http://www.anatel.gov.br/Portal/exibirPortalNoticias.do?acao=carregaNoticia&codigo=15193.

42   Many European countries have adopted policies to stimulate intramodal competition especially by obligating incumbent fixed line operators to provide wholesale access to their copper telephone lines (e.g. local loop unbundling). This has proven successful in some countries with early entrants first buying wholesale access and then after building up a customer base, investing in their own broadband infrastructure. Most developed countries have a high level of intermodal competition between ADSL and cable modem.

43   For example, telecommunication operators may not be allowed to provide television services, thus reducing the incentive to invest in broadband technology. Conversely, broadcasting firms may face restrictions on the provision of telephone or Internet access services.

44   For more on infrastructure sharing see ITU (2008c).

45   Information provided by the ITU, May 2009. See also the recently launched universal access and service module of the ITU, the infoDev ICT Regulation Toolkit (www.ictregulationtoolkit.org). The toolkit was developed to assist regulators in the design of effective and enabling regulatory frameworks by sharing analysis and information on key regulatory issues as well as best practices. The new module provides practical, relevant guidance and assistance in spreading access to ICTs and to broadband in particular.

46   See http://www.ucc.co.ug/rcdf/default.php .

47   During apartheid, not many townships had fixed line service and where they did exist, a lack of demand meant that existing exchanges have not been upgraded to support ADSL.

48   See GSM Association: Mobile broadband connects the unconnected; GSM Association Case Study Series. http://www.3gamericas.org/documents/cs_hspa_mtn.pdf .

49   See, for example, Microsoft: Egypt's PC for Every Home initiative provides skills, resources, and jobs never before available. http://download.microsoft.com/download/6/9/f/69f8c76b-198e-4114-9c12-f0b13e4d7e4e/UP_Egypt_narrative_v10_Ferm.pdf.

50   For an overview of the role of ICTs in the poverty strategies of different countries, see OECD (2003).

51   In terms of local fixed broadband access, ADSL delivered over telephone lines accounts for about 66 per cent of all connections. The next most popular is cable modem with some 20 per cent and then fibre with 12 per cent (Point Topic, 2009). Ethernet-based cable and power lines have also been used for broadband but their share of the global total is small.

52   There can be a significant gap between the number of actual and possible broadband lines based on fixed infrastructure. In India it is estimated that only around 20 per cent of telephone lines and 10 per cent of cable television connections are capable of supporting broadband. See Sinha S: What end-users desire from NGN? Next generation access. http://trai.gov.in/NGN/enduser.pdf.

53   Indicative speeds for DSL range from 0.246 to 24 Mbps, for cable modem from 1 to 150 Mbps and for fibre from 50 Mbps to 2.5 Gbps.

54   Although WiMAX has been primarily thought of as a fixed wireless technology, it also provides mobile service and has been adopted as an ITU IMT-2000 technology.

55   WiMAX Forum press release: WiMAX Forum® projects over 800 million people to have access to next generation WiMAX networks by 2010. 11 February 2009. http://www.wimaxforum.org/node/644.

56   Maravedis press release: Worldwide BWA/WiMAX subscriber base closing in on 2 million. 7 July 2008. http://www.maravedis-bwa.com/PressRelease-WiMAXCounts-QR.html.

57   Data from GSM Association.

58   Compiled from CDMA Development Group and UMTS Forum data.

[59]   In Europe, fixed 3G access accounts for between 1 per cent of all broadband subscribers in mature broadband markets (such as Belgium) to 17 per cent in new EU members (such as Slovakia) (European Commission, 2008).

[60]   In 2004, South Africa became the second country in Africa to launch WCDMA. Two of its mobile operators, Vodacom and MTN, introduced high speed HSDPA networks in 2006.

[61]   Reasons for delays in spectrum allocation may include a perceived lack of demand, that the spectrum is used for other purposes and uncertainty about what allocation method to adopt.

[62]   For example, Movistar in Argentina launched an HSDPA network in the 900 MHz band in mid-2007. It offers a flat rate 2 Mbps package with the service, some 4–5 times faster than EDGE. The network has been rolled out to around 150 localities. See Business News America (2009).

[63]   There are a number of initiatives to expand satellite's broadband capabilities and coverage. For example O3b Networks is building a satellite network encircling the world and that promises to offer low cost, fibre-like services. See http://www.o3bnetworks.com/advantage.html.

[64]   See Business Daily Africa: Fibre optic cables to cut EA Internet costs. http://bdafrica.com/index.php?option=com_content&task=view&id=801&Itemid=3388.

[65]   For example, the Pakistan Telecommunication Authority determined that the incumbent had significant market power in the international leased line market and ordered tariffs reduced by half. Pakistan Telecommunication Authority: Determination on PTCL bandwidth tariffs. http://www.pta.gov.pk/index.php?option=com_content&task=view&id=550&Itemid=569.

[66]   See http://www.apc.org/en/pubs/research/openaccess/africa/case-open-access-communications-infrastructure-afr.

[67]   The countries concerned are Botswana, Burundi, Central African Republic, Chad, the Democratic Republic of the Congo, Ethiopia, Lesotho, Malawi, Rwanda, Swaziland, Uganda, Zambia and Zimbabwe.

[68]   See International Finance Corporation (2008). Press release: IFC-financed East African EASSy cable project begins construction, helping provide broadband access for millions of Africans. 27 March. http://www.ifc.org/ifcext/pressroom/ifcpressroom.nsf/PressRelease?openform&8FBE3E547634C49785257419005052E1 .

[69]   See BBC News: Kenya awards internet cable deal. 12 October 2007. http://news.bbc.co.uk/2/hi/africa/7041103.stm.

[70]   See http://www.seacom.mu/intro.html.

[71]   See Total Telecom: Orange partners with ACE on African fibre link. 12 December 2008. http://www.totaltele.com/view.aspx?ID=433782.

[72]   See PT Telkom press release: Report of TELKOM share buyback crisis program. 13 January 2009. http://www.telkom.co.id/download/File/UHI/Release/sharebuybackengl.pdf .

[73]   See http://www.chinamobileltd.com/ir.php?menu=11&year=2008.

[74]   See http://www.trai.gov.in/WriteReadData/trai/upload/PressReleases/649/pr20feb09no16.pdf; http://www.trai.gov.in/WriteReadData/trai/upload/PressReleases/631/pr29dec08no110.pdf.; and http://www.trai.gov.in/WriteReadData/trai/upload/PressReleases/671/pr21apr09no38.pdf.

[75]   See http://www.ncc.gov.ng/subscriberdata.htm.

[76]   See Anatel: Dados de acessos móveis em operação e densidade, por unidade da federação, do serviço móvel pessoal. http://www.anatel.gov.br/Portal/verificaDocumentos/documento.asp?numeroPublicacao=220102&assuntoPublicacao=Dados%20de%20Acessos%20M%F3veis%20do%20SMP%20&caminhoRel=Cidadao-Telefonia%20M%F3vel-Dados%20do%20SMP&filtro=1&documentoPath=220102.pdf.

[77]   Frost and Sullivan: Social impact of mobile telephony in Latin America. http://www.gsmlaa.org/files/content/0/94/Social%20Impact%20of%20Mobile%20Telephony%20in%20Latin%20America.pdf.

[78]   Good Read: Business – Q&A; Tony Worthington, global head (telecoms, media and technology) at Standard Chartered Bank. http://spoonfeedin.blogspot.com/2008/11/business-q-worthington-global-head.html.

[79]   See Ericsson press release: Ericsson reports first quarter results. 30 April 2009. http://www.ericsson.com/ericsson/press/releases/20090430-1310016.shtml.

[80]   See France Telecom: Continental Europe, Africa, Middle East. Presented at the Investors Days. 5 March 2009. http://www.francetelecom.com/en_EN/finance/invest-analysts/invest-days/index.html.

[81]   See France Telecom press release: Orange to launch telecommunication services in Uganda. 20 October 2008. http://www.orange.com/en_EN/press/press releases/cp081020uk.html.

[82]   See TeliaSonera press release: TeliaSonera enters new high-growth emerging markets. 26 September 2008. http://www.teliasonera.com/press/pressreleases/item.page?prs.itemId=381770 .

[83]   "The countries we are in are not strongly tied to the international system so the effect (on our customers) is indirect." See Balancing Act no. 441: Minimum CAPEX, Maximum OPEX – Expresso's strategy for African expansion. http://www.balancingact-africa.com/news/back/balancing-act_441.html.

[84]   See http://www.zain.com/muse/obj/lang.default/portal.view/content/Investor%20relations/Press%20releases/Zain2008results.

[85]   See the World Bank: Financial crisis. http://www.worldbank.org/html/extdr/financialcrisis/.

[86]   See ZTE Corporation press release: China Development Bank provides ZTE $15 billion credit line. 23 March 2009. http://wwwen.zte.com.cn/main/News%20Events/Whats%20New/2009032364158.shtml.

[87]   See http://www.digitalcommunitiesblogs.com/international_beat/2009/02/global-economic-downturn-takes.php.

[88]   See Intelligent Enterprise (2009).

[89]   See Business Wire (2009).

[90]   See Business Wire (2009).

CHAPTER II

MAKING USE OF ICTs IN THE BUSINESS SECTOR

The extent to which improvements in ICT infrastructure and access translate into economic growth and development is greatly affected by the way such technologies are used in the productive sector. Indeed, only when ICTs are effectively applied can there be a significant positive effect on corporate turnover and productivity.[1] Thus, it is no surprise that countries are increasingly interested in measuring how ICTs are used as well as the related impacts. The need for such information has been accentuated by the economic crisis, as it could help policymakers understand how ICTs may contribute to economic recovery.

In many countries, however, ICT impact assessments are constrained by a lack of reliable and useful data. This applies not least to the area of ICT use by enterprises. For policymakers to be able to design and implement appropriate policies, access to reliable information is essential. Furthermore, internationally comparable indicators are needed to allow for cross-country benchmarking, monitoring of the digital divide and identifying good policy practices. Developing such indicators is a particular challenge for developing countries, many of which are at a nascent stage in terms of measuring ICT.

This chapter presents key findings from the 2008 UNCTAD global survey of national statistical offices (NSOs) on ICT usage by businesses and on the ICT sector.[2] The analysis confirms the existence of huge gaps both between and within countries in the use of different ICTs. Before presenting the data, however, section A reviews some evidence on how ICT use affects business performance. It also underlines limitations in the availability and comparability of relevant data and discusses the need for capacity-building. Section B then turns to the survey results, illustrating the significant divides in ICT use between enterprises of different sizes, between rural and urban areas and across industries. The final section discusses what governments can do to facilitate greater use of ICT in the business sector, not least in view of the economic crisis.

A. MEASURING ICT USE AND BUSINESS PERFORMANCE

1. Most studies show positive impact of ICT use

a. Growing evidence

Policymakers are increasingly interested in moving beyond the measuring of ICT diffusion to assessments of the impact of ICTs and related policies.[3] Nevertheless, progress has so far been slow in this area. A recent OECD paper concluded that "statistical standards have mostly contributed to measuring readiness and intensity while their contribution to measuring ICT impact has been limited".[4] With a view to address this challenge, the Partnership on Measuring ICT for De-

velopment (box II.1), of which UNCTAD is a founding member, recently set up a task group dedicated to measuring impact. This section offers a brief review of recent evidence on the impact of ICT use.

Most empirical studies of the impact of ICTs have found a positive correlation between the use of ICTs and corporate performance. Recent analyses (Eurostat, 2008) suggest that the positive effects may become stronger over time, possibly reflecting the expanding diffusion of ICTs and "that there are substantial adjustment costs in implementing IT" (Indjikian and Siegel, 2005: 689). This would imply that significant improvements in productivity growth should be expected mainly in the long run.

Impacts of ICT use on business performance, measured by productivity, can be assessed at three levels of aggregation: national (macro), sectoral and firm-level. Reflecting greater availability of data on ICT,

Box II.1. The Partnership on Measuring ICT for Development

UNCTAD is a member of the Steering Committee of the international, multi-stakeholder Partnership on Measuring ICT for Development.[a] One of the key achievements of the partnership has been the development of a core list of ICT indicators for the production of internationally comparable statistics. UNCTAD is responsible for the indicators related to the use of ICT by businesses and to the ICT sector.[b] The collaboration between partner agencies ensures that there is no duplication of work and that resources are utilized efficiently.

The main objectives of the partnership are to: (a) facilitate agreement on internationally comparable ICT indicators and develop methodologies to collect these indicators; (b) assist in building statistical capacity in developing economies for the production of ICT statistics; and (c) set up a global database on ICT indicators.

In 2008, the partnership created a Task Group on Impacts. Led by the OECD, it will examine how ICT impacts can best be measured and what data are needed. The goal is to provide countries with a set of statistical and analytical tools to carry out their own assessment of ICT impact. The need to measure the social and economic impacts of ICTs was the focus of a partnership panel at the WSIS Forum 2009. It was noted that while infrastructure and access indicators are widely available, indicators on ICT use (e.g. by households, individuals and businesses) are less frequent, especially in developing countries, but are of great importance for measuring impact. Participants further stressed the need for more harmonization of methodologies and standards for ICT measurement in order to ensure international comparability. This requires close cooperation between the members of the partnership, NSOs and other stakeholders.

The United Nations Economic and Social Council has acknowledged the work of the partnership to develop indicators and noted the need for further benchmarks and indicators to measure progress made towards achieving the targets in the outcome documents of the WSIS (resolution E/2008/31).

Source: UNCTAD.

[a] *In 2009, partners are: ITU; OECD; UNCTAD; the United Nations Educational, Scientific and Cultural Organization (UNESCO) Institute for Statistics (UIS); United Nations regional commissions (the Economic Commission for Latin America (ECLAC), the United Nations Economic and Social Commission for Western Africa (UN-ESCWA), the United Nations Economic and Social Commission for Asia and the Pacific (ESCAP) and the Economic Commission for Africa (ECA)); the United Nations Department of Economic and Social Affairs (DESA); the World Bank and Eurostat. The Partnership Steering Committee is composed of the ITU, UNCTAD and ECLAC. For further information, see http://measuring-ict.unctad.org.*

[b] *The ITU is responsible for the core indicators on ICT infrastructure, ICT access and use by households and individuals; the UIS is responsible for those on ICT in education; and the regional commissions and other regional organizations are developing the core indicators on ICT in government.*

most statistical studies on the impact of ICTs refer to developed countries.[5] Even in these cases, however, data limitations often make it difficult to obtain direct measures of businesses' use of ICT. Instead, many studies have relied on various proxy variables, such as investments in ICT or ICT capital.

Macro-level research generally shows a positive link between ICT use and growth in indicators such as GDP (OECD, 2004a) and foreign direct investment (FDI) (Lydon and Williams, 2005; Lewin and Sweet, 2005).[6] Investment in telecommunications infrastructure has been found to have a "growth dividend" in developed countries (OECD, 2009a), but there is little information on its effect in developing countries. In the case of the impact of (mobile) telephony penetration in developing countries, different levels in penetration and diffusion appear to explain some of the differences in economic growth (Waverman et al., 2005).[7] ICTs measured by fixed line and mobile phone penetration in Latin America were found to have a robust impact on economic growth.[8] Sectoral analyses similarly tend to include ICT investment or ICT capital as proxies for actual use of ICTs (UNCTAD, 2007a). They distinguish between industries that are more or less ICT-intensive. Information-intensive industries in developed economies tend to experience larger productivity gains from ICTs, but the way ICTs influence company performance even in the same industry can vary considerably (Eurostat, 2008).

For more accurate assessments of the impact of ICT use, firm-level data are required. Such information is rarely reflected in official statistics, partly due to confidentiality concerns, partly – especially in developing countries – because enterprise surveys seldom include questions related to ICT indicators. In developed countries, many NSOs have begun to conduct firm-level analyses (see e.g. OECD, 2004a; Eurostat, 2008). In some developing countries, such analyses have been carried out by private companies using a variety of data sources.[9]

Available firm-level evidence – by both public and private sources – indicates that the use of ICTs by businesses has a positive effect on labour productivity. A research project that linked firm-level data from 13 European countries found that ICT use – of computers, electronic sales and purchases, and measured by employee access to high speed Internet – had consistent, positive effects on labour productivity in manufacturing (Eurostat, 2008). The effect on services industries was higher in countries characterized by more intense market competition and with a critical mass in networks and ICT use. In knowledge-based services, giving workers access to broadband Internet connections appears to improve business performance. The same European research project indicated that ICTs have similarly been seen to have a strong effect as enablers of better links between enterprises and external suppliers and customers.

Many of the findings from studies undertaken in developed countries may be of relevance also to developing and transition economies. For example, research on SMEs in 14 African countries found a significant positive effect of ICT usage on company turnover as well as on labour productivity. This applied to SMEs in both the formal and informal sectors (Esselaar et al., 2007; Stork, 2006). In selected countries in Latin America, contributions of ICT capital to GDP growth rates were found to be in the order of 10 to 24 per cent to the rate of growth in GDP for the 1990–2004 period (ECLAC, 2007). However, varying circumstances in developed and developing countries must be taken into account when assessing the impact of ICT use. The magnitude of the ICT impact in a country depends on complementary factors, such as capacities and skills for adopting and applying the technologies in the productive sectors, and the quality of the national innovation systems, which is often lower in developing countries (Peres and Hilbert, 2009). The extent to which individual companies gain from enhanced access to ICT depends furthermore on company size, industrial sector, workforce skills, availability of relevant content and whether suppliers and customers are frequent users of ICTs.

b. Impact of the use of different ICTs

Various technologies can have different economic impacts depending on the development level of a country. In the following, special attention is given to the use of computers, the Internet, broadband and mobile phones.

(i) Computer use

Few studies based on developed country data have examined the impact of computer presence on labour productivity. In high-income economies, computer penetration in the business sector has typically already reached levels as high as 95 per cent. However, in developing countries the share of firms that use at least one computer for business purposes remains relatively low, especially among smaller companies and in rural areas (section II.B). Without computers, firms are unable to make full use of ICT in their administrative, productive or marketing processes. This, in turn, will limit their ability to engage in e-commerce activities.

Increased use of computers by developing country firms may have a more important effect than in developed country firms. For example, a study of the manufacturing sector in Thailand (UNCTAD, 2008a), showed that companies using computers had on average 10 times higher sales per employee than those without computers. When looking at the relationship between the intensity of computer use and labour productivity, an increase of 10 per cent in the share of employees using computers was associated with 3.5 per cent higher sales per employee in Thai manufacturing firms. For the same variable, the estimated coefficient in a Finnish study was only 1.8 (Maliranta and Rouvinen, 2003). Networking of computers and linking them to the Internet can further enhance the positive effects on labour productivity.

(ii) Internet and broadband use

There is growing evidence of the link between Internet use and business performance. The Internet enables online sales and purchases, often carried out through a website or an extranet, that can also have an effect on productivity. In the Netherlands and the United Kingdom, an increase in electronic sales appears to contribute significantly to labour productivity (Eurostat, 2008). In a number of European countries, fast-growing firms in manufacturing tend to engage more intensively in online sales and purchases. Thai manufacturing firms that use the Internet also reported higher labour productivity in the form of sales per employee. The positive impact was stronger for firms with a web presence (UNCTAD, 2008a).

Greater use of the Internet can also help to boost international and regional trade. One study noted that a 1 per cent increase in annual export growth in goods could be attributed to a reduction in the fixed costs of entry into foreign markets (Freund and Weinhold, 2004); the reduction in fixed costs was due to better market information made available through the Internet. An increase in the number of websites in a country in one year appeared to be related to export growth in the following year (a 10 per cent growth in web hosts led to a 0.2 per cent growth in exports).[10] Interestingly, despite the globalizing nature of the Internet, the im-

proved availability of market information through the Internet led mainly to more regional trade.[11]

Broadband is essential to enable enterprises to make full use of Internet-based services and applications (see chapter I). In the United States, for example, broadband users were 20 per cent more likely to make online purchases than narrowband users in 2004 (OECD, 2008a). In Sweden, where almost all companies have Internet access, the value added of Internet use was found to be dependent on the capacity of the companies' Internet connection (Statistics Sweden, 2008). Enterprises with a high speed connection were noted to make more use of the Internet, which in turn helped raise productivity.

As mentioned above, broadband connectivity appears to have a more positive effect on productivity in countries that already have a medium or high level of ICT use (measured by PC penetration). In 2008, broadband access was found to contribute 10 to 20 per cent of productivity growth in some OECD member countries (LECG, 2009). The magnitude of the positive relationship between broadband and productivity varies between industries and companies of different sizes, and also depends on whether or not the company is a multinational. In the United States, broadband penetration was found to be significantly related to non-farm employment growth in 2004–2005 (especially in finance and insurance, real estate and educational services), but not to GDP growth (Crandall et al., 2007).[12]

No empirical studies linking broadband subscriptions or general broadband use to productivity growth in developing countries were encountered while preparing this report. Even in developed countries, studies have focused on whether enterprises have broadband (or high speed) Internet access and the number of employees with such access, rather than on the actual use of such connections. The ability to dig further into the impact of actual broadband use on business performance is limited by difficulties to distinguish business from residential subscriptions in statistics.

(iii) Mobile phone use

Mobile phones have emerged as the most widespread ICT in the developing world (see chapter I). In most of the low- and lower-middle-income economies in Asia and the Pacific, mobile phones are used extensively for 2G applications, especially SMS, but also other data applications, such as m-commerce and m-banking (ITU, 2008b). In the near future, Internet-enabled phones may help deliver locally relevant information and services to entrepreneurs in developing countries, the way SMS and voice technology are already doing (Heeks, 2008).

Like other ICTs, mobile phones can affect the internal processes of a business (its value chain) and the way it relates to clients and suppliers (its value system) (Donner and Escobari, 2009). It has been suggested that mobile phones may generate similar effects on developing country economic growth as fixed line telephony did for developed countries in the second half of the twentieth century (Waverman et al., 2005). As mobile phones have presented a way to bridge the connectivity gap without expanding the networks of fixed lines, they are likely to have a greater impact on economic growth than in developed countries, where fixed lines were widely available when mobile phones were introduced.

Microenterprises and SMEs, many of which are in the informal sector in developing countries, appear to be the most affected by the adoption of mobile telephony (Donner and Escobari, 2009; Junqueira Botelho and da Silva Alves, 2007; Esselaar et al., 2007). In the United Republic of Tanzania, for example, one in four mobile subscribers used their phones for business purposes, which, among other things, helped reduce the need to travel (Vodafone, 2005). In the same study, a majority of microentrepreneurs in Egypt and South Africa indicated that mobile phones had contributed to increasing their profits, including by enhancing the flexibility of doing business (increased availability and possibility of placing/receiving remote orders). Microenterprises in the agriculture and fisheries sectors in Asia and Africa now use mobile phones to conduct sales and purchases and negotiate prices.

Mobiles have also become important for SMEs to manage customer relationships. In a study of SMEs in 11 African countries, 70 per cent used mobile phones for contacting customers and clients, while only 48 per cent used fixed lines (Esselar et al., 2007). The same study concluded that for many SMEs in Africa the mobile phone has overtaken computers as a tool for helping to run their business.

In India, too, the Warana Unwired project successfully replaced computers with mobile phones to make more efficient the exchange of information between sugar cane farmers in a cooperative and sugar processing plants (Veeraraghavan et al., 2009). Despite the wider

range of functionalities of computers, a needs assessment revealed that farmers were mainly interested in (and actually using) the specific function that allowed them to exchange information about the amounts of fertilizer and water needed, the validity of harvesting permits, harvest quantities and payment schedules. All of these could be transmitted more quickly and economically through SMS-enabled mobile phones.

Today, African countries are pioneering mobile banking and electronic transaction services. In Kenya, Safaricom's M-Pesa service allows previously "unbanked" microenterprises to transfer money (and make payments) via SMS through their mobile phones. As of May 2009, M-Pesa had 6.5 million subscribers and handled around $10 million in daily transactions.[13] Although it is unclear how many of these subscribers are microentrepreneurs, anecdotal evidence suggests that M-Pesa is widely used among these.[14] In India, Airtel's mChek offers similar services, and Nokia-owned Obopay is planning to do the same.[15] Mobile phones themselves can also be a source of income for small vendors in developing countries, such as through the sale of airtime or accessories, as in the Grameen Village Phones in Bangladesh.[16] At the same time, some characteristics of transactions among microenterprises may limit the gains from the use of mobile phones. For example, a study of the Nigerian cloth-weaving sector found that mobiles are unlikely to result in disintermediation, or in relocation of supply chains, since physical proximity is still required due to cultural issues of trust and knowledge transfer (Jagun et al., 2007).

2. More capacity-building needed to improve ICT data situation

To further the analysis of the impact of ICT on business performance in both developed and developing countries, there is a need for more and better firm-level data. The improved ability of countries to benchmark their levels of ICT use against each other would help them monitor the digital divide and identify measures to reduce it. Better data would also enable policymakers to identify obstacles to ICT adoption and implement relevant policy measures.

When they compile statistics related to the core indicators on ICT use by businesses (table II.I), UNCTAD recommends that countries include ICT questions in their enterprise surveys and in some cases in their

Table II.1. Core indicators on ICT use by businesses, 2008 revision

Code	Core indicator
B1	Proportion of businesses using computers
B2	Proportion of persons employed routinely usingcomputers
B3	Proportion of businesses using the Internet
B4	Proportion of persons employed routinely using a computer with access to the Internet
B5	Proportion of businesses with a web presence
B6	Proportion of businesses with an intranet
B7	Proportion of businesses receiving orders over the Internet
B8	Proportion of businesses placing orders over the Internet
B9	Proportion of businesses using the Internet by type of access (narrowband, broadband (fixed, mobile)) Response categories: • Narrowband • Fixed broadband • Mobile broadband
B10	Proportion of businesses with a local area network (LAN)
B11	Proportion of businesses with an extranet
B12	Proportion of businesses using the Internet by type of activity Response categories: • Sending or receiving e-mail • Telephoning over the Internet/VoIP or using video conferencing • Use of instant messaging, bulletin boards • Getting information about goods or services • Getting information from general government organizations • Interacting with general government organizations • Internet banking • Accessing other financial services • Providing customer services • Delivering products online • Internal or external recruitment • Staff training

Source: Partnership on Measuring ICT for Development (2009).

Figure II.1. Countries reporting data on "the proportion of businesses using the Internet", by region (per cent)

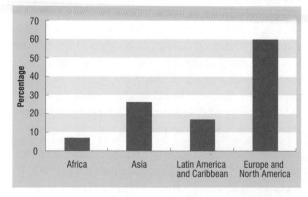

Source: Partnership on Measuring ICT for Development (2008).

economic censuses.[17] The collection of ICT data can also be carried out through stand-alone ICT surveys. All such efforts require the allocation of resources and the development of statistical infrastructure that is often insufficiently developed in developing countries. While most developed countries incorporate ICT statistics in their ongoing statistical programmes, the same is not true of developing economies, many of which run surveys on, at best, an ad hoc basis. From a geographical point of view, Europe is the only region that is well represented in business ICT use statistics. The availability of data is particularly weak in Africa, as is illustrated in figure II.1.

Patchy data from developing countries affects international comparability. Population frames and approaches to sampling often differ from one country to another. In some cases, reflecting different policy priorities, ICT surveys are confined to a particular sector rather than covering the whole economy. There may also be deficiencies in the availability of other business data that could support the analysis of ICT impact; for example, a lack of adequate business registers, information on employment by SMEs, their turnover, profitability, life span and economic activities (Esselar et al., 2007; UNCTAD, 2009a).

Nonetheless, there has been slow but steady progress in data availability and quality, with more countries reporting data on ICT use by businesses. In 2006, only three developing and transition economies were able to report fully comparable information. In 2008, in addition to data provided by Eurostat, the UNCTAD database comprised comparable information for 16 developing countries (but no LDC), eight countries with economies in transition and six non-European developed economies.[18] In addition, countries are increasing the number of ICT indicators collected through national surveys, as exemplified in table II.2. Despite progress made, more work is required to improve the data situation. For example, the core indicators on business use of ICT do not yet cover

Table II.2. Availability of core indicators on ICT use by businesses, selected countries, 2006 and 2008 (Number of indicators)

Country	2006 survey	2008 survey
Russian Federation	16	19
Singapore	16	19
Thailand	12	18

Source: UNCTAD Information Economy Database.

Box II.2. Mobile phone use by businesses

While the potential impact of mobile phones on business performance is gaining attention, the systematic collection of data has yet to begin. There are no core indicators related to the use of mobile phones in the business sector. Against this background, UNCTAD has proposed to add some indicators on mobile phone use by businesses to the partnership's core list (UNCTAD, 2009a), which could include the proportion of businesses: (a) using mobile phones; (b) receiving orders via mobile phones; (c) placing orders via mobile phones and (d) using mobile phones by type of activity (with response categories).

This would be followed by the development of model questions that NSOs could use to measure the way in which companies make use of mobile telephones.[a] Countries interested in collecting mobile phone indicators may also want to include questions on the use of fixed telephony, which would allow comparison between the two technologies.

Source: UNCTAD
[a] *Proposals on model questions for these indicators are contained in UNCTAD (2009a): 67.*

---

the area of mobile telephony, a technology that is of particular relevance for companies in developing countries (box II.2).[19]

UNCTAD recommends that countries adhere as much as possible to the definitions and methodological recommendations of the core indicators, in order to maximize international comparability, and that the core indicators are reflected when surveys are designed or redesigned. Countries should also try to make ICT surveys, or ICT modules in existing business surveys, part of their mainstream statistical programmes. There is a clear relationship between data availability and the requirement in the national statistical systems to conduct surveys (Partnership on Measuring ICT for

Development, 2008). UNCTAD can assist countries in this context (see box II.3).

In examining the availability of information on ICT use by businesses, there is generally more data from those developed and developing economies (particularly in Asia) that are relatively advanced in terms of ICT adoption by businesses. The gap related to ICT data availability can therefore be seen as yet another illustration of the digital divide. With due regard to the limitation on the availability and comparability of developing country ICT statistics mentioned above, the following section examines some of the information compiled annually by UNCTAD.

Box II.3. UNCTAD assistance in the area of measuring ICT

With the support of its development partners and in cooperation with the Partnership on Measuring ICT for Development, UNCTAD is helping developing and transition economies build capacities in the area of measuring ICT, namely ICT use by businesses and the ICT sector. In 2009, UNCTAD published a revised version of its *Manual on the Production of Information Economy Statistics,* which serves as a practical guide for NSOs. It takes a step-by-step approach and provides multiple country examples, best practices as well as model questionnaires to facilitate the planning, implementation and interpretation of relevant surveys. UNCTAD has also developed a special training course based on the *Manual*.

In addition, UNCTAD can provide advisory services to countries on their ICT data collection on demand. UNCTAD missions in individual countries in the Asia Pacific and North Africa have resulted, for example, in recommendations to improve coordination between data producers and users, strengthen the national statistical system to ensure the timely production of ICT data and align that system with international statistical standards.

UNCTAD has co-organized, with international and regional partners, regional workshops in Africa, Asia, Latin America and the Caribbean, that have brought together statisticians (data producers) and policymakers (data users), to ensure that ICT indicators are taken into account in the formulation of ICT for development policies, and that politicians understand the technical and resource needs to produce such information.

Data from developing countries on ICT use by business, on the ICT sector and on international trade in services are essential to review the impact of their ICT policies. In Africa, for example, 17 countries reported that they implement policies to promote e-business applications and 16 countries have policies that favour SMEs in the ICT sector (ECA, 2009), but there are practically no statistics to monitor and evaluate these policies. UNCTAD has been able to incorporate in its database information on ICT use by businesses and on the ICT sector from only two African countries: Egypt and Mauritius.

Further information on UNCTAD technical assistance on ICT measurement and the *Manual* are available at http://measuring-ict.unctad.org.

Source: UNCTAD.

B. WIDE GAPS PREVAIL IN ICT USE BETWEEN AND WITHIN COUNTRIES

There is great variation both between and within countries in the extent and nature of ICT use by businesses. Within countries, large enterprises consistently display higher levels of use than SMEs, and companies in urban areas mostly show greater use than those in rural areas. The degree of ICT use also varies considerably across industries. This section presents available survey data compiled by UNCTAD, Eurostat and the OECD on selected core indicators on ICT use by businesses (table II.1). A number of limitations to these data should be noted. First, while information is widely available for most developed economies, there are still considerable gaps among developing countries. Low-income countries are particularly poorly represented, which means that their situation is little studied.[20] Secondly, the ways in which countries collect and report data in this area need to be further harmonized. Consequently, international comparisons of the data should be interpreted with caution.

While there are insufficient data from developing and transition economies to make regional comparisons with developed economies, the latter generally tend to have higher levels of ICT use. There is a positive relationship between the income level of countries and ICT use by enterprises (figure II.2). However, the relationship shown in the figure is relatively weak, which partly reflects the absence of low-income countries in the UNCTAD Information Economy Database. It may also reflect that there are many other factors that determine the extent to which companies use technology, including the structure of the economy, the composition of the enterprise sector and the quality of infrastructure. The level of use reported by countries also depends on whether data refer to the economy as a whole (collected in rural as well as urban areas, and relating to a wide range of economic activities) or to a subset of the economy.

In Latin America, for example, while the use of computers by enterprises (with 10 or more employees) is relatively high, it is still far below European levels. Data from 2006 (or the latest available year) reveals a range of computer use between 50 and 80 per cent for selected countries (see annex table II.1). By compari-

Figure II.2. Computer use by enterprises and income level for selected countries, latest year (thousands of dollars and per cent)

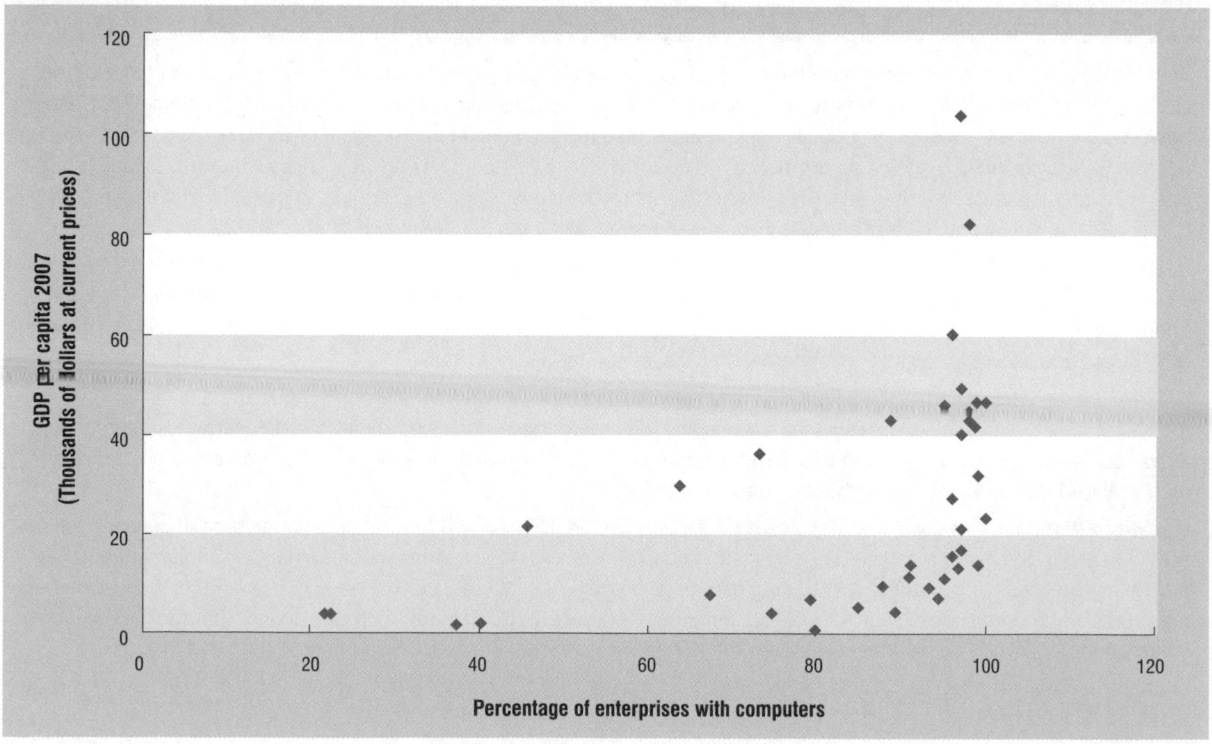

Source: UNCTAD Information Economy Database and IMF.

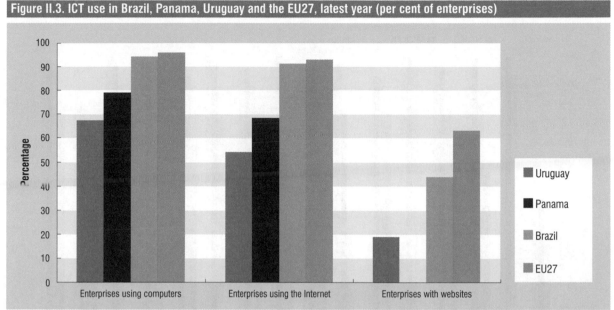

Figure II.3. ICT use in Brazil, Panama, Uruguay and the EU27, latest year (per cent of enterprises)

Source: UNCTAD Information Economy Database.

son, there was near universal (96 per cent) availability of computers in the European enterprises. While the use of computers for internal business operations has been evolving over many years in Europe, it started only recently in many Latin American countries. The digital gap between companies in developing and developed countries – as represented by Latin America and Europe – is even more significant when it comes to the use of the Internet or web presence (figure II.3). But as shown in the figure, there is considerable variation also within Latin America with regard to the use of the various ICTs. Companies in Brazil consistently show greater ICT use than their counterparts in Panama and Uruguay.

1. Large enterprises use more ICT

In both developed and developing countries, large enterprises generally use ICTs more than SMEs. This may be a result partly of their greater financial and human resources, and partly of their greater need for such technologies. This pattern is consistent for the use of computers and of the Internet as well as broadband.

Cross-country variation in computer use is depicted in figure II.4. Among the countries for which data are available, the largest gap exists between medium and large enterprises, on the one hand, and small and microenterprises, on the other.[21] In fact, with the exception of Azerbaijan, large enterprises in all the

economies included show usage levels of at least 96 per cent. However, variation across countries is much greater among smaller firms. In the case of microenterprises, the penetration ratio varies from 6 per cent in Egypt to 86 per cent in Cuba. For small enterprises the corresponding range was between 37 per cent in Azerbaijan and 96 per cent in Croatia.

With respect to Internet use, the picture is somewhat different. Even for the largest companies there is notable variation (figure II.5). For example, while virtually all large companies use the Internet in economies such as Brazil, Croatia, Hong Kong (China), the Republic of Korea, Singapore and Turkey, the corresponding level is much lower in Azerbaijan, Cuba and Kyrgyzstan. In the case of microenterprises, the gap is very wide – ranging from 2 per cent in Egypt to 62 per cent in Singapore and 75 per cent in developed countries on average. The situation in Cuba is conspicuous in that smaller enterprises report higher use of the Internet than large ones.

The extent to which companies have broadband access to the Internet shows still more variation (figure II.6). In this case, some developing and transition economies display higher levels of use than the average for developed countries. In the Republic of Korea,[22] a greater proportion of large, medium as well as small enterprises enjoy broadband access compared with the average for developed countries. For large companies, use levels were higher also in Croatia and

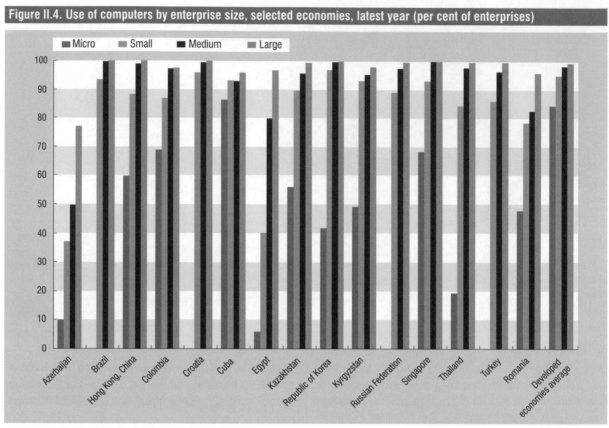

Figure II.4. Use of computers by enterprise size, selected economies, latest year (per cent of enterprises)

Source: UNCTAD Information Economy Database.

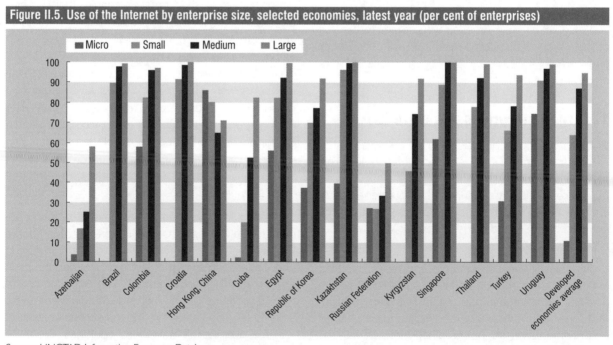

Figure II.5. Use of the Internet by enterprise size, selected economies, latest year (per cent of enterprises)

Source: UNCTAD Information Economy Database.

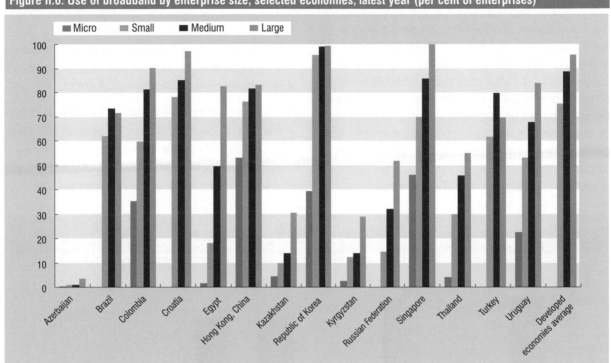

Figure II.6. Use of broadband by enterprise size, selected economies, latest year (per cent of enterprises)

■ Micro   ■ Small   ■ Medium   ■ Large

Source: UNCTAD Information Economy Database.

Singapore than the average for developed countries. By contrast, a very small proportion of companies in Azerbaijan, Kazakhstan and Kyrgyzstan benefit from high speed Internet access.

Consistently, microenterprises lag far behind. In the Republic of Korea, for example, 39 per cent of firms with less than four employees had broadband access in 2006, as did 96 per cent of firms with less than 10 employees. Even in developed countries, micro- and small enterprises show lower levels of use. In Finland, for example, the share of enterprises with 5–9 employees that had broadband access rose from 27 per cent in 2002 to 76 per cent in 2006. By comparison, that of enterprises with 100 or more employees increased from 00 per cent to 90 per cent. In addition, the digital divide in broadband access between enterprises in developed and developing countries is widened by price and actual speed (chapter I).

Low levels of ICT use by micro- and small enterprises in developing countries may partly reflect a lack of demand. In a survey of SMEs in 14 African countries, 45 per cent of enterprises responded that they had no need to own a computer (Esselar et al., 2007). The degree of formality of a business may also influence the likelihood of having an Internet connection, with

formal businesses tending to both have better access to the Internet and to use it more. It appears that the more formalized (and complex) a business operation, the more opportunities there are to use ICTs to support business processes.

2. ICT use is mostly higher in urban than in rural areas

The rural/urban divide is important from a development perspective. In developing countries, rural areas are typically less well connected. Where ICT infrastructure is available, "its use is often constrained due to inadequate supportive infrastructure, in particular electricity and, to a lesser extent, transport systems" (Africa Partnership Forum, 2008: 19). At the same time, especially in low-income economies, rural areas account for a large part of the business sector, in particular agricultural microenterprises and SMEs.[23] An improvement in the use of ICTs by businesses in rural areas can lead them to expand their markets and reduce costs, thereby increasing revenue and contributing to poverty alleviation. An inventory of projects aimed at using ICTs to optimize information flow to farmers in Africa showed how these can provide essential information to cut costs (FARA, 2009).

The digital divide between urban and rural areas in the use of ICT by businesses remains poorly documented. Few countries currently report data that allow for such a distinction to be made. There are at least two reasons for this. First, countries do not always have a clear definition of what constitutes urban and rural areas, but rather focus on collecting data disaggregated by areas based on population density or on political or administrative divisions (such as provinces). Secondly, some countries, because of a lack of resources to cover the whole national territory, or because of a perception that surveys on ICT use are not relevant to less developed (i.e. rural) areas of the country, simply do not collect data outside of urban centres. Only a handful of countries reports to UNCTAD on the different use of ICT by businesses in urban and rural areas. Among those that do, the pattern that emerges is not always straightforward (figures II.7 and II.8).

In the case of computers (figure II.7), the levels of use in Australia, Cuba, Kazakhstan, Kyrgyzstan and Mongolia are relatively similar in rural and urban areas. By contrast, rurally based enterprises in Azerbaijan and Egypt have much lower levels of computer use than

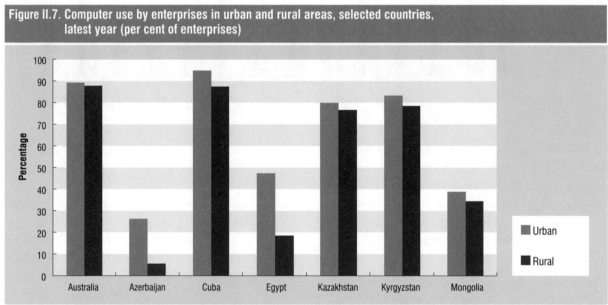

Figure II.7. Computer use by enterprises in urban and rural areas, selected countries, latest year (per cent of enterprises)

Source: UNCTAD Information Economy Database.

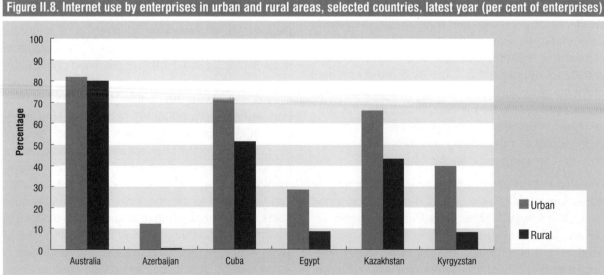

Figure II.8. Internet use by enterprises in urban and rural areas, selected countries, latest year (per cent of enterprises)

Source: UNCTAD Information Economy Database.

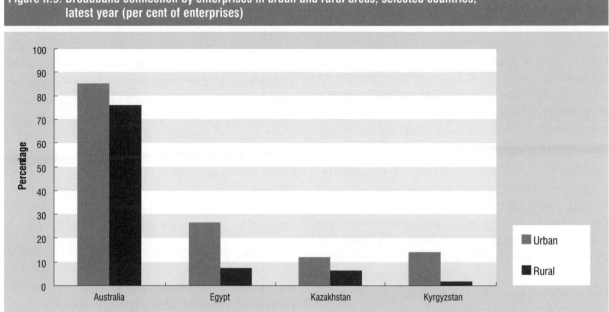

Figure II.9. Broadband connection by enterprises in urban and rural areas, selected countries, latest year (per cent of enterprises)

Source: UNCTAD Information Economy Database.

companies in urban regions. Turning to the Internet, among the countries included in figure II.8, only Australia displays similar use ratios for companies in urban and rural areas; in the remaining countries, rurally based companies consistently report lower levels of use. Even in developed countries such as the United States, a gap persists between urban and rural use of the Internet, but rural use has been rising: from 1997 to 2007, the proportion of farmers using the Internet for farm business went from 13 per cent to 55 per cent; also, in 2003 the volume of wholesale trade of farm products online had reached $3.7 billion, or 3 per cent of all wholesale farm product sales.[24]

Lower broadband penetration in rural areas (see figure II.9) may reflect less demand for the service (Crandall, 2008), higher prices than in urban areas or simply less access. In some developed countries (such as the United States) improved availability of rural broadband is reflected in growing use.[25] Policy measures can be taken to expand ICT access in rural areas – where the market is often not attractive enough for fully private initiatives due to issues of size and revenue – and to stimulate demand. However, such measures should respond to the actual needs of rural enterprises (see section C).

Based on the limited information available, the rural/urban divide appears to be more accentuated the more sophisticated the technology is. While the use of computers is relatively similar in many middle-income

economies, the gap is much wider in the areas of both Internet and broadband use. Data limitations make it difficult to draw any firm conclusions with regard to the use of ICTs in urban and rural areas of low-income countries, but it is likely that the divide is even more pronounced in those cases. This may constitute a particular challenge given that these are typically the economies with the greatest dependence on rurally based economic activities.

3. Sectoral differences in ICT use

The extent to which ICTs are used in the business sector varies also between industries. Spending on ICTs can be seen as an indicator of the aggregate levels of ICT use. At the end of 2007, global spending on ICTs stood at an estimated $3.4 trillion, of which $2.15 trillion was accounted for by the business sector (WITSA, 2008).[26] The single largest market segments in terms of ICT spending by the business sector were communications ($404 billion) and financial services ($334 billion). These were also the industries showing the highest ICT intensity, measured in terms of ICT spending over output. That ratio was 6.3 for communications and 2.3 for financial services. Meanwhile, the least ICT-intensive industry segments were manufacturing (0.41) and construction services (0.34) (WITSA, 2008). However, it is difficult to establish a direct relationship between ICT spending and ICT use due to the fragmentary data on the latter.

Most developed and several developing and transition economies have some information concerning the use of ICTs by companies in different industries. Currently, the UNCTAD Information Economy Database contains such data on at least one core indicator for about 60 economies. Nevertheless, the information is often not directly comparable. Countries do not always collect data on the same economic activities,[27] which means that averages by region or aggregate sector (i.e. primary, secondary, tertiary) can be misleading.

According to UNCTAD information for countries reporting relevant data, use of computers is on average the most widespread in real estate, renting and business activities, in which 91 per cent of enterprises use computers (see figure II.10).[28] This industry is followed by wholesale and retail trade (88), construction (87),[29] transport, storage and communications (86) and manufacturing (85). The same industries that lead in computer use are also the most frequent users of the Internet. Meanwhile, the lowest levels of computer and Internet use are observed for other community, social and personal service activities, where less than 75 per cent of enterprises used computers on average, and less than 70 per cent used the Internet.[30]

Obviously, overall averages mask huge differences between countries at different levels of development. For example, the degree of computer use by companies in the real estate industries ranged from 23 per cent in Azerbaijan to 100 per cent in Finland, although most economies included in the data set are at over 80 per cent. Similar variations can also be seen in the case of Internet use. To illustrate how much the sectoral pattern of ICTs can vary between countries at different levels of development, the Internet use situation is depicted below for three countries that report relevant data: Finland (figure II.11), Egypt (figure II.12) and Azerbaijan (figure II.13). It should be stressed that the industry coverage reported by each country differs significantly.

In Finland, Internet use is virtually ubiquitous across all industries included. Even in the one with the lowest penetration (transport), 94 per cent of all companies use the Internet. By contrast, in both Egypt and Azerbaijan, Internet use varies considerably across industries. For example, while 100 per cent of Egyptian companies in air transport were Internet users in 2008, the corresponding shares for community and social services, retail industries and post and telecommuni-

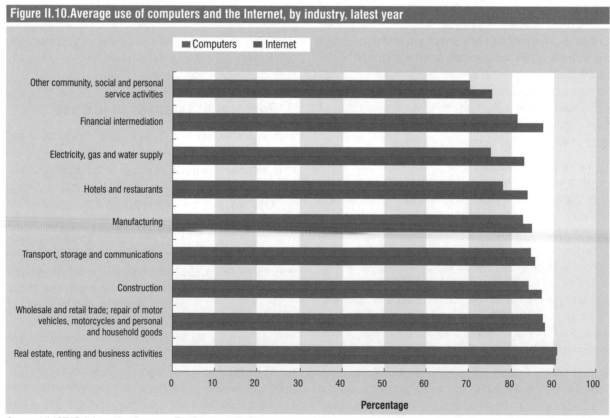

Figure II.10. Average use of computers and the Internet, by industry, latest year

Source: UNCTAD Information Economy Database.

cations were below 16 per cent. Meanwhile, in Azerbaijan Internet use is still relatively low overall; the top industries were financial mediation (47 per cent) and transportation and electricity supply (both 25 per cent). However, in construction, for example, only 8 per cent of enterprises made use of the Internet in 2006.

Such comparisons underline the importance of collecting firm-level data to understand how ICT is taken up in the business sector. Relying on aggregate data for the world as a whole can be very misleading. As most countries that report data on ICT use by businesses are high-income or upper middle-income economies, they strongly influence the aggregate picture. As illustrated above, the situation for countries at lower levels of income can be strikingly different. The analysis also illustrates that improved access to ICTs does not automatically translate into greater use across industries.

4. What do companies use the Internet for?

With regard to the Internet, it is relevant to study not only if companies use it, but also how it is utilized.[31] The

UNCTAD model questionnaire includes activities such as sending and receiving e-mails, using VoIP, Internet banking, providing customer services and delivering products online (see also table II.1). It is evident that the impact of Internet use on productivity, for example, can vary considerably depending on the way in which the Internet is used. For example, e-commerce is a type of Internet use that has seen strong growth in many countries, but for which there is still untapped potential.

Relatively few countries currently report data in this area (see annex table II.5). However, by highlighting the situation in a few economies, it is possible to shed some light on the wide gap between countries in terms of the nature of Internet use. In Finland, where broadband and Internet connectivity are among the highest in the world (see annex tables I.2 and I.3), more than nine out of 10 companies use the Internet for banking transactions and for interacting with public authorities (figure II.14). Other common areas of use include the monitoring of market developments and, to a lesser extent, receiving goods or services online. Various studies in developed countries have shown a wide range of business functions that can be supported by the use of the Internet (box II.4).

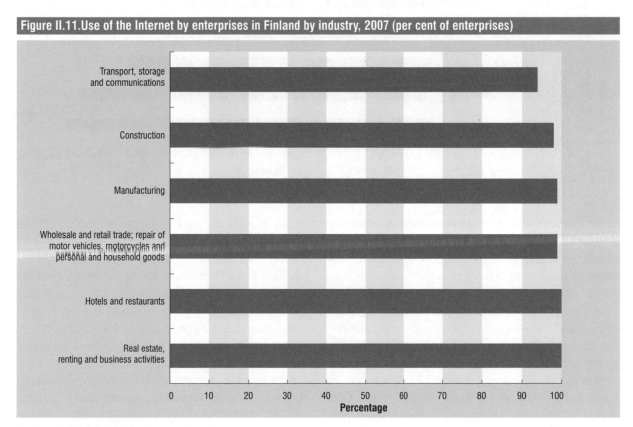

Figure II.11. Use of the Internet by enterprises in Finland by industry, 2007 (per cent of enterprises)

Source: UNCTAD Information Economy Database.

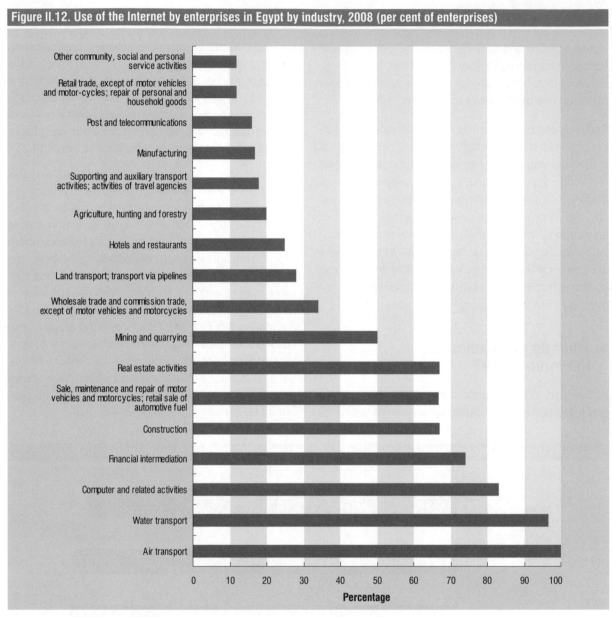

Figure II.12. Use of the Internet by enterprises in Egypt by industry, 2008 (per cent of enterprises)

Source: UNCTAD Information Economy Database.

By comparison, the situation in developing countries is quite different. According to the national surveys conducted in Egypt and the Republic of Korea, for example (figure II.15), the most common task conducted via the Internet is to send and receive e-mails. Only 3 per cent of the companies included in the Egyptian survey used the Internet to interact with public authorities, and only 6 per cent had started to do banking on the Internet. In the Republic of Korea, the share of companies using Internet banking is higher than in Egypt, but still far from the levels seen in Finland. One reason for this wide discrepancy is the important role played by microenterprises in the Republic of Korea

(more than 90 per cent of the target population). As shown above, while the level of Internet use is among the highest in the world among medium and large enterprises in the Republic of Korea, it is much lower for microenterprises there (figure II.5). From the perspective of benefiting more from Internet access, firms in developing countries could use available ICTs more intensively. In Latin America, for example, the adoption of Internet use by enterprises in the formal sector is high, but the way it is used still holds a large unexplored potential, in particular for integrating back and front office (ECLAC, 2009). To do this, Internet-based solutions that respond to market needs must become available,

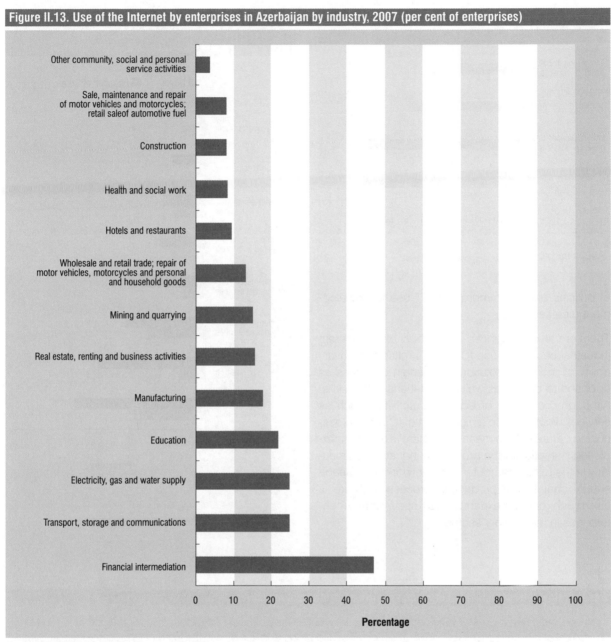

Figure II.13. Use of the Internet by enterprises in Azerbaijan by industry, 2007 (per cent of enterprises)

Source: UNCTAD Information Economy Database.

including through applications with local content, in local languages, and that are of relevance to SMEs. On the demand side, enterprises may still need to rethink some business and productive processes around new ICT tools, as well as invest in ICT skills development. This, in turn, requires resources and makes the success of ICT applications price sensitive.

In conclusion, the ICT data reviewed by UNCTAD confirm that there is still a gap in the use of ICT by businesses between developed countries and both developing and transition economies. Within coun-

tries, there are also digital divides between smaller and larger firms, both in the access to computers and Internet, and in the type of use they make of these technologies. The lag in broadband connections for both smaller enterprises and rural enterprises compound their disadvantage vis-à-vis larger and urban-based companies, and limit their capacity to make full use of the potential benefits of the Internet. Because microenterprises and SMEs constitute the majority of enterprises and are a key source of employment in the developing world, they should be an important focus

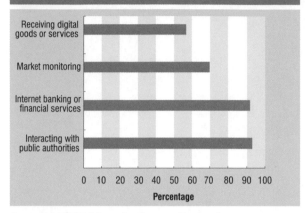

Figure II.14. Types of Internet use by enterprises in Finland, 2006 (per cent of enterprises)

Source: UNCTAD Information Economy Database.

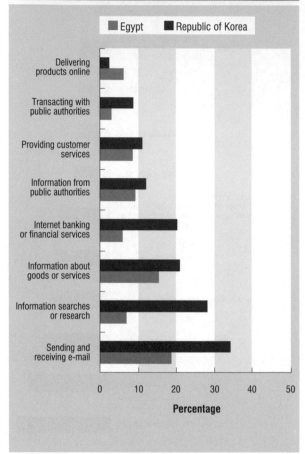

Figure II.15. Types of Internet use by enterprises in Egypt and the Republic of Korea, latest year (per cent of enterprises)

Source: UNCTAD Information Economy Database.

of policies aimed at improving ICT use for development (see section C).

There are also differences in the ability of the different industrial sectors to use ICTs. This reflects the availability of more ICT solutions for certain industries as opposed to others, as well as limitations in ICT skills. Although the nature of economic activities such as services would lead to a higher use of ICTs, the crosscutting nature of ICTs means that there is a large unexploited potential for the productive industries, particularly in the use of computers and networks to manage supply chains and production processes. There is also much room for expanding ICT use by smaller enterprises in the primary sector.

Box II.4. How Internet benefits European enterprises in different industries

The way the Internet is used varies not only by country but also by industry. An assessment of the use of ICT in European real estate enterprises found that intermediaries and property investors use the Internet to present offers and track the market, as well as manage client relationships; housing companies used Internet-based applications to manage facilities, do bookkeeping and facilitate owner and tenant relationships (E-Business Watch, 2003).[32] In the wholesale and retail trade sector, the Internet can take supply chain management to a higher level, as it enables real time, remote procurement, inventory management and logistics applications (E-Business Watch, 2008b). The transportation and logistics sector uses the Internet to exchange information between remote locations, but also increasingly for fleet control and monitoring (ibid.).

Both the retail trade sector and the transportation sector use the Internet to provide customer services, in particular by enabling online shopping, reservations, ticketing, check-in and after-sales services. In the construction sector, the Internet facilitates e-procurement. The European construction industry is starting to use the Internet for e-invoicing, which can yield efficiency benefits by becoming integrated with enterprise resource planning systems or be conducted in a web-based environment (E-Business Watch, 2006). In manufacturing, the Internet has become essential to remote supply chain management.

Source: UNCTAD.

C. IMPLICATIONS FOR POLICIES

In view of its potential positive contributions to growth and development, there are good reasons for governments to promote greater use of ICT in the business sector. The previous section highlighted some striking differences with respect to the nature and extent of ICT usage. Significant gaps were identified both between and within countries. Although it is up to each company to decide how ICTs could enhance its business performance, governments fill a critical function in terms of creating an environment that is conducive to greater use of ICTs, especially in developing countries. The role of governments in stimulating ICT use may be even more important in times of economic crisis (box II.5).

There are various ways in which developing country governments, with support from development partners, can promote greater use of ICTs by companies. Special attention should be given to SMEs, as they are lagging behind larger firms in terms of ICT uptake. In addition, SMEs often represent the backbone of developing economies and employ a large majority of the workforce. Despite recent progress in infrastructure and connectivity, there are still many bottlenecks that prevent entrepreneurs and small firms from using ICTs efficiently. Its use is often limited by low levels of ICT literacy, slow connection speed, a lack of local content and high costs of use. Moreover, in rural areas of many developing countries, even basic connectivity remains a challenge.

Countries in which the business sector has been keen to adopt ICTs have typically shown a strong policy commitment towards such technologies, emphasized the development of a competitive ICT infrastructure at least in urban areas, taken steps to build a workforce with the necessary skills and technological capabilities and adopted an enabling regulatory environment. Important areas of government intervention to encourage greater adoption and use of ICT in the business sector thus include: (a) making it a core element in a national ICT strategy; (b) improving ICT infrastructure in underserved areas; (c) building relevant skills; (d) promoting the development of local content; and (e) strengthening the legal and regulatory framework.

1. National ICT strategies

The formulation of a coherent and comprehensive national ICT strategy is an essential step towards raising awareness in both the public and private sectors about the opportunities created by ICTs (UNCTAD, 2003). During the past decade, more and more governments have developed and implemented national ICT strategies to boost their economic development. Fostering the uptake and use of ICTs in the business sector should constitute a core element of such strategies. However, there is no "one size fits all" solution for promoting ICT diffusion among enterprises. The strategy needs to be adapted to each country, reflecting different company needs; industry structures; demographic, geographical and cultural situations; and policy priorities. Moreover, even within a country, there can be great differences in ICT use.

Against this background, governments should ensure adequate coordination and involvement of all relevant stakeholders when designing and implementing the strategy. Consideration should furthermore be given to how effective the policy framework is in terms of achieving key objectives. The need for reviewing ICT plans on a regular basis and the importance of coordinated reviews among the different stakeholders involved cannot be overstated. Failure to monitor the implementation of ICT policy measures at an early stage can delay progress towards an inclusive information society. Developing countries should define, as part of their national ICT plans, mechanisms for ongoing policy review, assessment and monitoring. This is important to ensure that evolving ICT strategies are consistent with the development goals set out and to maximize the positive contributions of investments in ICT and in capability development. UNCTAD ICT Policy Reviews can serve as a useful tool in this context (box II.6) (see also UNCTAD, 2006b).

The importance of access to reliable data on the use of ICTs in the business sector is worth re-emphasizing. Without such information, policymakers are at a loss when formulating new or revising existing plans. Indicators must show to what extent ICTs are used as a tool to promote development. Governments need to better measure the impact of e-business, collect evidence, share experiences and good practices, and promote cross-fertilization among all relevant stakeholders. The core ICT indicators defined by the Partnership on Measuring ICT for Development are helpful in this process (see section II.A.2).

Box II.5. The economic crisis and ICT use

It is difficult to assess the impact of the crisis on ICT use. On the one hand, the general slowdown in the global economy impacts firms' capacities to raise capital for investments in ICTs. On the other hand, faced with shrinking demand, many companies view ICT investments – and greater use of ICT – as a way to reduce their operation costs. This may also involve increased use of offshoring (see chapter III). On balance, however, the needs to invest in ICT goods and services are un-likely to compensate fully for the slump in demand due to the downgraded economic prospects (see also OECD, 2009a). In fact, global spending on ICT as a share of world GDP has been on a downward trend since 2006, a trend that was accentuated by the cooling of economies (WITSA, 2008). This scenario appears to have been confirmed by the dramatic declines in ICT goods exports in the last months of 2008 and in early 2009 (chapter III).

The crisis is quickly spilling over from developed to developing countries, despite initial hopes that developing countries would be spared from the worst effects of the downturn. One reason is that today developing countries are more integrated into the global economy. For example, the average exports-to-GDP ratio of all developing countries rose from 26 per cent in 1995 to 52 per cent in 2007 (UNCTAD, 2009b: 9). In the case of Africa, it rose from 22 per cent to 52 per cent during the same period. Developing economies have been hurt by falling commodity prices, weaker demand for their exports, reduced access to credit and trade finance, less inward direct investment and shrinking remittances (ibid.: 3). As a result, many businesses in the South today face similar challenges as their peers in the North.

So far, it seems that the use of telecommunications has been relatively resilient, especially as compared with the signifi-cant declines in demand for various ICT goods (OECD, 2009a; ITU, 2009b; see also chapter I). For mobile telephony and Internet access, income elasticities have come down significantly (ITU, 2009b), suggesting that both consumers and firms are more reluctant to cut their expenditures on such items when incomes fall. Over the medium to long term, companies will continue to upgrade their ICT infrastructure as such technology is essential to their competitiveness. Recent surveys suggest that the crisis has made good use of ICT an even more important objective among companies.[a]

The impact is likely to be the most significant in those industries that have been the worst affected by the crisis, such as financial and real estate services. As noted in section B, these are among the most ICT-intensive industries and account for a large part of worldwide spending on ICTs. While financial services will be dramatically downsized by the crisis,[b] banks and other financial institutions are likely to face various new regulatory requirements, which in turn may require investment in new hardware, software and compliance solutions that will enhance ICT use even further.[c] Thus, even in the worst af-fected industries, ICT use is likely to expand over the medium to long term.

Some governments have identified enhanced ICT use as a strategy to quicken the recovery. Several developed countries have made ICTs an integral part of their economic stimulus packages, by both stimulating demand for ICT goods and con-tinuing to enhance the supply side (from infrastructure to spectrum). Measures aimed at supporting demand and shoring up the financial sector should help boost ICT use in that sector. Measures targeting the rolling out of broadband to areas with low connectivity may help alleviate some infrastructure bottlenecks. Innovation through ICTs is also being encouraged, including in education, energy (for example "smart power grids"), government, health care and transportation (OECD, 2009a). Similar initiatives have also been taken in developing countries (Nasscom, 2009; ECA, 2009; ECLAC, 2009). While the effect of these measures remains to be seen, economic policies are increasingly looking at the cost and efficiency benefits of ICT to support the path to recovery.

Source: UNCTAD.

[a] *See e.g. Reuters (2009).*
[b] *Between 2008 and 2009, as many as 15 banks left the Financial Times' listing of the world's 500 largest companies. The market value of the banks remaining on the list more than halved from $4.1 trillion in 2008 to $1.9 trillion in 2009. See Financial Times (2009).*
[c] *See Computerworld (2008).*

---

2. Improving infrastructure in underserved areas

Access to adequate infrastructure is a prerequisite for companies to adopt and use ICTs. Poor connectivity and limited access to electricity are important rea-sons for the limited use of ICTs in many rural areas of developing countries (UNCTAD, 2007b). As noted in chapter I, there also remain significant gaps between countries with regard to access to the Internet and especially broadband. The improvement of ICT infra-structure is therefore still high up on the development agenda (see e.g. UNCTAD, 2006b and 2007a).

While mobile telephones and their novel applications (such as m-banking) are becoming the most com-mon ICT support for SMEs in developing countries, they are only one technology among several that can meet different company needs. Government policies need to be flexible enough to respond effectively to different situations.[33] In certain cases, access to VoIP, community radios (in local language) or public Internet access points (such as Internet cafés, educational establishments and digital community centres) can be important for promoting ICT use by local companies.

The network infrastructure needs to be accessible, affordable and of good quality, which today often means high speed connectivity. To achieve efficient, low cost telecommunications and Internet access, countries typically have to reform and liberalize the sector and expose the incumbent to competition. Internet (and broadband) access is needed at both the national and international levels (chapter I). The expected increase in bandwidth for Africa may facilitate the creation and use of more value added applications and content for local SMEs, as well as cheaper access to broadband-enabled applications (Africa Partnership Forum, 2008). However, the impact of this new connectivity will partly depend on companies' capacity to use it.[34]

3. Creating skills

There is no way around proper ICT education and training if governments wish their companies to be competitive and connected to the global economy. Many developing countries, and especially LDCs, still lack the necessary capacity to take advantage of ICTs and should make the development of human resources a priority. People with ICT training generally have a higher chance of finding employment and can help companies and countries participate better in the knowledge-based economy. Governments can

enhance digital literacy by using the basic education system, beginning at primary school level, as well as by emphasizing lifelong learning through adult training programmes.

Public and private sectors, academia and training institutions, should ideally work together to develop national policies that focus on imparting the appropriate skills. This can be done, for example, by designing and delivering to students or entrepreneurs training programmes that meet industry's requirements. The provision of free Internet access in public schools, universities and libraries can broaden the use of technology and the Internet for entrepreneurs.

Governments can furthermore design special programmes to train entrepreneurs on how to best adapt their practices and methods to make use of ICTs and e-business. Entrepreneurs often lack human and financial resources and a basic understanding of the opportunities they could derive from ICTs. They may not see how investments required to use technology could be valuable and relevant to their business. Governments – at the central, regional and local levels – may also set an example in terms of ICT use, by taking the lead and providing online information and services, including e-procurement services. Such initiatives can help to raise awareness about ICTs as a tool to support business operations.

Attention should also be given to policies that can help retain and attract skilled professionals. The development of human resources, building up of capacities and continuous learning in the field of ICT and e-business are critical contributions to the change of mindset in companies and methods of doing business that are needed to make full use of ICTs.

Box II.6. UNCTAD ICT Policy Reviews

As part of its technical assistance work in the area of ICT for development, UNCTAD has developed a methodology for undertaking ICT Policy Reviews (ICTPRs) (UNCTAD, 2006b). This work benefits from the organization's experience with policy reviews in other areas, such as investment and science, technology and innovation. An ICTPR assesses the implementation of national ICT master plans. Each review focuses on the ICT environment, the main policy components of the master plan and the institutional framework and implementation mechanisms. Key policy areas targeted include infrastructure development, legal and regulatory framework, human skills, enterprise development, innovation, and trade and investment policies. The scope of the review is defined in consultation with the national counterparts on the basis of the objectives of the ICT plan under review as well as future policy orientations. Recommendations proposed by the ICTPR should serve as an input into the preparation of the next ICT plan. ICTPRs are demand-driven projects that require donor financing. The first UNCTAD ICTPR is currently under way in Egypt with the support of the United Nations Development Programme (UNDP).

Source: UNCTAD.

4. Developing local content

A lack of local content on the Internet and other forms of ICT (such as mobile devices) can limit the uptake of technologies. Even in developing countries that enjoy a relatively high level of connectivity, local content – i.e. information provided in local languages, reflecting the values, lifestyles and the needs of local communities – is often scarce. Meanwhile, such content can help create new business opportunities and improve access to information that is critical for SMEs, such as agricultural market information or local weather forecasts.

Increased production of local content requires that owners or originators have the incentives and resources to create, adapt or exchange such content. In many developing countries, individuals and organizations lack the financial and technical resources needed to create content suited to local needs. SME support policies should help companies provide content to both domestic and foreign consumers to promote local products and industries. While its importance has been raised in many international meetings and by donors and cooperation agencies, concrete initiatives and expertise in this area remain scarce (United Nations, 2009).

5. Strengthening the legal and regulatory framework

Governments can influence the extent to which companies use ICTs by helping to create an enabling environment for e-commerce and e-business. Governments should review their regulatory frameworks to accommodate electronic transactions and improve consumer and business confidence in them. The increasing use of ICTs for commercial and administrative activities, specifically in an Internet environment, requires laws and regulations to address a set of issues, such as the legal validity of electronic documents, e-signatures, privacy, intellectual property rights, cybercrime and building trust. Many developing countries need to adopt relevant and appropriate legal frameworks to unleash the full potential of the Internet. The provision of a predictable and supportive legal framework for e-commerce is an essential step to widen market access for SMEs at the regional and international levels. The international community provides guidance to developing countries wishing to implement legal reforms related to e-commerce, ensuring that there is a level of regional and international harmonization that could also encourage international trade through online channels (see box II.7).

Box II.7. Initiatives to facilitate the regional harmonization of cyberlaws

Several initiatives are underway in all developing regions for the regional harmonization of cyberlaws. Such initiatives are supported by regional institutions and international organizations such as UNCTAD, United Nations regional commissions, the Commonwealth Secretariat and the United Nations Commission on International Trade Law (UNCITRAL).

Regional harmonization is challenging as it has to take into account the different legal, social and economic systems of countries. Other hurdles include a lack of human resources and limited public awareness about the scope, application and potential benefits of making e-commerce more legally secure. To achieve harmonization of e-commerce legislation, countries need to review their own legislations; consider the state of legislation of the all countries in the same regional grouping; and discuss ways to harmonize, in particular in the light of existing regional trading agreements.

UNCTAD has been engaged since 2003 in technical cooperation with developing country governments and regional institutions in Africa, Asia and Latin America to prepare ICT legal frameworks (UNCTAD, 2007a). UNCTAD offers capacity-building activities, carries out comparative reviews of regional laws and assists in the drafting of cyberlaws and in the implementation process. For example, UNCTAD has been assisting the East African Community (EAC) in the preparation of a regional framework for cyberlaws. The new framework is expected to be endorsed by the EAC secretariat in 2009. UNCTAD has also supported activities in Latin America and the Caribbean, in coordination with the Asociación Latinoamericana de Integración (ALADI) and Mercosur, through training workshops and the preparation of a comparative study on existing cyberlaws.[a] In Asia, support has been provided to Cambodia and Lao People's Democratic Republic to build capacity and prepare cyberlaws in the framework of the ASEAN E-Commerce project (see (http://www.e-aseantf.org/).

UNCTAD works closely with United Nations regional commissions as well as UNCITRAL, which provides a basis for internationally harmonized e-commerce laws. Developing countries wishing to adopt modern legislation on electronic commerce might consider the adoption of UNCITRAL texts, starting with the Electronic Communications Convention.[b]

Source: UNCTAD.

[a] *See http://www.unctad.org/sp/docs//webdtlktcd20091_sp.pdf.*
[b] *Information on the UNCITRAL texts on electronic commerce is available at:*
 http://www.uncitral.org/uncitral/en/uncitral_texts/electronic_commerce.html.

NOTES

1   Some studies make a distinction between "useful connectivity" and normal connectivity, in this context highlighting the importance of how available ICTs are applied in practice (Waverman and Dasgupta, 2009).
2   The annual data collection process is carried out through the UNCTAD questionnaire on ICT usage by businesses and on the ICT sector, sent to NSOs through electronic mail.
3   See, for example, Economic and Social Council (2008).
4   See OECD (2009d).
5   For a review of 11 studies from 1996 to 2000, mostly in the United States, see Indjikian and Siegel (2005). Eurostat (2008) deals with studies from 13 European countries.
6   As noted above, however, such studies tend to rely on national accounts data on ICT investment (in some cases, software investment in particular) as a proxy for ICT use (Eurostat, 2008).
7   A developing country that had an average of 10 more mobile phones per 100 inhabitants between 1996 and 2003 would have enjoyed per capita GDP growth that was 0.59 per cent higher than an otherwise identical country (Waverman et al., 2005).
8   See e.g. presentation by Nauro F. Campos on the impact of ICTs on economic growth in Latin America, available at http://www.itu.int/osg/spu/dtis/documents/presentations/campos.ppt.
9   See e.g. Waverman and Dasgupta (2009) and Vodafone (2005).
10 It should be noted that this referred to the number of web hosts attributed to each country by counting top-level host domain names available from the Internet Software Consortium (http://www.isc.org), with the caveat that the domain name does not necessarily reflect the actual location of the website.
11 This would not apply to digital products. Trade in services, and in particular ICT-related services, are not part of the Freund and Weinhold analyses.
12 For a broader discussion on ICT, innovation and productivity, see chapter 12 of Eurostat (2008).
13 See http://wirelessfederation.com/news/15801-m-pesa-still-not-profitable-despite-high-growth-rate-safaricom-ceo/ .
14 See *International Herald Tribune* (2008).
15 See http://wirelessfederation.com/news/14114-airtel-mcheck-subscribers-reach-the-mark-of-1mn-india/ and http://wirelessfederation.com/news/11959-obapay-gazing-mobile-banking-in-india/ .
16 See http://www.grameen-info.org/index.php?option=com_content&task=view&id=540&Itemid=598 .
17 The core list of ICT indicators was developed by the Partnership on Measuring ICT for Development and endorsed by the United Nations Statistical Commission in 2007. For the full list of indicators and explanations on the latest revision, see Partnership on Measuring ICT for Development (2009).
18 For the 2008 survey, another 14 countries submitted data that were not comparable.
19 See UNCTAD (2009a).
20 Most economies for which data are available fall into the category of "high income level" as defined by UNCTAD; i.e. GDP per capita above $4,500. Middle-income countries are those with GDP per capita between $1,000 and $4,500; low-income countries are those with GDP per capita below $1,000.
21 Microenterprises refer to those enterprises with 0–9 employees; small enterprises refer to those with 10–49 employees; medium enterprises are those with 50–249 employees; and large enterprises have 250 employees or more (UNCTAD, 2009a).
22 The Republic of Korea is classified as a developing country, but is also an OECD member, has a high income level with a highly developed ICT infrastructure.
23 The value added of agriculture for low- and middle-income countries was 10 per cent of GDP in 2007 and 25 per cent for low-income countries alone. Agriculture often accounts for a very high share of total employment, as for example in Bangladesh (51 per cent) and the United Republic of Tanzania (82 per cent) (World Bank, 2007).
24 See http://www.ers.usda.gov/Publications/EIB47/EIB47_SinglePages.pdf.
25 See http://www.ers.usda.gov/Publications/EIB47/EIB47_SinglePages.pdf.
26 The remaining amounts were accounted for by consumers ($1 trillion) and government ($206 billion).
27 As defined by the International Standard Industrial Classification (ISIC) rev. 3.1.
28 It should be noted that only industries for which at least 10 countries report data have been included in this analysis.
29 The position of construction may appear to contradict the earlier observation that construction is among the least ICT-intensive industries. However, while the UNCTAD data show that a very high share of construction companies use computers, they do not say anything about the amounts spent on ICT equipment.
30 The pattern is similar for broadband, but the data are not displayed due to relatively few observations.
31 See the discussion on useful connectivity as part of the connectivity scorecard (Waverman and Dasgupta, 2009).
32 Although the report considers that overall ICT intensity in real estate services is low in comparison to other sectors.
33 See e.g. the summary of the discussion during the WSIS Forum 2009 on "e-Business and Poverty Alleviation", available at http://www.itu.int/wsis/implementation/2009/forum/geneva/al_c7_e_busn_pov_all.html.
34 For more on how to promote greater diffusion of various ICTs, see chapter I.

CHAPTER III

EVOLVING PATTERNS IN ICT TRADE

3

Information and communication technologies constitute an important part of world trade. Moreover, a growing share of exports of both ICT goods and services is accounted for by developing economies, especially in Asia. Trade patterns have already been affected by the current economic crisis, but the impact differs considerably between goods and services. While ICT goods are among those products that have been the most affected by the recession, IT and ICT-related services appear to be more resilient. Many companies see the offshoring of services as a way to reduce costs and improve their competitiveness.

The first part of this chapter looks at the evolution of trade in ICT goods over the past ten years with regard to geographical and product composition. Drawing on recent data, it also considers possible implications of the current crisis on the trade in ICT goods. The second part focuses on trade in IT and ICT-enabled services, highlighting the offshoring phenomenon. It notes that the economic crisis is likely to lead more companies in a broader range of industries to consider the possibilities from the offshoring of various business functions. This should imply new potential export opportunities for economies in many parts of the developing world.

A. TRADE IN ICT GOODS

1. Global shifts boost South–South trade

World trade in ICT goods has experienced ups and downs during the past decade. While ICT goods (box III.1) belonged to the most dynamic areas of world trade until 2000, they have subsequently expanded less rapidly than global trade as a whole (figure III.1). Between 1998 and 2007, the value of ICT goods exports rose from $813 billion to $1.73 trillion, representing 13.2 per cent of all merchandise trade. The share has diminished in recent years – from its peak of 17.7 per cent in 2000 – and the decline was accentuated in 2007, partly due to the commodity boom (WTO, 2008; UNCTAD, 2008b).[1] Despite the decline, ICT goods still account for a significant part of world trade.[2]

A salient feature of trade in ICT goods in the past decade has been a shift in its geographical composition with a spectacular rise in the market share of developing countries. Between 1998 and 2007, it increased from 38 per cent to 57 per cent (table III.1). This surge

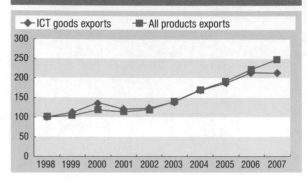

Figure III.1. World merchandise and ICT goods exports, 1998–2007 (index 1998 = 100)

Source: UNCTAD, based on based on COMTRADE data.

was almost entirely attributable to economies in developing Asia, which in 2007 accounted for 54 per cent of world exports of ICT goods. Other developing regions remain marginal players in ICT goods exports, with a combined share of less than 4 per cent of the world total in 2007. Economies in transition also account for a very small share.

Despite experiencing increased exports in absolute values, developed countries saw significant declines in their market shares. America's share fell by about

---

Box III.1. What are ICT goods?

ICT goods may be intended to fulfil the function of information processing and communication by electronic means, including transmission and display, or they may use electronic processing to detect, measure and/or record physical phenomena, or to control a physical process.[a] In 2003, the OECD Working Party on Indicators for the Information Society (WPIIS) proposed a list to facilitate the construction of internationally comparable indicators on trade in ICT goods. The products included were defined according to the Harmonized System nomenclature (1996 and 2002 versions), at the six-digit level of disaggregation. The list under HS-1996 contains 181 goods grouped in five categories: telecommunications equipment, computer and related equipment, electronic components, audio and video equipment, and other ICT goods (OECD, 2003).

In 2008, a new classification of ICT products was released, based on the United Nations Central Product Classification (CPC) (OECD, 2008b). This list contains not only ICT goods, but also ICT services, content and media. It is expected that when reporting trade data, countries will gradually migrate to this classification over the next few years.

In 2008, countries started to use the latest version of the Harmonized System, the HS-2007 classification. This posed significant challenges in terms of ensuring comparability over time as the new categories of products under the HS-2007 nomenclature do not necessarily correspond to those under HS-1996 or HS-2002 (OECD, 2009c). For example, the new classification may assign several lines to a product that was covered in a single category in HS-2002. Conversely, several goods under HS-2002 might have been regrouped under one or more different lines in the HS-2007 new classification.

The break in the time series warrants some caution in interpreting comparisons between 2007 and earlier years. However, the broader trends with regard to trade in ICT goods are unlikely to be affected. A comparative analysis undertaken by the OECD secretariat confirmed a downward trend in world exports of ICT goods in 2007 (OECD, 2008b and 2009b).

In the medium term, if countries are going to carry on with reporting trade under HS-2007, it will be necessary to agree upon a new list of ICT goods under HS-2007, in order to avoid the conversion issue mentioned above.

The analysis presented in this chapter uses COMTRADE data for some 176 economies, using the 1996 Harmonized System classification. A conversion table was designed to translate data from the HS-1992 classifications for countries that only reported according to that classification.

Source: UNCTAD.
[a] See http://stats.oecd.org/glossary/detail.asp?ID=6274.

Table III.1. Exports of ICT goods by source region, 1998, 2003 and 2007 (per cent)

	1998	2003	2007
Developed economies	61.84	50.84	42.43
America	18.40	13.15	10.58
Asia	12.13	9.88	6.67
Europe	31.03	27.60	25.01
EU-15	29.10	24.84	20.77
New EU members	1.24	2.26	3.72
Rest of Europe	0.69	0.51	0.51
Oceania	0.27	0.20	0.17
Developing economies	38.03	48.97	57.36
Africa	0.14	0.16	0.17
Latin America and the Caribbean	3.35	3.55	3.45
Asia	34.53	45.27	53.73
Oceania	0.00	0.00	0.00
LDCs	0.00	0.00	0.01
Transition economies	0.14	0.19	0.21
World	100.00	100.00	100.00
World ($ billion)	813.29	1,130.72	1,730.48

Source: UNCTAD, based on COMTRADE data.
See also annex table III.1.

Table III.2. Imports of ICT goods by main region, 1998. 2003 and 2007 (per cent)

Region	1998	2003	2007
Developed economies	66.47	57.54	52.57
America	23.87	19.48	17.07
Asia	5.43	5.61	4.49
Europe	35.94	31.31	29.84
EU-15	32.36	27.40	24.74
New EU members	2.14	2.81	4.08
Rest of Europe	1.44	1.10	1.01
Oceania	1.23	1.14	1.17
Developing economies	32.99	41.80	45.83
Africa	1.02	0.90	1.10
Latin America and the Caribbean	5.19	4.43	4.31
Asia	26.77	36.44	40.41
Oceania	0.02	0.03	0.02
LDCs	0.12	0.15	0.24
Transition economies	0.54	0.66	1.59
World	100.00	100.00	100.00
World ($ billion)	818.89	1,156.81	1,811.60

Source: UNCTAD, based on COMTRADE data.
See also annex table III.3.

eight percentage points, that of Asian developed economies by six percentage points and that of Europe also by six points over the period.[3] However, developments of exports from the European Union differed considerably between old and new EU members, with a large decline in the former and an increased market share for the latter (table III.1).[4]

Imports of ICT goods are also dominated by developed countries and economies in developing Asia. Compared with exports, changes have been smaller during the past decade. While the share of developing countries in world exports of ICT goods increased by almost 20 percentage points, their share of imports rose by a more modest 13 percentage points (table III.2). This rise was mainly linked to growing imports into developing Asia. The share of Latin America and the Caribbean fell while that of Africa was stable. Since 1998, the only developed countries for which the import share increased are the new EU members. Nonetheless, developed countries still receive more than half of all imports of ICT goods. In 2007, the top two destinations were United States and China, with

Figure III.2. Exports of ICT goods by main regions, 1998 and 2007 (per cent)

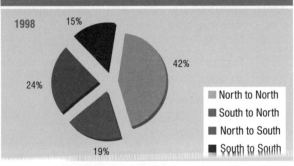

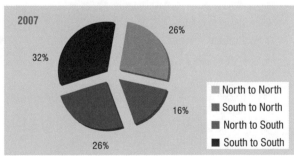

Source: UNCTAD, based on COMTRADE data.
Note. Economies in transition are included in the "South".

imports of about $273 billion and $255 billion, respectively (annex table III.3). Thus, both ICT exports and imports are dominated by the same geographic areas, with large parts of the world accounting for a marginal role in trade in ICT goods.

A result of the geographical shifts has been the growing importance of South–South trade (figure III.2). As late as 1998, trade between developed countries accounted for 42 per cent of world exports of ICT goods, compared with only 15 per cent for trade between developing economies. By 2007, this picture had been completely altered, with North–North trade accounting for only 26 per cent and South–South exports for more than 32 per cent. Nevertheless, exports of ICT goods from developed countries continued to expand during the period, from some $496 billion in 1998 to $732 billion in 2007.

2. A few economies dominate ICT goods trade

ICT goods exports are highly concentrated. The top five exporters – China, the United States, Hong Kong (China), Japan and Singapore – accounted for over half the world's exports of such goods in 2007 (table III.3), and the top 20 for more than 90 per cent.[5] The degree of concentration has increased since 2003, when the cumulative share of the top 5 exporters was about 46 per cent. With over $355 billion in exports of ICT goods, China is by far the largest exporter, responsible for more than 20 per cent of the total, more than twice the share of the second largest exporter (the United States). As shown in table III.3, most of the other top ten exporters are in Asia.

The growth of China's exports has been dramatic; its market share shot up from a mere 3 per cent in 1998 to 20 per cent in 2007 (figure III.3). In addition to China, most other exporters that have seen a significant increase in their market shares are in Asia or among the new EU members. Germany and the Netherlands are the only EU-15 countries appearing among the "winners" during the past decade. Hong Kong (China) and the Republic of Korea saw the second and third largest increases in market share. For all other exporters that gained market shares during the same period, the increases were smaller than one percentage point.

Table III.3. Top 20 exporters of ICT goods, 2007 (billions of dollar and per cent)			
Rank	Exporter	Exports of ICT goods ($ billion)	Share of global ICT goods exports (per cent)	Cumulative share (per cent)
1	China	355.57	20.46	20.46
2	United States	164.62	9.47	29.93
3	Hong Kong, China	148.08	8.52	38.46
4	Japan	112.20	6.46	44.91
5	Singapore	108.32	6.23	51.15
6	Germany	104.72	6.03	57.17
7	Republic of Korea	97.37	5.60	62.77
8	Taiwan, Province of China	85.34	4.91	67.69
9	Malaysia	73.19	4.21	71.90
10	Netherlands	70.62	4.06	75.96
11	Mexico	53.34	3.07	79.03
12	United Kingdom	37.56	2.16	81.19
13	Thailand	34.15	1.97	83.16
14	France	32.79	1.89	85.04
15	Ireland	23.53	1.35	86.40
16	Hungary	23.19	1.33	87.73
17	Canada	18.46	1.06	88.80
18	Czech Republic	17.95	1.03	89.83
19	Sweden	16.04	0.92	90.75
20	Italy	15.77	0.91	91.66

Source: UNCTAD, based on COMTRADE data.

Figure III.3. The 10 largest gains and losses in market shares of ICT goods exports, 1998–2007 (percentage points)

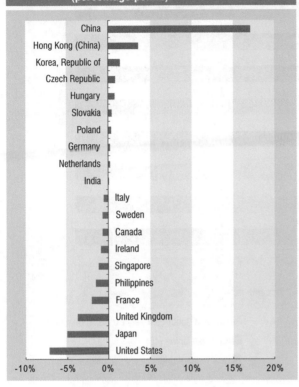

Source: UNCTAD, based on COMTRADE data. See also annex table III.2.

At the other end of the spectrum, the United States and Japan saw the greatest declines, as their market shares fell by 7 and 5 percentage points, respectively. Most other exporters that lost ground were among the EU-15 countries. Among the latter, the decline in market share was particularly pronounced in the cases of the United Kingdom (-3.7 per cent) and France (-2.1 per cent). In the United Kingdom, the decline was partly explained by fraudulent behaviour that had previously inflated export volumes (box III.2). The Philippines and Singapore also experienced a decline in their market shares.

The rise of China and the rest of East and South-East Asia as an export platform for ICT goods is the result of an increasingly integrated global production system. ICT goods production has gradually converged in locations that offer a combination of relatively high human capital in terms of skills and relatively low labour costs. Increased specialization and fragmentation of the production chain (Kierzkowski and Arndt, 2001; UNCTAD, 2002b) have spurred intense intra-industry and intra-firm trade not least within Asia – fuelling South–South interaction. In 2007, the two largest intra-Asian flows of trade in ICT goods were between China and Hong Kong, China. China exported ICT goods to a value of $93 billion to Hong Kong, China, while the reverse flows were worth about $88 billion. The third

---

Box III.2. The missing trader intra-community fraud in the United Kingdom

The decline in the exports of ICT goods from the United Kingdom was very sharp in 2007, even impacting aggregate figures at the world level. However, the decline was not so much related to the actual performance of the British ICT industry but to the reduction of criminal activities that had led to inflated figures for ICT goods exports. The problem, which was reported to the House of Lords in 2006 and 2007 (House of Lords, 2007) has been called the "missing trader intra-community" (MTIC) fraud.

In its basic form, an EU importer registers for permission to import goods from another EU member state and then goes into operation without paying the value added tax (VAT). The importer then sells the goods in his domestic market at prices inclusive of VAT, but without remitting the VAT to his national tax authorities, and disappears. In the "carousel version" of the MTIC fraud, the goods are not sold to a single consumer, but to a series of firms in the importing country. The goods are subsequently re-exported before being re-imported again by the "missing trader". The loss of VAT revenue becomes clear to the revenue authorities when the last firm in the domestic market claims for VAT refund from the treasury before re-exporting the consignment of goods.

Similar schemes have been observed in other EU countries, but the full extent of the fraudulent behaviour remains unknown. ICT goods have been particularly affected because they are high value, low volume goods and transporting them is hence relatively inexpensive.

The MTIC fraud has resulted in major distortions of trade data. Due to the re-exports in the carousel fraud, exports from the United Kingdom, and probably from several other EU countries, were grossly inflated for 2005 and 2006.

Corrective actions have been taken by the authorities and have helped to reduce the fraud significantly, with a substantial decline in ICT goods exports from the United Kingdom in 2007 as a result.

Source: UNCTAD.

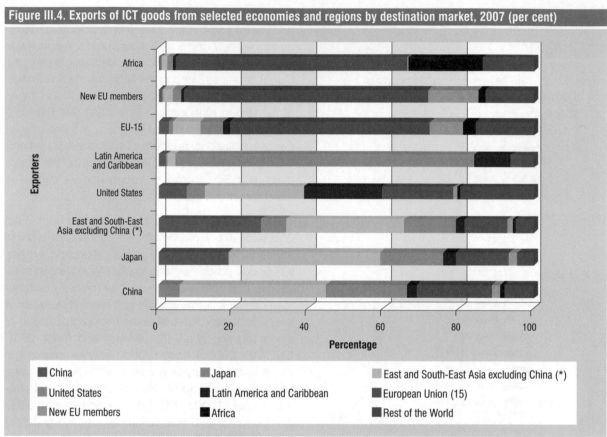

Figure III.4. Exports of ICT goods from selected economies and regions by destination market, 2007 (per cent)

Source: UNCTAD, based on COMTRADE data.
* East and South-East Asia excluding China includes: Hong Kong (China), Indonesia, Malaysia, the Philippines, Republic of Korea, Singapore, Taiwan Province of China and Thailand.

largest intra-Asian flow ($24 billion) consisted of exports from the Republic of Korea to China.

Among the main exporting economies and regions, the United States has the most diversified pattern of ICT goods exports, with no single dominant destination (figure III.4). For most other top exporters of ICT goods, intraregional trade predominates. With significant exports to the United States and to the EU, China has achieved a relatively high level of diversification, but regional exports (including to Japan) still account for close to 45 per cent of its total exports of ICT goods. All the other regions shown in figure III.4 rely heavily on a particular market. For example, exports from Africa are predominantly destined for the European market, while those from Latin America and the Caribbean are largely bound for the United States. Similarly, exports from the new EU members as well as those originating from the EU-15 are primarily sold within Western Europe.

Strong regional dependence can be seen also from mirror data on imports of ICT goods (figure III.5). Asian markets are supplied overwhelmingly from within Asia. For China, Japan and the rest of East and South-East Asia, close to 80 per cent of imports originated from Asia. The United States also sourced most (almost 65 per cent) of its imports from Asian suppliers and from neighbouring Latin America and Caribbean. In the case of both Europe and Africa, however, the EU-15 countries were the main source of imports. Latin America and the Caribbean countries imported their ICT goods mainly from the United States. But even in Africa, Europe and Latin America, at least 30 per cent of the imports originated from Asia.

3. Reliance on ICT goods is high in some countries

For a number of economies, ICT goods now constitute a significant share of total exports and thus account for important contributions to employment and production.[6] In about 20 economies, this share is higher than the world average (figure III.6). This is the case especially in some small economies, many of which have

Figure III.5. Imports of ICT goods of selected countries and regions by source economies and regions, 2007 (based on mirror trade) (per cent)

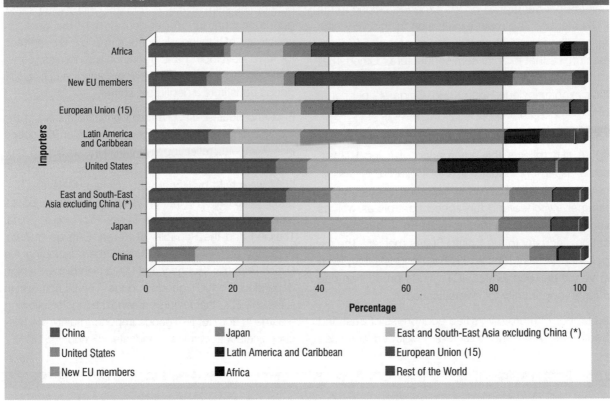

Source: UNCTAD, based on COMTRADE data.
* East and South-East Asia excluding China includes: Hong Kong (China), Indonesia, Malaysia, the Philippines, Republic of Korea, Singapore, Taiwan Province of China and Thailand.

Figure III.6. The 20 economics with the greatest reliance on ICT goods in total exports, 2007 (per cent)

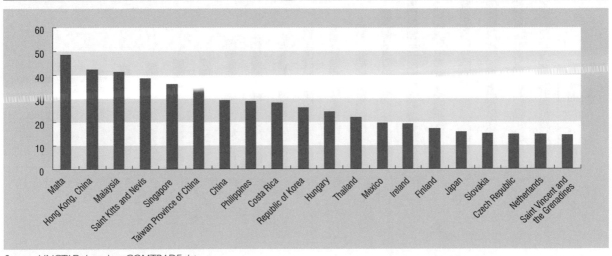

Source: UNCTAD, based on COMTRADE data.

attracted significant foreign investment into the ICT industry in recent years. In Malta, for example, almost half (49 per cent) of all goods exported belong to the ICT category. The main explanation to this very high ratio is the manufacturing facility owned by ST Micro-electronics that exports semiconductors.[7] Other small economies with high dependence on ICT goods in their exports include Hong Kong, China (42 per cent), Malaysia (41.5 per cent) and Singapore (36 per cent).

The position of Saint Kitts and Nevis (39 per cent) in figure III.6 reflects the emergence of a local small-scale assembly industry in the ICT area. It has experienced some success in exporting such items as dimmer switches and fan speed controls as well as various components for the cable TV and communications industry to the United States market.[8] The experience of Saint Kitts and Nevis suggests that, even in very small economies, ICT goods production can offer an opportunity for diversification.

A number of more diversified economies of East and South-East Asia and selected developed countries display a lower level of dependency on ICT goods, but are still above the world average. Even for large economies such as Japan and the United States, ICT goods account for 16 per cent and 14 per cent, respectively, of total goods exports in 2007. By contrast, for most developing and transition economies, especially among commodity exporters and the LDCs, ICT goods constitute a negligible share.

East and South-East Asia also dominate the list of the top 20 economies with the highest reliance on ICT goods in their imports, reflecting their role in the global ICT production system (figure III.7). The top four positions in 2007 were held by Hong Kong (China), Malaysia, Singapore and China, in that order. Other Asian economies featuring in the figure include Taiwan Province of China, Thailand and the Republic of Korea. Outside of Asia, Paraguay as well as new EU members including the Czech Republic, Hungary and Malta also display a high dependence on ICT goods imports. The oil-rich Sudan is the only LDC that features among the top 20, following a surge in 2007 of ICT goods imports (mainly line telephone sets with cordless handsets, HS code 851711).

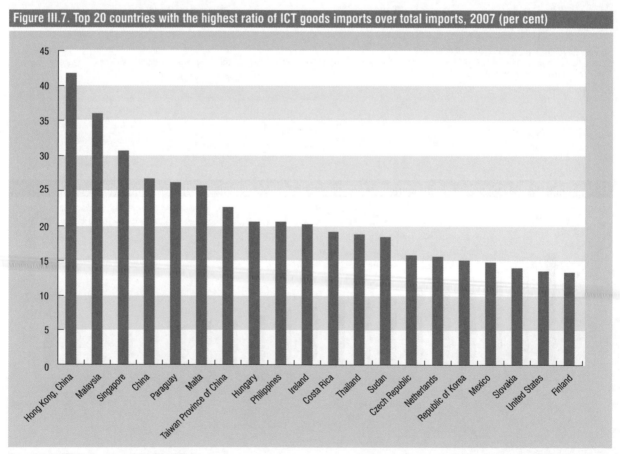

Figure III.7. Top 20 countries with the highest ratio of ICT goods imports over total imports, 2007 (per cent)

Source: UNCTAD, based on COMTRADE data.

Whereas Paraguay and Malta both exhibit very high ratios of ICT goods in total imports, the underlying reasons are very different for the two countries. As noted above, in the small island economy of Malta, ICT goods account for a very high share of exports. Malta's ICT goods imports were mainly made up of "other monolithic integrated circuits" (HS code 854230), which in 2007 accounted for close to 69 per cent of the island's ICT goods imports. By contrast, Paraguay – a landlocked economy largely dependent on agriculture and agro-processing exports – exports hardly any ICT goods and its ICT imports mainly consist of computer and related equipment (55 per cent), audio and video equipment (29 per cent) and telecommunications equipment (13 per cent).[9] Thus, in the case of Malta, imports reflect the fact that the country is a part of the global production system of a major TNC (ST Microelectronics); in the case of Paraguay, ICT goods are imported mainly to serve the local consumer market.

4. Shifts in the product composition

During the past decade, the product composition of ICT goods trade has changed in certain respects. Among the five categories of ICT goods (box III.1), telecommunications equipment was the most dynamic. Between 1998 and 2007, its share of world trade in ICT goods exports rose from 14 to 18 per cent (table III.4). At the same time, the category of computers and related equipment lost ground; its share falling from 34 to 25 per cent. Overall, electronic components were the largest subcategory of ICT goods in 2007.

The aggregate shifts mask changes at the product level. The rapid evolution of the semiconductor industry, for example, has resulted in the share of "other monolithic integrated circuits" rising by more than 12 percentage points, while that of "metal oxide semiconductors" dropped by almost 6 percentage points.

Table III.4. ICT goods exports, by main product category, 1998, 2003 and 2007 (per cent)

Subcategory	1998	2003	2007	Change 1998–2007 (percentage points)
Audio and video equipment	11.3	12.1	13.9	+2.6
Computer and related equipment	34.0	31.6	25.2	-8.8
Electronic components	32.8	34.3	33.8	+1.0
Other ICT goods	8.0	8.2	8.9	+0.9
Telecommunications equipment	13.9	13.8	18.2	+4.3
All ICT goods	100.0	100.0	100.0	na

Source: UNCTAD, based on COMTRADE.

Table III.5. Most exported ICT goods, 2007 (per cent)

Rank	Denomination*	HS code (1996)	Share of total ICT exports	Cumulative share
1	Other monolithic integrated circuits	854230	16.4	16.4
2	Parts and accessories of the machines of heading no. 84.71 (computers)	847330	8.1	24.5
3	Transmission apparatus incorporating reception apparatus (mobile phones)	852520	7.5	32.0
4	Portable digital automatic data processing machines, weighing not more than 10 kg (laptops)	847130	5.0	37.0
5	Parts of other electrical apparatus for line telephony (parts of telephone sets)	851790	4.3	41.4
6	Reception apparatus for television, whether or not incorporating radio-broadcast receivers or sound (colour TVs)	852812	4.1	45.5
7	Storage units (automatic data processing machines) (of computers, including peripherals)	847170	3.6	49.1
8	Parts for radio/tv, transmit/receive equipment	852990	3.5	52.6
9	Other electrical apparatus for line telephony	851780	3.4	56.0
10	Input or output units, whether or not containing storage units in the same housing	847160	2.9	58.9
	Total exports in ICT goods ($ billion)		1 730.48	100.0

Source: UNCTAD, based on COMTRADE.
* Abbreviated. HS code description augmented in parenthesis.

Similarly, while there has been an overall decline in the share accounted for by computers and their parts, the share of laptops has surged.

Although the entire list of ICT goods contains 181 items (at the six-digit level of HS-1996) the bulk of ICT goods trade is comprised of trade in just a few items. The ten most traded products made up almost 59 per cent of total exports of ICT goods in 2007 (table III.5).[10] The single most traded item was "other monolithic integrated circuits", with a share of 16.4 per cent. Other much traded goods include computer parts and accessories, mobile phones, laptop computers, parts of telephone sets, colour TVs and computer storage units. These items accounted in 2007 for almost half of world trade in ICT goods.

5. Implications of the crisis: a preliminary assessment

Time will tell how the most serious economic recession since the Great Depression will influence global trade in ICT goods. However, early indications suggest that there could be significant repercussions. Although official trade statistics for 2008 and early 2009 were not

yet available at the time of preparing this report, preliminary data indicate a dramatic decline in ICT goods exports. In the following, special attention is given to the performance of the top six exporters of ICT goods in 2007 (see table III.3): China, the United States, Hong Kong (China), Japan, Singapore and Germany.[11]

Data from TradeMap (www.trademap.org), a database of the International Trade Centre (ITC), show a significant fall in exports in ICT goods in the months following September 2008 (figure III.8). There appears to be an element of seasonality in the decline for the two first months of the year, followed by a recovery in March and another decline in April. Similar changes were observed in 2008, but at a higher level. While all countries included here experienced a decline, the magnitude of the fall varies considerably.

In the months leading up to the crisis, China's exports of ICT goods saw strong growth, reaching an all time high of $22 billion in October 2008. Exports then fell sharply, by nearly 50 per cent to $11.4 billion in January 2009. They recovered somewhat in March, before sliding again in April and May. Compared to the same period in 2008, Chinese exports of ICT goods were almost 25 per cent lower in May 2009 (table III.6). As it

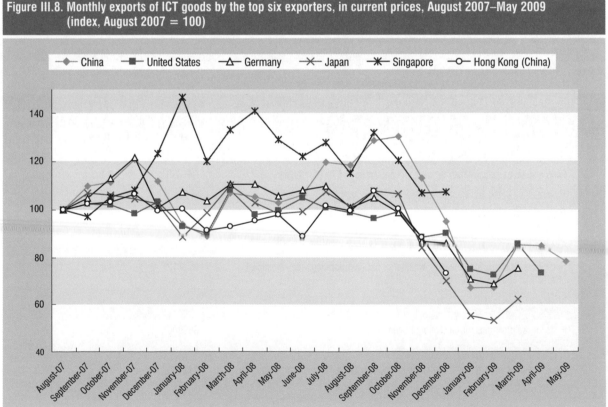

Figure III.8. Monthly exports of ICT goods by the top six exporters, in current prices, August 2007–May 2009 (index, August 2007 = 100)

Source: UNCTAD, based on the ITC TradeMap database.

Table III.6. Year on year variation in ICT goods exports by the world's top six exporters, August 2008-May 2009 (per cent)										
	2008						**2009**			
Exporters	**Aug.**	**Sept.**	**Oct.**	**Nov.**	**Dec.**	**Jan.**	**Feb.**	**Mar.**	**Apr.**	**May**
China	18.51	17.33	16.96	-6.46	-15.16	-28.53	-24.37	-20.38	-19.60	-24.06
United States	-1.42	-6.13	-2.84	-9.70	-12.67	-19.65	-19.49	-20.93	-25.36	n.a.
Germany	0.94	0.02	-12.49	-28.61	-14.61	-33.89	-33.65	-32.20	n.a.	n.a.
Japan	1.27	0.98	0.36	-19.74	-31.61	-37.83	-46.05	-43.38	n.a.	n.a.
Singapore	14.96	36.05	14.63	-1.48	-12.89	n.a	n.a	n.a	n.a.	n.a.
Hong Kong, China	-0.29	5.19	-2.82	-16.96	-26.24	n.a	n.a	n.a	n.a.	n.a.

Source: UNCTAD, based on ITC's TradeMap database.

is by far the largest source of such exports, China has seen the largest declines in absolute terms.

Exports of ICT goods from the United States were basically flat during the first three quarters of 2008. Sharp falls in January and February 2009 brought export volumes to approximately 20 per cent lower than the levels a year earlier. They recovered somewhat in March 2009 before falling again in April (figure III.8).

Germany's exports were also negatively affected by the crisis. In this case, the downward trend that started already in November 2007 accelerated in November 2008 (figure III.8). By March 2009, Germany's exports of ICT goods were one third below the level recorded in March 2008 (table III.6). Preliminary data from the Federal Statistical Office suggest that Germany's overall exports fell again in April and May.[12]

Of the top six exporters, Japan has experienced the steepest decline in relative terms, with its exports of ICT goods shrinking from $5.1 billion in October 2008 to $2.9 billion in March 2009. As in the cases of Germany and the United States, its exports had been stagnant in the months prior to the crisis. Despite a small recovery in Japan's ICT goods exports in March, they remained over 43 per cent below the level recorded a year earlier. Its export performance over this period suffered from a sharp appreciation of the Japanese yen against the United States dollar after September 2008. Indeed, despite some recovery, Japanese exports in April 2009 remained 39 per cent lower than in April 2008.[13]

Although Singapore's ICT goods exports in August and September 2008 remained considerably higher than a year earlier (table III.6), they have been on a downward trend since April 2008 (figure III.8). Data from International Enterprise Singapore show that exports continued to decline in early 2009. On a year-on-year basis,

electronic domestic exports were down by 38 per cent in January, 32 per cent in February and 26 per cent in March 2009.[14] Re-exports of electronic products were down even more. The decrease in electronic exports was largely due to lower exports of semiconductors, parts of personal computers and disk drives.

Finally, Hong Kong, China saw sizable reductions in its exports for November–December 2008 (table III.6). Although this economy had gained significant market shares in the beginning of the decade, its export performance had recently been stagnating. The role of Hong Kong, China as a gateway for trade into and out from China may mean that its trade performance will mirror that of China.

Beyond these top six exporters, the crisis has taken a toll also on smaller economies that rely on ICT goods in their exports (figure III.6). In Malta, for example, exports of ICT goods – in this case mostly semiconductors – fell sharply from a high of $135 million in September 2008 to $62 million in February 2009. They recovered somewhat in March, but remained at 25 per cent below the level a year earlier. Exports of ICT goods (mostly computers) from Costa Rica were also negatively influenced. Given the significant role of ICT goods in these countries' exports, such sharp reductions are likely to have serious repercussions on the two economies.

The downturn has hit many segments of the ICT goods. For example, in the first quarter of 2009, worldwide sales of servers were down 25 per cent compared with one year earlier.[15] Despite an upturn in April 2009, semiconductor sales were still down 25 per cent, year-on-year.[16] Even the demand for netbooks (small, cheap and underpowered laptops) dropped by 25 per cent in the first quarter, and sales of mobile phones were down about 9 per cent.[17] Storage software and

TV sales were down a more modest 5–6 per cent.[18] The main bright spot among the ICT goods has been smart phones (such as iPhones and BlackBerries), the demand for which was 12.7 per cent higher compared with the first quarter of 2008.[19] Many companies have suffered through declining profits and weakening demand, with frequent announcements of employment cuts as a result (table III.7).

It is too early to say how long it will take before the demand for ICT goods starts to pick up. Some data indicate that the fall in ICT goods trade may already have begun to bottom out in March 2009. Sales in semiconductors – an early indicator of developments in the ICT industry – increased in April 2009 and May 2009 by 6.4 per cent and 5.4 percent respectively.[20] Even though sales remained 25 per cent below the level a year before, they were higher than expected, boosted by growing demand for computer and mobile phones. On the other hand, the month of March often sees a seasonal increase in exports, and data for Germany and the United States do not appear to support an imminent turnaround.

At the time of preparing this report, there was considerable uncertainty with regard to the development of world trade during the rest of 2009 and for 2010. In June 2009, the World Bank predicted it to decline by as much as 9.7 per cent in 2009 (World Bank, 2009). Responses to a survey by the consultancy Gartner

of 900 chief information officers (CIOs) suggest that it will take a while before spending on ICT picks up. Some 42 per cent of the CIOs stated that they had lowered their budgets in the first quarter of 2009; only 4 per cent had seen increases.[21] Most respondents expected the economy to start bouncing back between the first and the third quarter of 2010. But even when the recovery begins, it is likely that ICT goods exports will remain well below their pre-crisis level for an extended period of time. In June 2009 the Semiconductor Industry Association forecast that semiconductors sales would be down 21.3 per cent in 2009 compared to 2008, and that sales would only slowly pick up in 2010 and 2011 (with a 6.5 per cent annual growth). If this turns out to be an accurate prediction, in 2011 sales in semiconductors would still be about 10 per cent lower than in 2008.

The fall in exports appears to have been particularly steep in economies whose exports were already stagnant or in decline prior to the crisis (Germany, Japan and the United States). This would imply that the crisis may accelerate a further shift in the geographic composition of ICT goods trade, with developing Asia reinforcing its market share. As more data become available over the course of 2009, a clearer picture will emerge. In any event, ICT goods exports have been much more severely affected than trade in IT and ICT-enabled services, which is the focus of the next section.

Table III.7. Examples of major employment reductions by ICT companies, October 2008–May 2009 (number of employees)

Company	Home country	Number of employees concerned	Date of announcement
Hewlett Packard	United States	24 600	October 2008
NEC	Japan	20 000	January 2009
Sony	Japan	16 000	December 2008
Panasonic	Japan	15 000	February 2009
AT&T	United States	12 000	December 2008
Pioneer	Japan	10 000	February 2009
Dell	United States	8 900	October 2008
Sprint Nextel	United States	8 000	January 2009
Sun Microsystems	United States	6 000	November 2008
Philips	Netherlands	6 000	January 2009
Ericsson	Sweden	5 000	January 2009
Microsoft	United States	5 000	January 2009
IBM	United States	5 000	March 2009
STMicroelectronics	United States	4 500	January 2009
Motorola	United States	4 000	January 2009

Source: Business Tech-CNET News (2009a).

B. OFFSHORING AND TRADE IN IT AND ICT-ENABLED SERVICES

IT and ICT-enabled services are growing in world trade. Increased broadband connectivity in a rising number of countries has facilitated the reorganization of the production of many services. Activities that once required face-to-face contact can now be split up into smaller components, which in turn can be undertaken in places offering the best locational advantages. The resulting offshoring of services has only just begun but is expected to continue to expand geographically and sectorally as well as across business functions. Moreover, the process is partly irreversible. Once companies learn to exploit the opportunities created by pooling services and locating them where they can be most efficiently produced, they are unlikely to return to "traditional" ways of organizing their business processes.

From a development perspective, the offshoring of services is an attractive proposition with potential benefits for all parties concerned. For the global economy as whole, it can generate efficiency gains from international specialization and trade. Importing companies and countries can access services at lower cost and focus on activities where they enjoy a comparative advantage. For the exporters of the services, offshoring can imply the creation of attractive employment opportunities, industrial diversification, export revenues, knowledge transfers and economic upgrading (UNCTAD, 2004; ECLAC, 2009). Meanwhile, as shown below, new countries are emerging on the radar screen as offshoring locations. Unsurprisingly, many governments are now seeking to design effective policies to boost related exports by local and foreign firms.

Measuring and understanding offshoring are no easy tasks, however. There is a lack of internationally agreed definitions of offshoring and there are many data limitations. An additional challenge is that the phenomenon is rapidly evolving. This section starts by reviewing different sources of data to gauge how offshoring of services was evolving until the current crisis erupted. It highlights the main industries and countries involved by reviewing various sources of information. After discussing the role of ICTs in the context of offshoring, the section turns to the implications of the crisis, distinguishing between the more immediate impacts and longer-term consequences. The overall picture that emerges is considerably more optimistic than in the case of ICT goods.

1. Recent trends

a. Defining the phenomenon

The offshoring of services grew rapidly during the past decade. While the phenomenon still accounts for a modest contribution to world trade, more and more companies in a growing number of industries and countries are embracing the opportunities created by ICTs for the specialization and internationalization of services. Offshoring of services occurs in different ways (figure III.9). It can be done internally by moving the production from a parent company to its foreign affiliates (often referred to as "captive offshoring"). It may also involve the international outsourcing of services to a third party services provider – domestically or foreign-owned.

The scope of activities that are affected by offshoring continues to expand. There is no internationally agreed approach to categorize the kinds of services that can be offshored, but it is common to make a distinction between IT services and ICT-enabled services (table III.8). The latter group covers front office services, back office services and various forms of knowledge process offshoring (KPO). Some activi-

Figure III.9. Offshoring and outsourcing

Location	Internalized production	Externalized production (outsourcing)
Domestic	Production kept in-house at home	Production outsourced to third party service provider at home
Foreign (offshoring)	Production by own foreign affiliate "captive offshoring"	Offshore outsourcing to third party provider abroad

Source: UNCTAD (2004): 148.

Table III.8. Categories of services affected by offshoring

Service category	Examples of service activities
IT services	Programming, systems integration, application testing, IT infrastructure management and maintenance, IT consulting, software development and implementation services, data processing and database services, IT support services, data warehousing, and content management and development
ICT-enabled services	
Front office services	Call centres and customer contact centres (inbound and outbound)
Back office services	Data entry, human resources, payroll, finance and accounting, procurement, transcription
KPO	Financial analysis, data mining, engineering, research and development, insurance claims processing, architectural design, remote education and publishing, medical diagnostics, journalism

Source: UNCTAD.

ties relate to specific industries while most are generic and relevant for businesses in virtually all industries. The skills involved range from relatively low levels of qualification (data entry, certain call centres) to very high levels (research and development, design, medical testing and financial analysis). As companies have grown more accustomed to the practice, supplier capabilities have improved and the quality of the fibre optic network has expanded, the offshoring of services with higher added value has gradually become more common (see e.g. KPMG, 2008).

The extent to which different services are exposed to offshoring varies considerably. Offshoring of traditional IT services such as programming and applications development are approaching a high level of maturity (table III.9). Today, companies considering offshoring these services can choose among many suppliers and locations, and the growth in adoption rates has started to taper off. Most business processes are found at an earlier stage of offshoring maturity, experiencing fast growth as more and more companies are still exploring the opportunities that offshoring can offer. Among these functions, customer contact services are the most mature, and knowledge services the least. The third stage comprises functions that are only just

emerging as candidates for offshoring, including, for example, procurement and legal process services.

Within the worldwide spending on technology products and related services, IT services represent the largest segment. Market analysts estimate global spending on IT services in 2008 to be worth about $557 billion, and spending on business processes outsourcing some $115 billion (IDC, 2008).[22] While only a small share of these expenditures involves international sourcing (offshoring), that part is growing. During the period 2004–2008, for example, the value of IT and ICT-enabled services sourced in a foreign location grew more than three times faster than the overall growth in outlays related to such services (ibid.). Global exports resulting from the offshoring of IT services and business processes have been estimated at $89 billion to $93 billion in 2008, up from $30 billion to $35 billion five years earlier (figure III.10). However, as these numbers do not include all cross-border sourcing occuring among the high-income countries, they underestimate the total value of offshoring.[23] In 2008, the market share of IT services was estimated to be about 60 per cent.

The preferred method of offshoring depends on the type of activity. While reliable data are lacking in this

Table III.9. Offshoring maturity levels of different service activities, selected examples

Level of maturity	Examples of services	Features
Already reaching maturity	IT services, such as programming and application development and maintenance	Decelerating adoption rates but continued growth in scope Clearly established players and locations Accepted business models and standards
Emerging rapid growth	Customer contacts Infrastructure management Finance and accounting Human resources Remote infrastructure monitoring Knowledge services	Accelerating adoption rates and increased scope and scale penetration Suppliers becoming established Market consolidation Location options with varying characteristics increasing Fewer, better established models leading to lower risk in choosing the appropriate design
Pioneer stage	Procurement Legal process offshoring	Untapped value proposition, early but few adopters Limited number of suppliers in few locations Multiple business models and unclear standards

Source: UNCTAD, based on information from Everest Research Institute, April 2009.

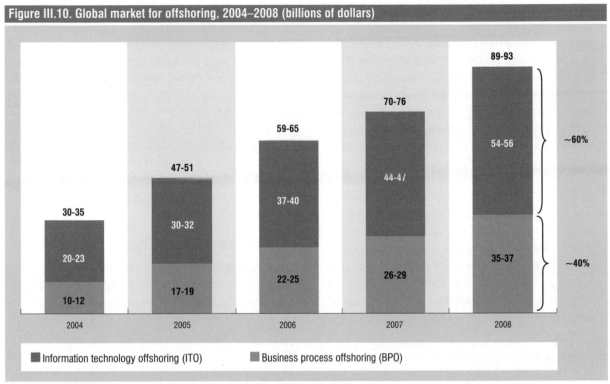

Figure III.10. Global market for offshoring, 2004–2008 (billions of dollars)

■ Information technology offshoring (ITO)   ■ Business process offshoring (BPO)

Source: UNCTAD, based on information from the Everest Research Institute.

area, "captive solutions" (i.e. services undertaken in-house in a foreign location) tend to be more important in the case of ICT-enabled services than in IT services (Boston Consulting Group, 2007). In India, for example, local service providers account for an estimated 70–75 per cent of the sales of IT services, foreign "captives" for 10–15 per cent and foreign third party providers also for a 10–15 per cent share. In the case of ICT-enabled services, the share of local Indian providers was estimated to be about 45–50 per cent, that of foreign captives 30–35 per cent and that of foreign third party providers 20–25 per cent (Nasscom, 2009).[24]

In countries with less developed local supplier capabilities than India, the relative importance of foreign affiliates (captive or third party providers) is often considerably higher. For example, even in a mature location such as the Philippines, foreign companies account for the bulk of ICT-enabled services exports. It is estimated that in 2008, around 90 per cent of such exports reported to the Board of Investment was accounted for by foreign companies.[25] In South Africa, more than half of all employees working with exports of business process services for the financial sector worked for foreign-owned companies (Everest Research Institute, 2008c). Similarly, in many locations in Latin America

and the Caribbean, foreign companies dominate. For example, a 2009 survey found their share of jobs related to the offshoring of business services to be 59 per cent in Honduras, 63 per cent in Saint Lucia, 82 per cent in Saint Vincent and the Grenadines and 90 per cent in El Salvador (ECLAC, 2009).

The use of offshoring varies also by industry. Financial services companies have been the leaders in this area, accounting for an estimated 40–45 per cent of the global offshoring market (Everest Research Institute, 2008c: 20). Among the next most important industries are high technology/telecommunications, manufacturing and retail.[26] The high proportion of offshoring related to financial services makes it particularly relevant to consider the implications of the global economic crisis (section III.B.3).

b. Mapping the new geography of offshoring

Comprehensive official data on the spread and magnitude of ICT-enabled offshoring in different countries simply do not exist.[27] To obtain a fairly accurate picture of the phenomenon, it is necessary to rely on a multitude of different sources. One review summarized the situation as follows (Arora et al., 2006: 96):

There are numerous problems with the current state of data. Definitions used in reporting offshoring's growth and impact are inconsistent with one another. All of the obvious metrics that could be used to measure offshoring have limitations. Government statistical organizations ... provide the greatest promise in providing good data because of their highly trained staffs and long traditions of quality, reliability, and objectivity. Governments collect data, however, in connection with existing policy issues, and the offshoring phenomenon is sufficiently different that existing government data sources turn out to be not very useful. Trade organizations and consulting firms are not disinterested parties, and these organizations are often unwilling to make public the methods and assumptions by which they arrive at their results so it is not surprising that there is some skepticism in the economic community about the credibility of their results. For many parts of the world, little or no data is being gathered.

The *Information Economy Report 2009* uses various data, including balance-of-payments statistics, data related to FDI projects, company information and market analysis. At the same time, the international community should take steps to address deficiencies in the current data situation. The lack of reliable and credible information increases the risk that the offshoring phenomenon is either exaggerated or underestimated, leading to misinformed policy responses. In order to encourage the development of better data, UNCTAD intends to initiate new work related to the measuring of offshoring (box III.3).

When the exporting of IT and ICT-enabled services first started to take off, a few countries quickly emerged as the key players. Among developed countries, Canada and Ireland were the front-runners, as were India and the Philippines among developing countries. Since then, many other countries have entered the scene. Global service providers today seek to offer flexible solutions to their clients by tapping into different knowledge pools, language skills and time zones. As a result, while the early movers remain the globally leading destinations for offshoring, various regional alternatives are now considered as attractive locations for specific services.

(i) Balance of payments data

Official statistics on trade in services are compiled by the International Monetary Fund (IMF) balance-of-payments data. Using such information to examine the offshoring of services has both benefits and limitations. An advantage is that data are available for a large group of countries. A limitation is that balance-of-payments data do not distinguish between the different modes of services supply, making it difficult to isolate trade flows that are related to cross-border supply facilitated by ICTs.[28] Another disadvantage is that they do not specifically identify "IT services" or "ICT-enabled services". Balance-of-payments data can be seen as an upper limit for any estimated value of offshored services (WTO, 2005).

In this report, the same definition of trade in IT and ICT-enabled services is used as in previous *Information*

Box III.3. New UNCTAD initiative to improve the measurement of ICT-enabled offshoring

The lack of consistent and reliable data makes it difficult to measure the magnitude of offshoring. It also limits the possibility for countries to benchmark their performance in terms of attracting services that are offshored. Currently, international comparisons have to rely on information and studies prepared by private consultancy firms, using varying methodologies and country coverage. Governments have expressed dissatisfaction with this lack of data, which makes it more difficult to design and assess policies. For example, at the seventh ITU World Telecommunication/ICT Indicators Meeting in Cairo on 3–5 March 2009, Egypt's Minister of Communications and Information Technology called upon the international community to work together to improve the situation. Several international organizations have also highlighted the poor data situation (ECLAC, 2009; OECD, 2004b and 2007; WTO, 2005). More generally, the United Nations Economic and Social Council has called upon the Partnership on Measuring ICT for Development to develop better benchmarks in the area of ICTs (resolution E/2008/3, para. 29).

As the organization within the partnership responsible for indicators related to trade in ICT, UNCTAD will seek to advance the work on developing better methods to capture the nature and magnitude of services offshoring. A first step will be to take stock of the various approaches currently used by national and international organizations and institutions, including in the private sector. UNCTAD will explore the interest of statisticians and policymakers with experience in the subject matter in participating in a working group whose task will be to assess existing methods against the needs of policymakers. Ultimately, the working group should propose concrete steps to improve the situation. A first meeting of the group would be organized in 2010.

Source: UNCTAD.

Table III.10. World trade in services and in IT and ICT-enabled services, 1990, 1995, 2000–2007 (billions of dollars and per cent)										
Item	1990	1995	2000	2001	2002	2003	2004	2005	2006	2007
Total services	826.7	1234.9	1524.0	1529.0	1640.5	1891.5	2288.2	2557.2	2878.1	3410.4
IT and ICT-enabled services	269.0	441.7	648.8	665.7	723.1	856.1	1033.4	1163.3	1354.3	1635.1
IT and ICT-enabled services as % of total services	32.5	35.8	42.6	43.5	44.1	45.3	45.2	45.5	47.1	47.9

Source: UNCTAD, based on data from IMF. See also annex table III.5.
Note: IT and ICT-enabled services include the following categories of services: communication; insurance; financial; computer and information; royalties and license fees; other business services; and personal, cultural and recreational services.

Economy Reports (see UNCTAD, 2002a and 2006b). Accordingly, the following categories of services are included: communication services; insurance services; financial services; computer and information services; royalties and license fees; other business services; and personal, cultural and recreational services.[29] One reason for such a broad definition is technology convergence. It has become increasingly difficult to distinguish between, for example, computer-related services, business services, value added telecommunications services and software services. Using the broad definition, world trade in IT and ICT-enabled services amounted to $1.635 trillion in 2007 (table III.10). Between 2000 and 2007, such services grew in importance as a share of total services trade – from 42.6 to 47.9 per cent.

The United States was by far the largest exporter of such services in 2007; its exports amounted to $270 billion (figure III.11). The United Kingdom was a clear second. While most of the top 15 exporters are developed countries, India had the fifth largest, China the tenth largest and Hong Kong, China the thirteenth largest exports in the world.

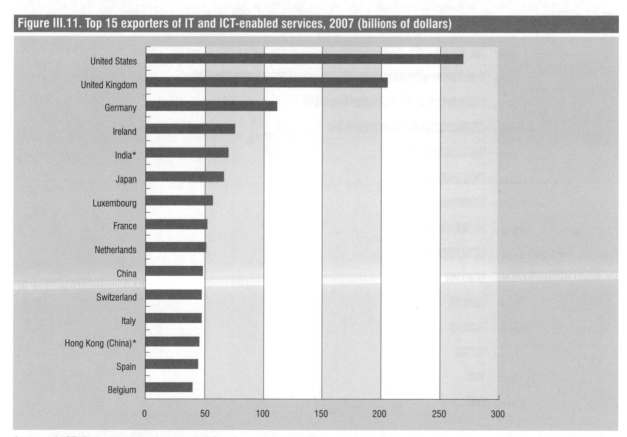

Figure III.11. Top 15 exporters of IT and ICT-enabled services, 2007 (billions of dollars)

Source: UNCTAD, based on data from the IMF. See also annex table III.4.
*Note: * The 2007 export values for India and Hong Kong, China are estimates. The values were derived based on the growth rate for "other services" between 2006 and 2007.*

Judging from balance-of-payments data, the most dynamic exporters of IT and ICT-enabled services have mainly concentrated in selected developing countries in Asia, Russian Federation and some EU countries. Between 2000 and 2007, India and Ireland reported the largest export market share gains (figure III.12). India's exports of such services rose from $10 billion to an estimated $69 billion, increasing its market share from 1.6 to 4.2 per cent. In the case of Ireland – the world's fourth largest exporter in 2007 – its market share grew by 2.4 percentage points to 4.6 per cent. Other dynamic developing and transition economy exporters included Argentina, China, Kuwait, Russian Federation and Singapore.

At the opposite end of the spectrum, the largest declines were observed for the United States, followed by Japan, France and Canada (annex table III.5). Despite increasing its total exports of IT and ICT-enabled services from $127 billion to $270 billion, the market share of the United States fell by three percentage points to 16.5 per cent in 2007. Several other devel-

oped countries also experienced declines as did the developing economies of Egypt, Hong Kong (China), Malaysia, Mexico, Saudi Arabia, Taiwan Province of China and Turkey.

(ii) Data on FDI projects related to selected ICT-enabled services

As noted above, much of the offshoring of services involves FDI. Information on the number of new FDI projects can offer insights into the international locations of offshoring projects that involve foreign investment. Such data are privately collected and available only for the period 2003–2008.[30] Special attention is given here to FDI projects related to such business processes as customer contact services (front office services) and back office services, proxied by the location of "shared services centres".[31] Unsurprisingly, the patterns that emerge differ from those based on balance-of-payments data. First, the coverage of services is much narrower. Secondly, these FDI data do

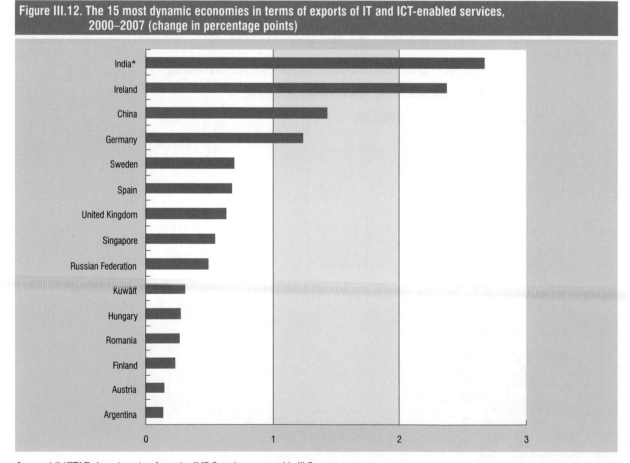

Figure III.12. The 15 most dynamic economies in terms of exports of IT and ICT-enabled services, 2000–2007 (change in percentage points)

Source: UNCTAD, based on data from the IMF. See also annex table III.5.
Note: * India's export value for 2007 was estimated based on the growth rate for "other services" between 2006 and 2007.

not capture projects involving outsourcing of services to local companies. Thirdly, the analysis is based on the number of projects, rather than on the volume of exports.

Most FDI projects related to customer contact and shared services centres are undertaken by companies based in developed countries. During the period 2003–2008, two countries – the United States and the United Kingdom – accounted for more than half of the 847 known FDI-related contact centre projects and more than two thirds of the 481 known shared services centre projects.[32] Less than 8 per cent of the projects were undertaken by companies from the South. The predominance of developed country firms partly reflects that cost reduction is still the main driver for the establishment abroad of many business processes (UNCTAD, 2004).

Contrary to common perceptions, however, customer contact and shared services centres are not only set up in the South. In fact, during the 2003–2008 period, the majority of the known contact centre FDI projects, and almost half (44 per cent) of all shared service centre FDI projects, were implemented in developed countries (table III.11). Savings can be achieved not only by seeking out lower-cost locations, but also by consolidating operations and reducing the cost of infrastructure, training and management. Developed host countries that attracted a large number of customer contact centre projects included Canada, France, Germany, Ireland and the United States. In the case of shared service centres, developed country destinations often chosen included the Czech Republic, Hungary, Ireland, Poland and the United Kingdom.[33] Differences between the two categories reflect the particular importance attached to English language skills in the case of front office services.

Among developing countries, Asia's strong position as a preferred host region is confirmed in the FDI project data. That region accounted for two thirds of all customer contact centre projects in developing countries, and almost 90 per cent of all shared services centre projects in the South. India and the Philippines were the front-runners for both types of projects. Outside Asia, several countries have emerged as destinations. In Africa, Morocco attracted the largest number of projects during 2003–2008, followed by South Africa and Egypt. In Latin America, Costa Rica was the top recipient – with seven new contact centres and 10 shared service centre projects – followed by Argentina and Brazil.

There appears to be a tendency among transnational corporations (TNCs) to diversify their customer contact and shared services projects into new locations. A comparison of the number of projects undertaken in the principal developing country regions suggests that the share of Latin America and the Caribbean increased between 2003–2005 and 2006–2008, while the share of developing Asia and Oceania fell (table III.12). The shift was more pronounced for customer contact centres, where Asia's share shrank from 74 per cent to 57 per cent. Latin America and the Caribbean saw its share of customer contact centre projects grow from 16 per cent to 33 per cent, and its proportion of shared services centres increase from 5 per cent to 11 per cent. Greater geographical diversity in customer contact services reflects companies' desire to cover multiple time and language zones.

That Latin America and the Caribbean is increasingly important as an offshoring destination has been corroborated in other studies (e.g. ECLAC, 2009; A.T. Kearney, 2007). The bulk of services offshored to this region has been in relatively low skilled contact centres, but exports of higher value added service activities have also grown in some places, including Uruguay (box III.4). Reasons that have been cited for investing in this region include proximity to the United States, language capabilities (especially English and Spanish) and the existence of talent and technology hubs in some areas with low attrition rates. Oftentimes, a presence in Latin America and the Caribbean can serve as a complement to service activities in Asia and other parts of the world as companies seek to ensure flexible service delivery round the clock.

(iii) Market analysis data

Market analysis firms represent a third source of information. As noted above, the global market for the offshoring of IT and ICT-enabled services was estimated at around $500 billion in 2008, of which IT services accounted for 60 per cent (figure III.10). A closer examination of these data confirms the trend towards geographical diversification, at least in the case of ICT-enabled services. In 2004, five countries – Canada, China, India, Ireland and the Philippines – accounted for as much as 95 per cent of the total market for business process offshoring; by 2008, their combined share had shrunk to 80 per cent as new attractive locations had emerged (figure III.13). Among new major destinations are Malaysia and Singapore in Asia; Czech Republic, Hungary, Poland and Romania

Table III.11. Number of FDI projects related to selected ICT-enabled services, 2003-2008 (Number of projects)

By host region/economy	Customer contact centres							Shared services centres						
	2003	2004	2005	2006	2007	2008	03-08	2003	2004	2005	2006	2007	2008	03-08
World	176	149	141	144	119	118	847	75	80	99	114	60	53	481
Developed economies	105	69	83	97	61	46	461	35	28	43	51	31	22	210
Canada	30	13	13	10	1	1	68	3	1	1	1	-	-	6
United Kingdom	14	13	14	13	11	7	72	3	2	6	5	2	2	20
France	1	1	10	20	7	2	41	1	-	1	2	-	1	5
United States	6	3	5	7	10	5	36	1	-	1	2	2	1	7
Ireland	11	5	8	5	1	3	33	7	4	7	2	1	1	22
Germany	5	5	4	6	5	4	29	-	-	-	1	1	-	2
Spain	2	5	1	6	5	3	22	1	6	2	2	3	-	14
Poland	3	3	2	3	8	2	21	3	2	8	13	3	8	37
Czech Republic	2	1	3	4	1	-	11	6	3	4	4	1	2	20
Hungary	3	1	3	2	1	1	11	5	4	3	7	5	1	25
Australia	5	5	1	-	-	6	17	-	-	1	1	3	-	5
Romania	-	1	2	3	3	6	15	-	1	2	3	4	3	13
Other	23	13	17	18	8	6	85	5	5	7	8	6	3	34
Developing economies	71	80	52	47	57	70	377	39	52	55	62	28	31	267
Africa	5	8	7	4	9	5	38	2	2	1	-	4	1	10
Morocco	1	6	3	2	2	1	15	-	-	-	-	3	1	4
South Africa	1	-	1	2	2	1	7	1	-	-	-	-	-	1
Egypt	1	-	1	-	2	2	6	-	-	1	-	-	-	1
Tunisia	-	1	1	-	2	1	5	-	-	-	-	-	-	-
Other African countries	2	1	1	-	1	-	5	1	2	-	-	1	-	4
Latin America and the Caribbean (LAC)	11	12	10	12	21	24	90	2	1	4	6	4	3	20
Argentina	-	1	2	2	4	3	12	-	-	-	2	-	-	2
Brazil	2	3	1	2	-	3	11	-	-	1	1	-	1	3
Colombia	-	-	2	1	4	3	10	-	-	-	-	-	-	-
Costa Rica	2	-	-	1	3	1	7	-	1	3	3	2	1	10
Mexico	2	-	3	-	1	3	9	-	-	-	-	1	1	2
Chile	-	1	-	2	1	1	5	2	-	-	-	-	-	2
Uruguay	-	2	1	-	1	3	7	-	-	-	-	-	-	-
El Salvador	1	2	-	-	1	1	5	-	-	-	-	-	-	-
Other LAC economies	4	3	1	4	6	6	24	-	-	-	-	1	-	1
Asia and Oceania	55	60	35	31	27	41	249	35	49	50	56	20	27	237
India	26	32	8	10	6	8	90	24	38	34	40	5	10	151
Philippines	10	16	10	14	7	19	70	-	0	0	6	7	7	20
China	9	6	3	2	4	4	28	2	-	5	3	3	5	18
Singapore	1	2	2	2	2	1	10	3	2	1	4	-	1	11
United Arab Emirates	4	1	1	-	-	1	7	-	-	-	2	1	-	3
Malaysia	4	1	-	-	1	2	8	3	3	1	2	3	3	15
Other Asian economies	1	2	11	3	7	6	30	3	3	3	-	1	1	11
Transition economies	-	-	6	-	1	2	9	1	-	1	1	1	-	4
Russian Federation	-	-	4	-	1	-	5	1	-	-	-	-	-	1
Other transition economies	-	-	2	-	-	2	4	-	-	1	1	1	-	3

Source: UNCTAD FDI/TNC database.
Note: The table mentions developing and transition economies with at least five projects during the 2003–2008 period, and developed economies with at least 20 projects.

Table III.12. FDI projects in developing countries related to customer contact centres and shared services centres, 2003–2005 and 2006–2008, by host country (percentage share of all projects in developing economies)

Host region	Customer contact centres		Shared services centres	
	2003–2005	2006–2008	2003–2005	2006–2008
Developing economies	100	100	100	100
Africa	10	10	3	4
Latin America and the Caribbean	16	33	5	11
Asia and Oceania	74	57	92	85

Source: UNCTAD FDI/TNC database.

Box III.4. Uruguay – an emerging offshoring destination

Uruguay has emerged as an attractive regional offshoring destination in Latin America. In 2006, more than 750 companies were involved in the exporting of business services worth more than $500 million and employing almost 18,000 people (box table III.4.1). Uruguay has one of the highest incomes per capita in Latin America and boasts a well-educated population and a relatively high level of ICT readiness. According to the ICT Development Index, it was the third highest ranked country in Latin America, just after Argentina and Chile (ITU, 2009a).

Most companies involved in offshoring benefit from either of two regulatory incentive schemes: duty free zones (DFZs) or special incentives for the ICT and audiovisual service industries. Under both schemes, companies can enjoy fiscal exemptions from domestic taxes (value added and rental taxes) and the elimination of import tariffs (on inputs and investment goods and equipment). Under the special sectoral regimes, fiscal incentives apply only to export sales. Foreign affiliates dominate in DFZs, and domestic companies are the main beneficiaries of the special incentives for ICT and audiovisual services. In general, foreign affiliates are more export-oriented than domestic firms.

In the past few years, Uruguay has attracted a number of TNCs. In IT and consulting services, Tata Consultancy Services (India) is the leading investor. Its centre in Uruguay employs more than 800 people and exports make up 90 per cent of its sales (ECLAC, 2009). In the case of call centres, two foreign affiliates of Sabre and RCI (both from the United States) together employed more than 1,000 people in 2006. Outside the DFZs, there are several important domestic companies, such as Quanam, CSI and Memory, which export consulting and professional services and software mainly to the regional market. In the audiovisual industry, the main actors are domestic firms – such as Metropolis and Salado Films – associated with TNCs.

Although official data are lacking, the exports of business services have continued to expand. In 2007–2008, at least four new foreign contact centres were established, including by IBM (United States) and Grupo Konecta (Spain). It remains to be seen how the current economic crisis will influence the industry's prospects in the country. There are some concerns that new protectionist measures will be adopted, with potential negative effects on exports from Uruguay. However, there is little so far to indicate any significant slowdown in the offshoring activity in the country. In fact, two main projects of new areas for offshoring services are being developed in Uruguay, with the creation of at least 4,000 new jobs as a result.

Source: UNCTAD, based on Vaillant (2008) and Vaillant and Lalanne (2009).

Box table III.4.1. Exports of business services and related employment, Uruguay, 2006 (millions of dollars, number of workers and per cent)

Category of services	Firms (numbers)	Exports (millions of dollars)	Export orientation (per cent)	Employment (workers)
Duty Free Trade Zones	258	200	66	3,601
IT services	45	85	81	556
Consulting services	141	45	78	822
Call centre services	2	58	100	1,022
Other business services	70	90	93	1,201
Particular regimes	500	220	40	14,000
ICT services	300	120	40	10,000
Audiovisual services	200	100	40	4,000
Total	758	500	58	17,601

Source: Vaillant (2008) and Vaillant and Lalanne (2009).

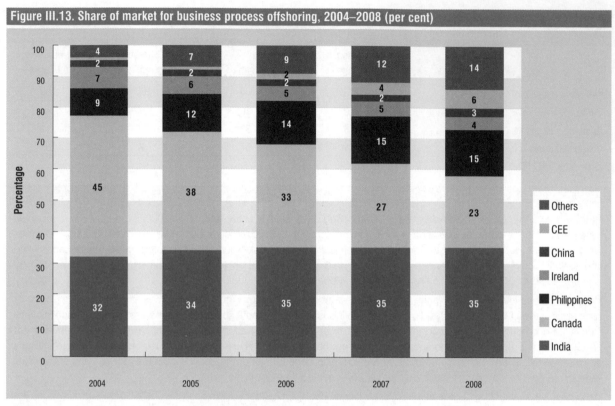

Figure III.13. Share of market for business process offshoring, 2004–2008 (per cent)

Source: UNCTAD, based on data from the Everest Research Institute.

in Europe; and Latin American economies such as Argentina, Brazil and Mexico.

In the case of IT services, fewer new locations have been able to challenge the position of the more established countries. India remains the preferred choice for exports of such services, with a market share in 2008 of about 55 per cent, according to data from the Everest Research Institute (figure III.14). Canada accounted for another 18 per cent and new EU members for about 6 per cent. Brazil, China and Mexico were the main countries in the "others" category.[34] For the provision of IT services, having a presence in different time zones and different language areas is less important than for many business processes. English is the dominant language, and the choice of location is primarily determined by the cost and availability of appropriate skills. Another important advantage of India is the possibility to scale up projects relatively quickly.[35]

In summary, the review of the three different sources of data shows that a new geography of offshoring is emerging. As part of its rapid growth in the past few years, a number of countries in Africa, Asia, Europe and Latin America and the Caribbean are today per-

ceived as attractive candidates for the production of various business services. This trend is particularly visible in the case of voice-based services, where companies look to develop global supply capabilities covering many language areas and time zones. Meanwhile, the scope of services affected by offshoring is continuously evolving, which means that countries should carefully assess in what areas they represent a competitive export location.

2. How important is the quality of ICT infrastructure?

For countries seeking to promote exports of IT and ICT-enabled services, the quality of the ICT infrastructure is important. Whereas in the early days of offshoring, relatively few locations could offer acceptable connectivity, the spread of ICTs has allowed many more countries to be seen as potential destinations. Today, good ICT infrastructure is regarded as a necessary but not sufficient condition to attract export-oriented services projects. When assessing the ICT infrastructure, the quality and costs of international telecommunication connectivity are particularly important, although requirements vary for different services.

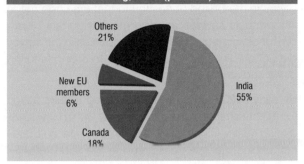

Figure III.14. Share of market for information technology offshoring, 2008 (per cent)

Others 21%

New EU members 6%

Canada 18%

India 55%

Source: UNCTAD, based on data from the Everest Research Institute.
Note: 100 per cent = $54–56 billion

With regard to international telecom connectivity, companies look for redundancy in bandwidth, i.e. multiple providers or cables supporting international connectivity. Rather than a country-level minimum threshold, requirements centre on whether there is redundancy and if there are multiple providers supporting bandwidth delivery. For example, Costa Rica was already supporting offshore services when it had only one fibre optic bandwidth pipe into the country. This has since developed and there are now multiple pipes into the country.[36]

When considering the quality of international telecom connectivity, companies typically look at various reliability metrics (such as extent of down time) to assess the stability and quality of the infrastructure available. For example, in the United States, quality of connectivity is often required to be high enough to ensure that the service can be delivered up to 99.999 per cent of the time; in an offshore location, the equivalent threshold is typically 99.9 per cent.[37]

Requirements are particularly strict for certain types of services. For remote IT infrastructure management, extremely high standards are required, and only locations with very reliable infrastructure can be considered. For voice-based services, reliability is also important but less critical than in the case of remote IT infrastructure management. In the case of voice-based customer contact centres, it is difficult to rely on satellite technology, as latency becomes an issue, which in turn means that fibre optic links are usually required.[38] Given the importance of fibre optic connectivity for voice-based services, the spread of submarine cables in Africa (chapter I) should make more countries potentially interesting as locations for contact centres. For data traffic, there can be more

flexibility, making it possible in certain situations to rely on satellite connections.

There are no absolute metrics (e.g. minimum international telecom bandwidth) at a country level as location decisions typically involve highly company- and site-specific criteria. This is primarily because requirements differ across companies, e.g. in terms of the size of the centre. For companies processing very large quantities of data, the extent of bandwidth may be more important than the reliability of the connections.

Finally, the cost aspect is important. The two main cost items are wages and connectivity costs. When connectivity costs are kept relatively high by local telecom operators, it can slow the growth of services exports and/or reduce the scope for paying higher compensation to employees.

3. Implications of the crisis: a mixed picture

Exporters of IT and ICT-enabled services appear to have weathered the global economic crisis considerably better than ICT goods exporters. One reason for this is that companies see offshoring of services as one way to reduce their production costs and enhance their competitiveness. In the short term, the volume of offshoring of services is influenced by two opposing forces. On the one hand, services exports may decline due to a general slowdown in economic activity. This applies especially to services offshored by the financial industry, in which some companies may disappear altogether.[39] On the other hand, as the recession adds pressure on companies across industries to reduce production costs, some will choose to source more services, and new services, from lower cost locations.[40] In the longer term, and as the global economy recovers, both the volume and the scope of offshoring are likely to grow significantly.

The analysis in this section draws on field research, media reports and information presented by leading companies in the industry. It examines the immediate impact as well as the medium- and longer-term growth prospects to expand the scale and scope of offshoring to new business segments and geographies. Special attention is given to developments in India as it is the largest developing country exporter of IT and ICT-enabled services. When this report was prepared, there was still considerable uncertainty with regard to the depth and longevity of the global economic downturn. Moreover, the availability of official data for recent months is generally limited, which means that the analysis has to rely on private sector market estimates and forecasts. Thus, predictions of future outcomes should be regarded as tentative.

a. Short-term and long-term effects differ

The prospects for the modalities of continued export-oriented growth in IT and ICT-enabled services are being re-examined in the light of the global economic downturn. Most firms are facing a deceleration of growth in demand, but optimism appears to prevail regarding the long-term prospects for the IT and ICT-enabled services industry.

As the impact of the global economic slowdown has slowly started to become clearer, projections for spending on IT and ICT-enabled services have gradually been revised downwards. IT organizations worldwide are trimming their budgets and cutting back on discretionary spending (Gartner, 2009).[41] The speed and severity of the response by businesses and consumers alike to these economic circumstances should result in a market slowdown in 2009 that will be worse than the 2.1 per cent decline in IT spending in 2001 when the "dot com" bubble ended. In the short term, reduced spending on ICT should have a chilling effect on the demand for offshoring. In India, for example, prior to September 2008, exports of IT and ICT-enabled services were projected to grow by 21–24 per cent in 2008/09 in dollar terms; by February 2009 this estimate had been reduced to a 16–17 per cent growth rate reflecting substantially lower growth in export earnings from October 2008 to March 2009 (Nasscom, 2009). Other analysts agree that growth in IT offshoring will remain moderate in 2009 and 2010, and that economic uncertainty, increased competition, price cuts in smaller projects and recession will continue through the first half of 2009, with revenues starting to improve in the second half of 2009 and in 2010 (Forrester, 2009).

The effects of the crisis on corporate behaviour will evolve over time. In India, the eruption of the crisis was followed in October–December 2008 by a slowdown in revenue growth, but both revenue and employment continued to grow. This first phase was characterized by increased caution among buyers. The issuing of new major services contracts was basically frozen and some contracts were cancelled altogether. Buyers of IT and ICT-enabled services held back on discretion-

ary spending but less so on services related to maintenance. A November 2008 survey of 100 companies based in the United States found that the crisis made labour costs savings an even more important objective for offshoring. Otherwise, companies in the survey did not predict significant changes to their offshoring plans and strategies (Lewin et al., 2009).

By early 2009, companies had started to take action to limit the effects of the crisis, mainly with a view to reducing costs. According to the survey of United States companies, actions considered in the short term included benchmarking offshoring contracts, closer scrutiny of service provider invoices, assessments of service provider performance and evaluations of current offshore sourcing locations to determine whether other centres might be more advantageous (Lewin et al., 2009). In India, there have been examples of buyers cancelling or postponing new offshoring contracts due to budget cuts, and some have sought to renegotiate existing agreements. In fact, some of the slower revenue growth among vendors in India reflects increased pressure by buyers to cut billing rates. Billing rates have declined by 5–30 per cent as a result of renegotiations of old contracts or the issuing of new ones (Gartner, 2009).

Several market analysts forecast that the export revenue growth of IT and ICT-enabled services will rebound relatively quickly. At the time this report was prepared, the rebound was expected to occur in the second half of 2009 or early 2010. Many buyers who delayed contracts as an immediate reaction to the global economic crisis will find it increasingly difficult to postpone decisions any further, resulting in new contracts (Mitra, forthcoming). Moreover, greater pressure to cut costs and the maturing of existing as well as new applications may imply that many firms will consider expanding the scale and scope of their offshoring activities.

Given the current focus on cutting costs, more firms in the developed countries may be expected to expand their offshore operations in the medium and long term. For companies in industries with limited experience with offshoring, the crisis may act as a trigger for them to explore the opportunities provided by sourcing services from abroad. According to some studies, the greatest potential for more offshoring is likely to be in health care, retail, retail banking, ICT and insurance industries (ECLAC, 2009). Existing users of offshoring as well as new ones are also likely to show increased interest in sourcing a wider range of business functions in order to reduce costs.[42] In the medium to long run, this should translate into larger volumes of offshoring activity. When the economic cycle eventually improves, a surge in IT and ICT-enabled services exports can be expected. By then, more companies will have been exposed to offshoring.

b. Effects vary by industry segment and type of firm

Some segments of the offshoring industry in India appear to have been more affected than others.[43] In the case of IT services, non-discretionary services such as mandatory operations and maintenance have been less affected than discretionary services such as consulting. Similarly, application development work has been more affected than application management. While companies have been reluctant to upgrade or attempt to develop new applications, application management and maintenance are essential services that are more difficult to scale down. In the case of ICT-enabled services, a mixed picture emerges. Some vendors have been severely hit and others less so. Again, discretionary spending has been the most affected. This may imply more negative effects for front office (customer care/marketing) services than for back office services (e.g. accounting, human resources, and payroll), although data to confirm this have yet to emerge. Knowledge process offshoring, including research, product development and engineering, appears to have been badly affected as companies have cancelled or delayed related work both at home and offshore. Many firms will eventually commit to offshore more work in this area as such investments are essential to ensure their future competitiveness.

The effects of the crisis also vary between industries. As noted above, the financial services industry accounts for the largest share of services sourced offshore (section III.B.1). Consequently, the strategic responses by banks, insurance companies and other financial services significantly influence the overall impact. In 2008, the total value of outsourcing deals involving financial services dropped by 28 per cent to its lowest level since 2001 (TPI, 2009). Some observers believe that financial institutions in Europe and the United States reduced their volume of newly awarded outsourcing contracts by nearly 30 per cent in 2008 compared with 2007.[44] In India, banking, financial services and insurance have remained the largest industry segment for IT and ICT-enabled services exports, accounting for 41 per cent of all such exports in 2008/09 (Nasscom,

2009). Other industries significantly affected by the slowdown include travel, retail, telecommunication, manufacturing and engineering services. Less affected industries include IT and ICT-enabled services for the health sector and public administration.[45]

All of these business segments, including banking, financial services and insurance, are, however, expected to resume growth as the global economy recovers. Some indications, especially for the medium or long term, paint quite a positive picture. Some forecast that offshoring of business processes by financial services companies will increase an impressive 25 times its current market size over the next five years.[46] Moreover, for some major financial groups, offshoring may form one element of a strategy to get out of the current crisis. For example, as part of its global restructuring efforts, Citigroup in November 2008 announced that it would add 1,000 people to its front office and back office service functions in the Philippines.[47] Similarly, JP Morgan Chase announced plans to increase its outsourcing to India by 25 per cent in 2009 to nearly $400 million. It also stated that it would manage the integration of two companies it had acquired (Washington Mutual and Bear Sterns) from India in order to bring down the cost of harmonizing the different IT systems.[48]

The crisis will have dissimilar effects on different service providers. Those with a relatively high exposure to clients in the financial sector and to the United States market may be the most vulnerable in the short term (Everest Research Institute, 2008b). Some predict that, while the more established companies are well supplied with liquidity and may see the current crisis as an opportunity to reappraise their operations, smaller companies may be more affected. SMEs typically have fewer clients and often depend more on service niches characterized by a relatively high degree of discretionary IT spending, i.e. expenditures that have been cut back the most during recent months. Moreover, smaller suppliers are often more exposed to the volatility of demand, exchange rates and the credit crunch. But it is difficult to generalize with regard to the impact on large versus smaller firms. Some SMEs may also enjoy certain advantages, especially if they are able to offer lower cost solutions than the large vendors.

c. Implications for different exporting countries

While the lack of data makes it hard to assess the impact on different country exporters of IT and ICT-enabled services, some tentative conclusions can be made.

First, countries that mainly export their services to the United States and the United Kingdom may be the most vulnerable to potential negative effects in the short term. This may include companies in Latin America and the Caribbean as well as those in Asian economies such as India and the Philippines. For example, in 2008/09, four fifths of India's IT and ICT-enabled services exports went to the United States and the United Kingdom; the United States accounted for 81 per cent of all ICT-enabled services exports from the Philippines in 2006. In the medium- to long-term perspective, this may become less of an issue. The United States and other English-speaking developed economies are likely to continue to dominate IT spending and the purchasing of offshore services for the foreseeable future. Indeed, even after the crisis, five out of every six new large deals won by Tata Consultancy Services have been from the United States.[49] This market will grow rapidly again but it is hard to foresee if the growth will reach levels similar or even higher than what was typical prior to the global economic slump.

Secondly, despite the expected sustained importance of anglophone countries as importers of IT and ICT-enabled services, much of the incremental growth in offshoring is likely to come from other developed countries as well as from various emerging economies. The fact that the current economic crisis is global in nature implies that companies in most economies may have to consider the offshoring option to protect their cost competitiveness. This means that countries servicing languages areas other than English may find new business opportunities. In China, for example, 50 per cent of ICT service exports are already delivered to Japan and the Republic of Korea.[50] Emerging offshore locations in Latin America and Africa are likely to continue to gain strength as companies look for complementary assets in terms of skills and time zones. Global specialized service providers are continuously oooking new locations from which to serve various major language areas. For African economies that will become connected to submarine fibre optic cables in the near future, new possibilities will emerge to serve foreign locations with voice-based services, provided the right framework conditions are created.

Thirdly, India has long been the preferred location in the area of IT and ICT-enabled services. It has managed to upgrade its supplier capabilities and is continuously expanding the range of services that can be exported. The decline in demand may be a mixed blessing for India-based exporters. On the one hand

it is already translating into lower profit margins and reduced growth. On the other hand, it has provided some breathing space in an otherwise overheated market that was until recently characterized by high labour attrition and rising wage costs. In turbulent times, India may also benefit from its reputation as a location that is "tried and tested" (Mitra, forthcoming).

Latecomers in Africa, Asia and Latin America and the Caribbean will have to continue to improve their locational advantages and identify the niches in which they can compete most effectively. Key issues to address include the costs and quality of broadband connections, the availability of human resources in the areas targeted and the effective promotion of existing opportunities to potential investors. To the extent that countries choose to offer financial or fiscal incentives to lure investors into the production of ICT-enabled services, it is important to adapt the incentive schemes to the nature of such projects – with more emphasis on costs related to human resources than on capital investments (UNCTAD, 2004). At the same time, countries should be cautious not to be too generous when offering incentives as it may fuel a race to the bottom among potential destinations. Those locations that have already emerged on the radar screen for services with low added value may aim to move gradually towards more sophisticated service production. The challenge in this case is to develop the kinds of human resources as well as the regulatory framework (protection of intellectual property and private data) necessary to be able to compete with alternative locations.

In summary, long-term growth prospects for the offshoring of IT and ICT-enabled services are promising for early starters (such as India) as well as many other emerging locations. As the global offshoring business is poised to grow, there should be room for more countries to develop a sizeable export-oriented services industry if they can meet companies' needs for complementary assets in terms of skills and time zones. The scope of industries and business functions that become subject to offshoring is also expected to expand in the longer term. A recent assessment of the long-term prospects of the offshoring industry suggest that as much as 80 per cent of its incremental revenue until 2020 is expected to come from new industries (such as the public sector, health care, media and utilities), customers (especially SMEs) and countries (Nasscom and McKinsey. 2009).

NOTES

[1] While the prices of all manufactured goods rose by 35 per cent from 2002 to 2007, those of commodities increased by 113 per cent and those of crude petroleum by 185 per cent over the same period (UNCTAD, 2008b).

[2] By comparison, the share of fuels in world merchandise trade was 15 per cent in 2007, and those of agricultural and automotive products were 8.3 per cent and 9 per cent, respectively (WTO, 2008).

[3] Developed economies in America include Bermuda, Canada and the United States. Developed economies in Asia include Israel and Japan.

[4] The 12 new EU members are Bulgaria, Cyprus, the Czech Republic, Estonia, Hungary, Malta, Latvia, Lithuania, Poland, Romania, Slovakia and Slovenia.

[5] Imports in ICT goods are less concentrated than exports of ICT goods; the top ten importers accounted for close to 65 per cent of world imports in 2007.

[6] The ratios of ICT goods exports and imports over total exports and imports are two of the core indicators defined by the Partnership on Measuring of ICT for Development. They have been included to allow for international comparisons of the ICT trade performance of different nations (see annex table III.4).

[7] Malta's exports of ICT goods comprise almost exclusively one product, "other semiconductor devices" (HS-1996 code 854150). It accounted for 92 per cent of the country's exports of ICT goods in 2007.

[8] See e.g. http://www.caribbeannetnews.com/article.php?news_id=15078.

[9] At the product level (6 digits HS-1996), the largest item in Paraguays's imports of ICT goods were laptops (portable digital automatic data processing machines, weighing not more than 10 kg (HS-1996 code: 847130)). This product category accounted for 23.8 per cent of Paraguay's total ICT goods imports in 2007.

[10] In 2006, the top 20 products accounted for 75 per cent of ICT goods trade (OECD, 2009a).

[11] Data availability for these economies varies. At the time of drafting, information for Hong Kong (China) and Singapore was available up to December 2008; for Germany and Japan up to March 2009; for the United States up to April 2009; and for China up to May 2009.

[12] See *Statistisches Bundesamt Deutschland* (2009a and 2009b).

[13] Ministry of Finance, Trade statistics of Japan, April 2009. http://www.customs.go.jp/toukei/suii/html/time_e.htm.

[14] See various press releases from IE Singapore at www.news.gov.sg.

[15] See *Business Tech-CNET News* (2009b).

[16] See *Business Tech-CNET News* (2009c).

[17] See *Business Tech-CNET News* (2009d).

[18] See *Business Tech-CNET News* (2009e and 2009f).

[19] See *Business Tech-CNET News* (2009d).

[20] See http://www.sia-online.org/cs/papers_publications/press_release_detail?pressrelease.id=1612 and http://www.sia-online.org/cs/papers_publications/press_release_detail?pressrelease.id=1629.

[21] See *Business Tech-CNET News* (2009g).

[22] Spending on IT outsourcing grew by 7.2 per cent in 2008, as companies continued to focus on their core activities and contract external service providers for various IT activities (IDC, 2008).

[23] The Everest Research Institute does not include all types of cross-border exports. While new EU member countries' (e.g. the Czech Republic or Romania) exports of services to countries into other European countries is captured, Everest does not include, for example, the Austrian shared services centre of a company exporting to Germany and Switzerland.

[24] In the case of customer contact centres, some 130,000 of a total of 280,000 operators in India are in captive centres. See Cybermedia (2008).

[25] Communication to UNCTAD by the Board of Investment of the Philippines, April 2009.

[26] In the case of India, these industries represent as much as 86 per cent of the total market for offshored services (Nasscom, 2009).

[27] For a discussion on statistical shortcomings in this area see e.g. Amiti and Wei (2004), van Welsum and Reif (2005), Kirkegaard (2005; 2007), and UNCTAD (2004).

[28] The four modes are cross-border supply, consumption abroad, commercial presence and presence of natural persons.

[29] Other studies have applied a more narrow definition that includes only computer and information services and other business services (see e.g. OECD, 2004b; van Welsum, 2004). This definition does not include telecommunication services and many other service activities affected by offshoring, such as remote education, medical diagnostics and financial analysis. In addition, fewer countries report data that fit the narrow definition. Against this background, and in order to ensure consistency with data published in earlier *Information Economy Reports*, this report uses the broad definition of IT and ICT-enabled services.

[30] The database has been compiled by the company OCO Consulting. It includes new and expansion FDI projects worldwide, both announced and realized. Each project identified is cross-referenced against multiple sources and the company website. The usual caveat on completeness and accuracy of information applies.

[31] According to Wikipedia, "Shared Services refers to the provision of a service by one part of an organization or group where that service had previously been found in more than one part of the organization or group. Thus the funding and resourcing of the service is shared and the providing department effectively becomes an internal service provider."

[32] The UNCTAD FDI/TNC database.

[33] The new EU member States of Czech Republic, Hungary, Poland and Romania have attracted a growing share of such projects in the past three years. Indeed, these four countries accounted for more than half of all shared services centre projects in developed countries during 2006–2008.

[34] Some reports suggest that India's share of the market for the offshoring of product and software development may be declining. A study led by the Fuqua School of Business, Duke University, found that India's share of the total market dropped from 68 per cent in 2002 to 50 per cent during the 2005–2007 period. According to the same study, China accounted for the largest increase in market share. See *Cyber Media Online Ltd.* (2008).

[35] See e.g. *CIO* (2009).

[36] Communication by the Everest Research Institute, 9 April 2009.

[37] Interview with Teleperformance, 6 April 2009.

[38] Normally, customers can accept up to 280 milliseconds of latency. In order for satellites to meet this objective, the voice transmission has to be optimal. With fibre optic connections, even from a distant geographic location such as the Philippines, latency does normally not exceed 150 milliseconds. Interview with Teleperformance, 6 April 2009.

[39] In the wake of the crisis, Bear Sterns was taken over by JP Morgan, Merrill Lynch by Bank of America and Wachovia by Wells Fargo.

[40] A survey of 150 ICT companies in the United States found that 60 per cent of their IT departments saw offshore outsourcing as a way to reduce costs. See Team International (2008).

[41] See also IDC (2009) and Everest Research Institute (2008b).

[42] Company interviews.

[43] This assessment is mainly based on Nasscom's *Strategic Review 2009*, presentations given by industry leaders at the Nasscom 2009 Leadership Forum, Mumbai, India, February 2009, as well as articles published in the *Economic Times of India*, *Business Standard*, *Dataquest* and interviews with industry managers and equity market analysts.

[44] See *Yale Global Online* (2009).

[45] According to Tata Consultancy Services, in addition to financial services, offshoring by companies in manufacturing, telecommunications and high-technology industries has also been very affected by the crisis. Retail, utilities and pharmaceuticals were among the least affected. See www.tcs.com/investors/Documents/Analyst%20Conference%20Calls/Transcript_TCS_Q3FY09_Earnings_Call.pdf.

[46] See Everest Research Institute (2008a).

[47] See *Asia News Network* (2008).

[48] See *Coreadvisor.com* (2009).

[49] See http://www.tcs.com/investors/Documents/Analyst%20Conference%20Calls/Transcript_TCS_Q3FY09_Earnings_Call.pdf.

[50] See *Yale Global Online* (2009).

REFERENCES

Africa Partnership Forum (2008). ICT in Africa: boosting economic growth and poverty reduction. Paper prepared for the tenth meeting of the Africa Partnership Forum. Tokyo. 7–8 April.

Agency for Telecommunications and Postal Services (2008). *Annual Report for 2007*.

Alexander H (2008). The telehealth promise: better health care and cost savings for the 21st century. AT&T Center for Telehealth Research and Policy. Galveston.

America Móvil (2008). *Annual Report 2007*.

Amiti M and Wei S-J (2004). Fear of service outsourcing: is it justified? NBER working paper 10808. National Bureau of Economic Research. New York.

Arora A et al. (2006). The economics of offshoring. In: Association for Computer Machinery. *ACM Job Migration Task Force, Globalization and Offshoring of Software*. https://www.acm.org: 71–100.

Asia News Network (2008). Citigroup to expand in the Philippines. 24 November.

A.T. Kearney (2007). Destination Latin America: a near-shore alternative. http://www.atkearney.com/shared_res/pdf/Near-Shore_Latin_America_S.pdf.

Boston Consulting Group (2007). Estudios de competividad en clusters de la economía chilena, documento de referencia offshoring. https://www.corfo.cl.

Business Tech-CNET News (2009a). Press release: Tech layoffs: the scorecard. 13 May.

Business Tech-CNET News (2009b). Press release: Server sales drop 25 per cent worldwide. 28 May.

Business Tech-CNET News (2009c). Press release: April chip sales: good news, bad news. 1 June.

Business Tech-CNET News (2009d). Press release: Smartphone sales shine in first quarter. 20 May.

Business Tech-CNET News (2009e). Press release: TVs sales continue to decline. 19 May.

Business Tech-CNET News (2009f). Press release: Storage software takes a revenue hit. 8 June.

Business Tech-CNET News (2009g). Press release: Gartner: 42 per cent of CIOs cut their budgets. 10 June.

Business News America (2009). Movistar expects to offer 3.5G in 74 per cent of country by end-H1. 23 February.

Business Wire (2009). IDC forecasts worldwide IT spending growth of 0.5 per cent in 2009. 25 February.

CIO (2009). India is losing its share of offshoring market, says Gartner. 21 April.

Computerworld (2008). Financial crisis: tech innovation at risk. 8 October.

Coreadvisor.com (2009). JPMorgan to up outsourcing to India by 25 per cent. 8 March.

Crandall R (2008). Broadband policy: growth, jobs and investment. Presented at the Innovation and Regulation Chair Conference on Telecommunications Infrastructure and Economic Performance. Paris. 16–17 October.

Crandall R et al. (2007). The effects of broadband deployment on output and employment: a cross-sectional analysis of U.S. data. *Issues in Economic Policy*. 6.

Cyber Media Online Ltd. (2008). Offshore outsourcing: this is not the end. 11 December.

Cybermedia (2008). Press release: Domestic call centre industry growth to accelerate to 65 per cent in 07–08, to touch Rs 8500. 12 February. http://www.cybermedia.co.in/press/pressrelease76.html.

Donner J and Escobari M (2009). A review of the research on mobile use by micro and small enterprises (MSEs). Paper presented at the International Conference on Information and Communications Technologies and Development. Doha. 17–19 April.

Eastern Caribbean Telecommunications Authority (2007). *Annual Telecommunication Sector Review*.

E-Business Watch (2003). ICT and e-business in the real estate sector. European e-Business Market Watch Sector Report 14 (II). http://www.ebusiness-watch.org/studies/sectors/real_estate/documents/Real-Estate_2003_II.pdf.

E-Business Watch (2006). ICT and e-business in the construction industry. Sector Report 7. http://www.ebusiness-watch.org/studies/sectors/construction/documents/Construction_2006.pdf.

E-Business Watch (2008). ICT and e-business impact in the transport and logistics services industry. Impact Study 05/2008. http://www.ebusiness-watch.org/studies/sectors/transport_services/documents/Study_04-2008_Transport.pdf.

ECA (2009). Implementing the World Summit on the Information Society Action Lines in Africa – analysis of country reports. Prepared for the first session of the Committee on Development Information, Science and Technology. Addis Ababa. 28 April–1 May.

ECLAC (2007). Monitoring eLAC2007: progress and current state of development of Latin American and Caribbean information societies. LC/W 151. Santiago.

ECLAC (2009). *Foreign Investment in Latin America and the Caribbean.* United Nations publication. Santiago.

Economic and Social Council (2008). Resolution 2008/3. Paragraph 29.

Ericsson (2007). White paper: the evolution of EDGE.

Esselaar S et al. (2007). ICT usage and its impact on profitability in 13 African countries. *Information Technologies and International Development.* 4 (1): 87–100.

European Commission (2008). Broadband access in the EU: situation at 1 July 2008. European Commission, Information Society and Media Directorate-General. Brussels.

European Regulators Group (2005). Broadband market competition report. ERG Secretariat. Brussels. http://www.erg.eu.int/doc/publications/erg_05_23_broadbd_mrkt_comp_report_p.pdf.

Eurostat (2008). *Final Report – Information Society: ICT Impact Assessment by Linking Data from Different Sources.* Luxembourg.

Everest Research Institute (2008a). Global sourcing in banking, capital markets and insurance.

Everest Research Institute (2008b). Market vista report: Q3 2008.

Everest Research Institute (2008c). Ready to compete: South Africa's BPO capabilities in the financial services sector.

Financial Times (2009). FT Global 500 2009. 29 May.

Forrester (2009). Predictions 2009: ePurchasing market. http://www.forrester.com/Research/Document/Excerpt/0,7211,44129,00.html.

Forum for Agricultural Research in Africa (FARA) (2009). *Inventory of Innovative Farmer Advisory Services.* http://www.iicd.org/files/Innovative-Farmer-Advisory-Systems-Feb09.pdf.

Freund CL and Weinhold D (2004). The effect of the Internet on international trade. *Journal of International Economics.* 62 (2004): 171–189.

Gartner (2009). Gartner Dataquest Market Databook, March 2009 update. http://www.gartner.com/DisplayDocument?ref=g_search&id=923118&subref=simplesearch.

Heeks R (2008). ICT4D 2.0: the next phase of applying ICT for development. *Computer.* 41 (6): 26–33.

House of Lords (2007). *Stopping the Carousel: Missing Trader Fraud in the EU, Report with Evidence.* London, The Stationery Office Limited.

Hunsberger K (2006). A country connects. *PM Network.* http://www.highbeam.com/doc/1P3-1060921271.html.

IMF (2009). *World Economic Outlook Update.*

Indjikian R and Siegel DS (2005). The impact of investment in IT on economic performance: implications for developing countries. *World Development.* 33 (5): 681–700.

INEGI (2007). *Encuesta Nacional sobre Disponibilidad y Uso de las Tecnologías de la Información en los Hogares.*

Intelligent Enterprise (2009). Forrester slashes IT spending forecast. 1 April.

International Data Corporation (IDC) (2008). Worldwide IT spending 2008–2012. http://www.idc.com.

IDC (2009). Economic crisis response: worldwide IT spending 2008–2012 forecast update. http://www.idc.com.

International Herald Tribune (2008). Africa: mobile banking prospects remain positive. 3 October

International Telecommunication Union (ITU) (2008a). *Measuring Information and Communication Technology Availability in Villages and Rural Areas.* Geneva, ITU.

ITU (2008b). *Asia-Pacific Telecommunication/ICT Indicators 2008.* Geneva, ITU.

ITU (2008c). Trends in telecommunication reform 2008: six degrees of sharing. http://www.itu.int/ITU-D/treg/publications/Trends_exec_A5-e.pdf.

ITU (2009a). *Measuring the Information Society.* Geneva, ITU.

ITU (2009b). *Confronting the Crisis: Its Impact on the ICT Industry.* Geneva, ITU.

ITU and UNCTAD (2007). *World Information Society Report 2007: Beyond WSIS.* Geneva, ITU.

Jagun A et al. (2007). Mobile telephony and developing country micro-enterprise: a Nigerian case study. Development Informatics Working Paper Series paper 29. University of Manchester. Manchester.

Junqueira Botelho A and da Silva Alves A (2007). Mobile use/adoption by micro, small and medium enterprises in Latin America and the Caribbean. Background paper. DIRSI. Lima.

Kirkegaard JF (2005). Outsourcing and offshoring: pushing the European model over the hill, rather than off the cliff. Working Paper Series WP 05-1. Institute for International Economics. Washington.

Kirkegaard JF (2007). Offshoring, outsourcing, and production relocation: labour market effects in the OECD countries and developing Asia. Working Paper Series WP 07-2. Peterson Institute for International Economics. Washington.

Kierzkowski H and Arndt S (2001). *Fragmentation: New Production Patterns in the World Economy.* Oxford, Oxford University Press.

KPMG (2008). *Knowledge Process Outsourcing: Unlocking Top-Line Growth by Outsourcing "the Core".* Mumbai, KPMG.

LECG (2009). How broadband impacts economic productivity. Presentation at Expert Roundtable, LECG and Nokia Siemens Network. 4 March.

Lewin A et al. (2009). Getting serious about offshoring in a struggling economy. *Shared Services News.* 19–23.

Lewin D and Sweet S (2005). *The Economic Impact of Mobile Services in Latin America: a Report for the GSMA, GSM Latin America and ACHIET.* London, Indepen and Ovum.

Lydon R and Williams M (2005). Communications networks and foreign direct investment in developing countries. *Communications and Strategies.* 58 (2nd quarter): 43–60.

Maliranta M and Rouvinen P (2003). Productivity effects of ICT in Finnish business. Discussion Paper 852. The Research Institute of the Finnish Economy. Helsinki.

Malaysia Communications and Multimedia Commission (2008). *Communications and Multimedia Selected Facts and Figures, Q3 2008.*

Mitra R (forthcoming). *The Crisis and Beyond: India and the Transformation of Global Sourcing of Services.* Washington, World Bank.

MTN Group Limited (2009). *Final Audited Results for the Year Ended 31 December 2008.*

Nasscom (2009). *Strategic Review 2009.* New Delhi, Nasscom.

Nasscom and McKinsey (2009). *Perspective 2020: Transform Business, Transform India.* New Delhi, Nasscom.

New York Times (2008). Google sees surge in iPhone traffic. 14 January.

Orbicom (2002). *Monitoring the Digital Divide.* Montreal, Orbicom. http://www.orbicom.ca/projects/ddi2002/ddi2002.pdf.

Organization for Economic Cooperation and Development (OECD) (2001). *Understanding the Digital Divide.* Paris, OECD.

OECD (2003). Information and communication technology (ICT) in Poverty Reduction Strategy Papers (PRSPs). CCNM/GF/DCD/KE(2003)4. Paris, OECD.

OECD (2004a). *The Economic Impact of ICT: Measurement, Evidence and Implications.* Paris, OECD.

OECD (2004b). *OECD Information Technology Outlook.* Paris, OECD.

OECD (2007). *Offshoring and Employment: Trends and Impacts.* Paris, OECD.

OECD (2008a). *Broadband Growth and Policies in OECD Countries.* Paris, OECD.

OECD (2008b). *Information Technology Outlook 2008.* Paris, OECD.

OECD (2009a). The impact of the economic crisis on ICTs and their role in the recovery. Paper prepared for the Working Party on the Information Economy. DSTI/ICCP/IE(2000)1. Paris.

OECD (2009b). International trade in ICT: measuring recent trends. DSTI/ICCP/IIS(2009)4. Paris.

OECD (2009c). Information Economy Product definitions based on the Central Product Classification (Version 2). DSTI/ICCP/IIS(2008)1/FINAL. Paris.

OECD (2009d). Implementing the Seoul Agenda. Discussion points for the Round Table on ICT Measurement: assessment and proposals by member countries. DSTI/ICCP/IIS/RD(2009)1: paragraph 13. Paris.

OPTA (2005). *Annual Report.*

Ovum (2007). UMTS900 – benefits and issues: a summary report to GSMA February 2007. Ovum Consulting. London. http://gsmworld.com/documents/umts900_exec_sum.pdf.

Partnership on Measuring ICT for Development (2008). *The Global Information Society: a Statistical View.* Santiago, United Nations.

Partnership on Measuring ICT for Development (2009). Revisions and additions to the core list of ICT
    indicators. Note prepared for the United Nations Statistical Commission's fortieth session. 24–27 February.

Peres W and Hilbert M, eds. (2009). *La Sociedad de la Información en América Latina y el Caribe – Desarrollo
    de las Tecnologías y Tecnologías para el Desarrollo.* Santiago, United Nations.

Pew Research Center (2009). Luxury or necessity? The public makes a U-turn: a Social and Demographic
    Trends Report. http://pewresearch.org.

Point Topic (2009). *World Broadband Statistics Report, Q4.*

Qualcomm (2004). CDMA2000 for wireless in local loop networks. http://www.cdg.org/resources/white_papers/
    files/WLL_VK1.pdf.

Reuters (2009). IT seen as playing increasingly critical role for companies during economic crisis. 31 March.

Statistisches Bundesamt Deutschland (2009a). Press release: German exports in April 2009: -28.7 per cent on
    April 2008. 9 June.

Statistisches Bundesamt Deutschland (2009b). Press release: German exports in May 2009: -24.5 per cent on
    May 2008. 9 July.

Statistics Sweden (2008). Yearbook on productivity 2008. Papers presented at the Saltsjöbaden Conference.
    October. http://www.scb.se/statistik/_publikationer/OV9999_2008A01_BR_X76BR0802.pdf.

Stork C (2006). ICT and performance. In: Stork C and Esselaar S, eds. *Towards an African e-Index: SME e-
    Access and Usage.* Johannesburg, Axius Publishing: 129–136.

Tata Communications (2009). Strategy update and Q3 FY09 consolidated earnings. http://www.
    tatacommunications.com/downloads/investors/analyst/Analyst_Presentation_Q3%202008-09.pdf.

Team International (2008). Industry report: IT offshore outsourcing: early predictions for 2009. http://www.
    teaminternational.com/knowledge_center_outsourcing_predictions_2009.html.

Technology Partners International (TPI) (2009). The TPI Index: an informed view of the state of the global
    commercial outsourcing market fourth quarter and full year of 2008. http://www.tpi.net/pdf/index/4Q08_TPI_
    Index_Presentation.pdf.

Uganda Communications Commission (2007). *Review of Sector Taxation Policies and Determining the
    Elasticity of Penetration and Price of the Various Telecommunication Services in Uganda.* Kampala, Uganda
    Communications Commission.

UNCTAD (2002a). *E-Commerce and Development Report 2002.* United Nations publication. New York and
    Geneva.

UNCTAD (2002b). *World Investment Report 2002, Transnational Corporations and Export Competitiveness.*
    United Nations publication. New York and Geneva.

UNCTAD (2003). *E-Commerce and Development Report 2003.* United Nations publication. New York and
    Geneva.

UNCTAD (2004). *World Investment Report 2004: the Shift towards Services.* United Nations publication. New
    York and Geneva.

UNCTAD (2005). *The Digital Divide: ICT Development Indices 2004.* United Nations publication. New York and
    Geneva.

UNCTAD (2006a). *The Digital Divide: ICT Diffusion Index 2005.* United Nations publication. New York and
    Geneva.

UNCTAD (2006b). *Information Economy Report 2006: the Development Perspective.* United Nations
    publication. New York and Geneva.

UNCTAD (2007a). *The Information Economy Report 2007–2008: Science and Technology for Development: the
    New Paradigm of ICT.* United Nations publication. New York and Geneva.

UNCTAD (2007b). *The Least Developed Countries Report 2007: Knowledge, Technological Learning and
    Innovation for Development.* United Nations publication. New York and Geneva.

UNCTAD (2008a). *Measuring the Impact of ICT Use in Business: the Case of Manufacturing in Thailand.* United
    Nations publication. New York and Geneva.

UNCTAD (2008b). *Trade and Development Report 2008: Commodity Prices, Capital Flows and the Financing of
    Investment.* United Nations publication. New York and Geneva.

UNCTAD (2009a). *Manual for the Production of Statistics on the Information Economy 2009 Revised Edition.*

United Nations publication. New York and Geneva.

UNCTAD (2009b). Global economic crisis: implications for trade and development. TD/B/C.I/CRP.1. Geneva.

United Nations (2009). Progress made in the implementation of and follow-up to the World Summit on the Information Society outcomes at the regional and international levels. Report of the Secretary-General to the General Assembly and the Economic and Social Council. A/64/64–E/2009/10.

van Welsum D (2004). In search of "offshoring": evidence from U.S. imports of services. Birkbeck Working Papers in Economics and Finance 0402. School of Economics, Mathematics and Statistics. Birkbeck.

van Welsum D and Reif X (2005). The share of employment potentially affected by offshoring – an empirical investigation. DSTI Information Economy Working Paper, DSTI/ICCP/IE(2005)8/FINAL. OECD. Paris.

Vaillant M (2008). Nuevas oportunidades para economías pequeñas y remotas: Uruguay como exportador de servicios. Serie Estudios CI 89. División de Comercio Internacional de la CFPAI

Vaillant M and Lalanne A (2009). Zonas francas en Uruguay: actividad económica, comercio exterior y plataforma para la exportación de servicios. Serie Documento de Trabajo. CEPAL. Montevideo.

Veeraraghavan R et al. (2009). Warana unwired: replacing PCs with mobile phones in a rural sugarcane cooperative. *Information Technologies and International Development*. 5(1): 81–95.

Vodacom (2007). *Form 20-F*.

Vodafone (2005). Africa: the impact of mobile phones. The Vodafone Policy Paper Series 3.

Waverman L et al. (2005). The impact of telecoms on economic growth in developing countries. The Vodafone Policy Paper Series 2. 10–23.

Waverman L and Dasgupta K (2009). *Connectivity Scorecard 2009*. London, LECG and Nokia Siemens Networks.

World Bank (2007). *World Development Indicators 2007*. Washington, World Bank.

World Bank (2009). *Global Development Finance 2009: Charting a Global Recovery*. Washington, World Bank.

World Information Technology and Services Alliance (WITSA) (2008). *Digital Planet 2008*. Vienna, VA: WITSA.

World Trade Organization (WTO) (2005). *World Trade Report 2005*: *Exploring the Links between Trade, Standards and the WTO*. Geneva, WTO.

WTO (2008). *International Trade Statistics 2008*. Geneva, WTO.

Yale Global Online (2009). Economic crisis complicates offshoring of services. 9 February.

STATISTICAL ANNEX

Annex tables

Annex table I.1. Mobile subscriptions and penetration, 2003, 2007 and 2008

Region/Economy	Mobile subscriptions (millions)			Compound annual growth rate (CAGR) (%)	Penetration (subscriptions per 100 inhabitants)			Change in penetration
	2003	2007	2008	2003 – 2007/2008	2003	2007	2008	2003 – 2007/2008
Developed economies								
America								
Bermuda	0.04	0.06	..	13.62	57.10	93.74	..	36.63
Canada	13.22	19.92	21.46	10.17	41.68	60.41	64.41	22.73
United States of America	158.72	255.40	270.33	11.24	54.30	84.67	88.91	34.61
Asia								
Israel	6.67	8.90	9.26	6.77	98.64	124.11	128.60	29.95
Japan	86.66	100.52	105.83	4.08	67.96	78.67	82.72	14.76
Europe								
Andorra	0.05	0.07	..	7.18	71.75	82.37	..	10.62
Austria	7.09	9.83	10.58	8.32	87.88	117.92	126.60	38.72
Belgium	8.07	10.83	11.83	7.96	77.80	101.56	110.18	32.38
Bulgaria	2.78	10.14	10.79	31.15	37.06	131.98	141.96	104.90
Cyprus	0.55	0.75	0.83	8.54	76.57	95.20	103.67	27.10
Czech Republic	9.71	13.05	13.41	6.67	96.46	126.75	128.00	31.54
Denmark	4.77	6.24	6.59	6.70	88.39	114.39	119.44	31.05
Estonia	1.05	1.61	..	11.30	77.73	120.17	..	42.44
Faroe Islands	0.03	0.05	0.05	11.59	62.87	107.71	107.44	44.57
Finland	4.75	6.12	..	6.57	90.96	115.60	..	24.64
France	40.39	53.27	55.79	6.67	67.43	86.33	89.84	22.42
Germany	64.84	97.15	107.25	10.59	78.59	118.17	130.69	52.10
Greece	9.96	16.23	18.08	12.65	90.53	145.04	160.49	69.96
Hungary	7.94	10.13	10.77	6.28	76.88	100.73	107.39	30.51
Iceland	0.28	0.33	..	4.09	96.56	105.22	..	8.65
Ireland	3.42	5.10	5.27	9.04	85.00	117.88	116.72	31.72
Italy	55.92	89.75	91.57	10.37	97.28	150.81	152.39	55.11
Latvia	1.22	2.21	3.30	22.03	52.86	97.01	145.95	93.09
Liechtenstein	..	0.03	..	..	..	82.99	..	..
Lithuania	2.17	4.57	5.02	18.28	62.82	135.84	149.91	87.09
Luxembourg	0.53	0.68	..	6.39	118.35	143.74	..	25.40
Malta	0.29	0.37	0.39	5.89	72.66	90.49	93.55	20.89
Netherlands	13.64	18.32	19.63	7.56	83.73	111.67	119.08	35.36
Norway	4.16	5.26	5.16	4.37	90.89	110.97	107.41	16.51
Poland	17.36	40.62	44.03	20.46	44.98	106.56	115.48	70.49
Portugal	9.35	13.45	14.91	9.78	89.56	126.08	140.24	50.68
Romania	6.90	22.90	26.50	30.88	31.75	106.37	123.27	91.53
Slovakia	3.68	5.80	5.73	9.26	68.42	107.43	105.87	37.46
Slovenia	1.74	1.85	2.06	3.44	87.10	91.61	100.32	13.22
Spain	37.51	48.40	52.37	6.90	89.29	107.87	114.21	24.92
Sweden	8.80	10.37	10.46	3.51	98.05	112.98	112.95	14.90
Switzerland	6.19	8.10	8.57	6.73	84.58	107.36	111.79	27.22
United Kingdom[c]	52.98	73.80	75.42	7.32	89.02	120.22	122.41	33.38
Oceania								
Australia	15.46	21.47	23.49	8.73	77.52	102.16	109.90	32.38
New Zealand	2.60	4.36	..	13.80	64.83	103.10	..	38.27
Developing economies								
Africa								
Algeria[c]	1.45	21.45	26.00	78.19	4.56	62.34	75.64	71.08
Angola[b, c]	0.33	3.80	6.70	82.60	2.30	22.32	38.29	35.99
Benin	0.24	1.81	2.89	64.96	3.36	20.05	30.99	27.63
Botswana	0.52	1.43	1.66	26.01	29.71	73.71	87.17	57.46
Burkina Faso	0.23	1.61	2.51	61.75	1.85	10.90	16.52	14.67
Burundi[a, b, c]	0.06	0.27	0.48	49.63	0.90	3.17	5.42	4.52
Cameroon	1.08	4.54	5.71	39.60	6.48	24.45	30.18	23.71
Cape Verde	0.05	0.15	0.21	31.23	11.63	30.97	41.54	29.91
Central African Republic[a]	0.04	0.29	0.53	67.92	0.97	6.78	12.07	11.11
Chad	0.07	0.92	1.33	82.97	0.80	8.52	12.02	11.22
Comoros[b]	0.00	0.04	0.09	115.89	0.25	4.77	10.91	10.66
Congo	0.33	1.33	2.17	45.68	10.34	35.40	56.27	45.93
Côte d'Ivoire	1.24	7.05	8.91	48.43	6.87	36.60	45.38	38.51
Democratic Republic of the Congo	1.26	5.54	10.64	53.14	2.29	8.85	16.44	14.15
Djibouti	0.02	0.07	..	30.57	3.58	8.35	..	4.77

Region/Economy	Mobile subscriptions (millions)			Compound annual growth rate (CAGR) (%)	Penetration (subscriptions per 100 inhabitants)			Change in penetration
	2003	2007	2008	2003 - 2007/2008	2003	2007	2008	2003 - 2007/2008
Egypt	5.80	30.07	41.27	48.08	8.45	39.82	53.71	45.27
Equatorial Guinea	0.04	0.22	0.28	45.97	8.98	43.35	52.92	43.93
Eritrea[b]	0.00	0.07	..	0.00	0.00	1.44	..	1.44
Ethiopia	0.05	1.22	1.95	107.15	0.07	1.64	2.60	2.53
Gabon	0.30	1.17	1.33	34.61	23.09	87.86	98.21	75.12
Gambia[a]	0.13	0.57	0.90	47.25	9.53	33.36	51.31	41.78
Ghana	0.80	7.60	11.57	70.63	3.74	32.39	48.32	44.58
Guinea	0.11	1.37	2.20	81.63	1.44	14.64	23.03	21.59
Guinea-Bissau	0.00	0.33	0.42	218.52	0.10	19.23	23.94	23.84
Kenya	1.59	11.35	17.11	60.81	5.02	30.23	44.37	39.35
Lesotho	0.10	0.46	0.61	43.62	4.38	22.71	30.25	25.86
Liberia[a]	0.05	0.56	0.75	71.74	1.48	15.01	18.95	17.47
Libyan Arab Jamahiriya [a, b]	0.13	4.50	..	143.98	2.30	73.05	..	70.75
Madagascar	0.28	1.79	3.02	60.95	1.71	9.11	14.93	13.22
Malawi	0.14	0.96	1.58	63.55	1.29	6.91	11.07	9.78
Mali	0.25	2.54	3.28	67.36	2.30	20.62	25.81	23.51
Mauritania	0.35	1.51	..	44.02	12.75	48.33	..	35.58
Mauritius	0.46	0.94	0.97	16.00	37.87	74.24	76.39	38.52
Morocco	7.33	20.03	22.82	25.49	24.59	64.15	72.19	47.60
Mozambique[b]	0.43	2.90	3.34	50.73	2.28	13.53	15.30	13.02
Namibia	0.22	0.80	1.28	41.66	11.63	38.57	60.70	49.08
Niger	0.06	0.90	1.66	94.72	0.52	6.33	11.27	10.75
Nigeria	3.15	40.01	62.99	82.06	2.28	26.50	41.58	39.31
Réunion	0.57	..	0.88	9.19	74.74	..	111.86	37.13
Rwanda	0.13	0.68	1.27	56.87	1.60	6.98	12.72	11.12
Sao Tome and Principe	0.00	0.03	0.05	60.30	3.37	19.37	31.84	28.47
Senegal	0.78	4.12	5.39	47.10	7.55	36.79	42.48	34.92
Seychelles	0.05	0.08	..	11.83	59.46	90.55	..	31.10
Sierra Leone	0.11	0.78	0.97	53.51	2.28	13.23	16.17	13.89
Somalia[a, b]	0.08	0.60	..	68.18	0.76	6.90	..	6.14
South Africa	18.03	43.84	47.63	21.45	38.88	91.61	97.54	58.67
Sudan	0.55	7.46	9.45	76.86	1.62	20.04	23.97	22.34
Swaziland	0.09	0.38	0.52	42.61	8.43	33.29	45.20	36.77
Togo[b]	0.24	1.19	..	48.68	4.87	18.08	..	13.20
Tunisia	1.91	7.84	8.57	34.99	19.33	76.70	82.08	62.75
Uganda	0.78	5.16	7.46	57.24	3.12	18.25	23.38	20.26
United Republic of Tanzania	1.04	8.25	11.64	62.07	2.95	20.73	28.29	25.34
Zambia	0.24	2.49	3.41	69.83	2.15	20.88	28.02	25.86
Zimbabwe	0.38	1.27	..	35.37	3.22	9.54	..	6.31
Asia								
Afghanistan	0.20	4.80	7.01	103.69	1.00	19.02	24.85	23.85
Bahrain	0.44	1.12	1.45	26.81	64.27	146.81	189.66	125.39
Bangladesh	1.37	34.37	44.64	100.87	1.01	24.10	30.89	29.88
Bhutan[c]	0.01	0.15	0.25	100.39	1.09	22.99	37.49	36.39
Brunei Darussalam	0.16	0.34	..	19.98	45.27	86.73	..	41.46
Cambodia[c]	0.64	2.43	3.50	40.47	4.80	16.85	23.81	19.01
China	269.00	547.29	641.23	18.97	20.82	41.37	47.99	27.17
Hong Kong, China	7.19	9.63	10.34	7.53	106.89	139.17	148.21	41.33
India	26.15	233.63	346.89	67.70	2.47	20.45	29.24	26.77
Indonesia	18.80	92.10	141.96	49.83	8.74	40.85	60.58	51.84
Iran, Islamic Republic of	3.38	26.11	43.35	66.61	5.10	37.04	60.03	54.92
Iraq	0.07	11.47	16.71	200.67	0.27	39.54	56.66	56.39
Jordan	1.33	4.77	5.45	32.70	25.49	83.37	89.12	63.63
Kuwait	1.42	2.77	3.22	17.76	55.76	83.53	110.17	54.41
Lao People's Democratic Republic	0.14	1.03	1.46	59.91	2.47	17.53	24.55	22.09
Lebanon	0.80	1.26	1.67	15.89	22.86	30.74	40.37	17.51
Macao, China	0.36	0.79	0.93	20.70	81.51	151.07	168.98	87.47
Malaysia	11.12	23.25	27.13	19.51	44.20	85.69	97.82	53.62
Maldives	0.06	0.35	0.43	46.65	22.01	113.45	137.63	115.62
Mongolia	0.32	0.95	..	31.39	12.98	36.16	..	23.18
Myanmar	0.07	0.27	..	42.55	0.15	0.56	..	0.42
Nepal	0.05	2.50	4.24	142.66	0.21	9.46	14.74	14.52
Occupied Palestinian territory	0.48	1.00	..	20.14	13.27	24.89	..	11.63

Region/Economy	Mobile subscriptions (millions)			Compound annual growth rate (CAGR) (%)	Penetration (subscriptions per 100 inhabitants)			Change in penetration
	2003	2007	2008	2003 - 2007/2008	2003	2007	2008	2003 - 2007/2008
Oman	0.59	2.50	3.22	40.24	25.35	91.14	121.45	96.10
Pakistan	2.62	76.88	89.91	102.74	1.75	46.91	53.85	52.09
Philippines	22.46	54.97	66.40	24.21	27.69	62.06	74.07	46.37
Qatar	0.38	1.26	1.74	35.82	59.20	148.24	203.29	144.09
Republic of Korea	33.59	43.50	45.61	6.31	70.30	89.77	93.81	23.51
Saudi Arabia	7.24	28.40	28.71	31.73	32.87	118.33	113.53	80.65
Singapore	3.58	5.62	6.34	12.13	85.25	122.46	131.01	45.76
Sri Lanka	1.39	7.98	11.08	51.40	7.24	39.72	57.14	49.91
Syrian Arab Republic	1.14	6.91	7.69	46.50	6.52	35.60	37.62	31.10
Taiwan Province of China	25.80	24.29	23.95	-1.47	113.97	105.79	103.98	-10.00
Thailand	21.89	52.21	62.00	23.15	35.00	79.47	96.40	61.40
Timor-Leste[a]	0.02	0.08	0.13	44.27	2.67	6.75	10.48	7.82
Turkey	27.89	61.05	65.90	18.77	40.84	86.49	92.15	51.31
United Arab Emirates[c]	2.97	7.59	8.00	21.90	73.57	169.12	177.68	104.11
Viet Nam	2.81	35.21	67.47	88.81	3.46	41.36	78.31	74.85
Yemen	0.73	3.77	4.89	46.42	3.61	16.83	21.21	17.60
Latin America and the Caribbean								
Antigua and Barbuda[a]	0.04	0.11	..	29.47	50.89	135.42	..	84.53
Argentina	7.84	40.40	46.51	42.76	20.71	102.20	117.02	96.31
Bahamas[b]	0.12	0.32	..	26.70	38.55	94.59	..	56.05
Barbados	0.14	0.26	..	16.47	51.55	94.01	..	42.47
Belize	0.06	0.14	..	24.26	22.07	46.30	..	24.23
Bolivia, Plurinational State of	1.28	2.98	..	23.50	14.19	31.26	..	17.07
Brazil	46.37	120.98	150.64	26.57	26.36	64.01	78.11	51.75
Chile	7.27	13.96	14.80	15.28	46.08	84.08	88.26	42.19
Colombia	6.19	33.94	41.36	46.23	14.78	77.27	85.69	70.90
Costa Rica[b]	0.76	1.70	1.94	20.75	18.12	37.98	42.67	24.55
Cuba	0.04	0.20	0.27	44.13	0.39	1.76	2.43	2.04
Dominica	0.02	0.09	..	40.31	29.54	124.36	..	94.82
Dominican Republic	2.12	5.51	7.21	27.73	24.44	60.28	75.02	50.58
Ecuador	2.39	9.94	10.77	35.09	18.41	71.86	77.18	58.77
El Salvador	1.15	6.23	6.95	43.31	17.65	88.96	95.86	78.21
French Guiana	0.09	..	0.19	16.88	48.09	..	95.96	47.87
Grenada	0.04	0.10	..	22.86	40.28	90.92	..	50.64
Guadeloupe[b]	0.31	0.43	0.45	7.93	70.35	..	101.14	30.79
Guatemala	2.03	11.90	13.64	46.30	17.44	89.15	99.63	82.18
Guyana	0.12	0.33	..	28.94	13.36	42.99	..	29.63
Haiti[a, b]	0.32	2.00	..	58.11	3.84	23.17	..	19.33
Honduras	0.38	4.18	6.13	74.47	5.53	55.58	79.56	74.03
Jamaica	1.63	2.14	..	7.15	61.47	78.97	..	17.50
Martinique	0.29	..	0.41	7.05	75.09	..	103.24	28.16
Mexico	30.10	68.24	75.30	20.13	29.51	64.36	70.83	41.32
Nicaragua	0.47	2.12	3.04	45.46	8.86	38.16	53.61	44.75
Panama	0.69	3.01	..	44.40	22.21	90.14	..	67.93
Paraguay[c]	1.29	4.28	5.00	31.14	22.70	69.91	80.15	57.45
Peru	2.93	15.42	20.95	48.20	10.79	56.23	74.24	63.45
Puerto Rico[b]	1.63	2.20	..	7.76	42.08	55.82	..	13.74
Saint Kitts and Nevis	0.02	0.07	..	35.33	46.12	142.50	..	96.38
Saint Lucia	0.10	0.17	..	15.11	60.14	99.05	..	38.91
Saint Vincent and the Grenadines	0.07	0.11	..	12.62	57.55	102.97	..	45.43
Suriname[b]	0.17	0.35	..	20.13	34.65	66.67	..	32.01
Trinidad and Tobago	0.37	1.51	..	42.51	28.54	116.05	..	87.51
Uruguay	0.50	3.00	3.51	47.79	14.59	90.39	105.21	90.62
Venezuela, Bolivarian Republic of	7.02	23.82	27.08	31.02	27.30	86.76	97.86	70.56
Oceania								
Fiji	0.11	0.38	0.69	44.57	13.57	45.90	82.23	68.66
French Polynesia	0.07	0.18	..	24.43	29.29	67.31	..	38.01
Kiribati[a, b]	0.00	0.00	..	13.62	0.67	1.05	..	0.38
Marshall Islands[b, c]	0.00	0.00	..	4.02	1.11	1.23	..	0.12
Micronesia, Federated States of	..	0.03	..	..	..	24.66	..	..
New Caledonia	0.10	0.18	..	16.08	42.62	73.48	..	30.86

Region/Economy	Mobile subscriptions (millions)			Compound annual growth rate (CAGR) (%)	Penetration (subscriptions per 100 inhabitants)			Change in penetration
	2003	2007	2008	2003 - 2007/2008	2003	2007	2008	2003 - 2007/2008
Northern Mariana Islands	..	0.02	..	..	..	24.25	..	..
Papua New Guinea[a, b]	0.03	0.32	..	80.01	0.53	4.98	..	4.44
Samoa	0.01	0.09	..	68.68	5.76	45.54	..	39.78
Solomon Islands	0.00	0.01	0.03	78.55	0.33	2.62	5.32	4.99
Tonga[a]	0.00	0.05	..	85.14	4.02	46.84	..	42.82
Vanuatu	0.01	0.02	0.04	37.26	3.76	10.61	16.41	12.65
Transition economies								
Albania[c]	1.06	2.32	2.50	18.61	34.65	73.35	77.94	43.29
Armenia	0.11	1.87	2.58	87.59	3.46	57.98	86.22	82.76
Azerbaijan	1.06	4.27	5.79	40.49	12.74	49.89	67.79	55.05
Belarus	1.12	7.14	8.25	49.16	11.32	73.72	85.67	74.34
Bosnia and Herzegovina	1.05	2.45	3.84	29.62	27.40	63.78	100.00	72.60
Croatia	2.55	5.11	5.89	18.21	57.47	115.07	132.95	75.48
Georgia	0.52	2.76	3.54	46.66	11.43	62.72	81.27	69.84
Kazakhstan	1.41	12.28	13.63	57.33	8.93	81.22	87.76	78.84
Kyrgyzstan[c]	0.09	2.17	3.00	100.52	1.78	41.28	55.80	54.02
Montenegro	0.42	1.21	1.40	27.28	67.73	193.24	234.65	166.93
Republic of Moldova	0.35	1.88	2.21	44.37	9.76	52.70	61.89	52.13
Russian Federation	36.23	169.79	187.50	38.93	25.12	117.10	132.25	107.12
Serbia	3.28	8.45	9.98	24.92	43.85	114.51	135.74	91.89
Tajikistan	0.05	2.13	2.88	127.11	0.73	31.64	42.07	41.34
The former Yugoslav Republic of Macedonia	0.61	1.95	2.26	30.05	29.17	95.15	110.39	81.21
Turkmenistan	0.01	0.40	1.07	158.97	0.19	8.14	21.27	21.08
Ukraine	6.46	56.20	54.82	53.36	13.62	121.13	119.54	105.92
Uzbekistan	0.32	5.88	10.40	100.52	1.25	21.50	37.45	36.20

Source: UNCTAD on the basis of ITU and national sources.
[a] *Estimates for 2003.*
[b] *Estimates for 2007.*
[c] *Estimates for 2008.*

Annex table I.2. Internet users and penetration, 2003, 2007 and 2008

Region/Economy	Internet users (millions)			CAGR (%) 2003 - 2007/2008	Penetration (users per 100 inhabitants)			Change in penetration 2003 - 2007/2008
	2003	2007	2008		2003	2007	2008	
Developed economies								
America								
Bermuda	0.04	0.05	..	9.33	55.52	78.11	..	22.60
Canada [c]	16.40	19.20	20.00	4.05	51.70	58.22	60.04	8.34
United States of America	160.16	183.62	190.78	3.56	54.79	60.88	62.74	7.95
Asia								
Israel	1.90	3.05	3.10	10.29	28.08	42.52	43.06	14.97
Japan [c]	77.30	88.11	88.50	2.74	60.62	68.95	69.17	8.56
Europe								
Andorra	0.01	0.06	..	55.66	13.90	70.97	..	57.07
Austria	3.73	4.21	4.51	3.85	46.20	50.58	53.92	7.72
Belgium	3.70	5.24	..	9.08	35.67	49.11	..	13.43
Bulgaria	0.65	1.86	1.90	23.86	8.66	24.16	24.93	16.27
Czech Republic	2.42	3.92	4.73	14.32	24.08	38.07	45.20	21.11
Cyprus	0.13	0.23	0.24	13.75	17.35	28.82	29.69	12.34
Denmark	2.80	3.24	3.38	3.83	51.86	59.42	61.17	9.31
Estonia	0.49	0.66	0.68	6.63	36.49	48.93	50.70	14.21
Faroe Islands [c]	0.03	0.03	0.03	3.58	53.97	61.94	63.55	9.58
Finland	2.55	3.10	3.26	4.99	48.90	58.51	61.13	12.23
France	21.90	29.30	31.38	7.46	36.56	47.49	50.52	13.96
Germany	39.00	45.48	47.62	4.07	47.27	55.32	58.03	10.76
Greece	1.37	2.83	3.28	19.05	12.45	25.27	29.09	16.64
Hungary	1.90	4.01	4.52	18.94	18.39	39.87	45.10	26.71
Iceland	0.16	0.20	0.21	4.94	57.02	64.64	65.66	8.64
Ireland	1.26	1.86	2.09	10.67	31.30	42.92	46.31	15.00
Italy	12.59	17.03	18.86	8.42	21.90	28.61	31.39	9.48
Latvia	0.43	0.97	1.07	19.87	18.72	42.72	47.28	28.55
Liechtenstein	0.01	0.02	..	11.10	38.00	56.55	..	18.55
Lithuania	0.70	1.26	1.37	14.43	20.14	37.46	40.74	20.60
Luxembourg	0.18	0.28	0.29	10.53	39.20	58.59	59.39	20.18
Malta [d]	0.09	0.14	0.16	10.85	23.21	34.34	37.57	14.36
Monaco	0.02	0.03	..	4.46	64.42	76.43	..	12.01
Netherlands	8.50	10.21	10.54	4.40	52.19	62.21	63.96	11.76
Norway	2.20	2.89	3.06	6.79	48.03	60.94	63.65	15.62
Poland	8.00	12.94	14.45	12.55	20.73	33.95	37.89	17.16
Portugal	1.75	3.21	3.37	14.02	16.76	30.12	31.72	14.96
Romania	1.60	4.02	4.81	24.60	7.36	18.66	22.35	14.99
Slovakia	1.38	2.35	2.79	15.18	25.59	43.58	51.54	25.96
Slovenia	0.56	0.83	0.88	9.56	27.95	41.30	42.90	14.96
Spain	12.13	17.90	19.81	10.31	28.88	39.89	43.21	14.33
Sweden	4.98	5.37	5.96	3.69	55.44	58.49	64.41	8.97
Switzerland	2.82	3.85	4.01	7.28	38.59	50.99	52.34	13.74
United Kingdom	26.70	32.48	34.74	5.41	44.86	52.91	56.39	11.53
Oceania								
Australia	8.80	11.24	11.93	6.28	44.13	53.47	55.82	11.69
New Zealand	2.00	2.30	2.35	3.28	49.89	54.40	55.05	5.17
Developing economies								
Africa								
Algeria [b]	0.50	3.00	3.50	47.58	1.57	8.72	10.18	8.61
Angola [b]	0.10	0.35	0.40	31.95	0.70	2.06	2.29	1.59
Benin [d]	0.07	0.30	0.35	37.97	1.00	3.32	3.76	2.76
Botswana	0.04	0.08	0.10	20.11	2.27	4.13	5.25	2.98
Burkina Faso	0.05	0.35	0.40	52.81	0.39	2.37	2.63	2.24
Burundi [d]	0.01	0.07	..	49.53	0.20	0.82	..	0.63
Cameroon [d]	0.10	0.50	0.75	49.63	0.60	2.70	3.96	3.36
Cape Verde [b, c]	0.02	0.04	0.05	20.11	4.36	8.29	10.00	5.64
Central African Republic [d]	0.01	0.03	0.04	42.29	0.14	0.69	0.79	0.65
Chad [d]	0.01	0.06	0.07	47.58	0.12	0.56	0.63	0.51
Comoros	0.01	0.02	..	31.61	0.63	1.79	..	1.16
Congo	0.02	0.04	0.04	21.67	0.47	0.93	1.04	0.57
Côte d'Ivoire [d]	0.30	1.25	1.50	37.97	1.67	6.49	7.64	5.98
Democratic Republic of the Congo	0.08	0.25	0.30	31.95	0.14	0.40	0.46	0.33
Djibouti [d]	0.01	0.02	..	32.44	0.97	2.40	..	1.43
Egypt	2.70	8.62	11.69	34.06	3.93	11.42	15.21	11.28
Equatorial Guinea [d]	0.00	0.01	..	47.72	0.45	1.97	..	1.52
Eritrea [d]	0.03	0.15	..	56.51	0.60	3.09	..	2.49

Region/Economy	Internet users (millions)			CAGR (%)	Penetration (users per 100 inhabitants)			Change in penetration
	2003	2007	2008	2003 - 2007/2008	2003	2007	2008	2003 - 2007/2008
Ethiopia[d]	0.08	0.30	0.35	36.08	0.11	0.41	0.47	0.36
Gabon[d]	0.04	0.15	0.18	37.97	2.69	11.27	12.96	10.27
Gambia[a]	0.01	0.05	0.06	36.81	0.88	3.15	3.28	2.40
Ghana	0.30	1.20	1.40	36.08	1.40	5.11	5.85	4.44
Guinea[d]	0.04	0.10	..	25.74	0.52	1.07	..	0.55
Guinea-Bissau	0.02	0.04	0.04	21.67	1.17	2.06	2.29	1.12
Kenya[a, c]	0.50	2.77	3.00	43.10	1.58	7.38	7.78	6.21
Lesotho	0.02	0.06	..	31.61	0.88	2.99	..	2.11
Liberia	0.00	0.02	0.03	52.81	0.09	0.53	0.63	0.55
Libyan Arab Jamahiriya	0.16	0.30	0.32	14.87	2.89	4.87	5.09	2.20
Madagascar[d]	0.07	0.25	0.20	31.20	0.13	1.27	1.36	0.93
Malawi	0.04	0.18	..	48.49	0.34	1.26	..	0.91
Mali[d]	0.05	0.10	..	18.92	0.46	0.81	..	0.35
Mauritania[b, c]	0.02	0.08	0.09	43.10	0.55	2.40	2.81	2.26
Mauritius[b]	0.15	0.20	..	7.46	12.29	15.86	..	3.58
Morocco[b, c]	1.00	7.00	7.50	49.63	3.35	22.42	23.73	20.38
Mozambique[d]	0.13	0.40	0.50	30.92	0.69	1.87	2.29	1.60
Namibia[d]	0.07	0.15	0.18	21.91	3.38	7.23	8.33	4.95
Niger[d]	0.02	0.04	0.04	17.32	0.16	0.25	0.27	0.12
Nigeria[b, c]	0.75	4.00	5.00	46.14	0.54	2.65	3.30	2.76
Réunion	0.18	..	..	..	23.81	..	..	..
Rwanda	0.03	0.07	0.08	21.67	0.36	0.72	0.80	0.44
Sao Tome and Principe[d]	0.01	0.01	..	16.36	4.19	7.10	..	2.91
Senegal[a, c]	0.15	0.65	0.70	36.08	1.45	5.80	5.52	4.07
Seychelles[d]	0.02	0.03	..	20.86	18.12	37.63	..	19.52
Sierra Leone	0.01	0.02	0.03	22.67	0.18	0.34	0.42	0.24
Somalia[b]	0.03	0.25	..	69.90	0.30	2.87	..	2.57
South Africa	1.76	2.59	3.22	12.83	3.80	5.40	6.59	2.79
Sudan[b, c]	0.20	1.80	2.30	62.98	0.59	4.83	5.83	5.24
Swaziland	0.03	0.07	0.08	24.26	2.59	6.13	6.97	4.38
Togo	0.28	0.53	0.50	12.70	5.50	7.97	7.39	1.89
Tunisia	0.63	1.72	2.80	34.76	6.37	16.84	26.82	20.45
Uganda[a]	0.15	2.00	2.30	72.63	0.60	7.07	7.21	6.61
United Republic of Tanzania[b, c]	0.25	0.60	0.75	24.57	0.71	1.51	1.82	1.11
Zambia	0.07	0.50	..	62.33	0.64	4.19	..	3.55
Zimbabwe[d]	0.35	0.55	0.60	11.38	2.97	4.12	4.45	1.48
Asia								
Afghanistan[d]	0.02	0.50	..	123.61	0.10	1.98	..	1.88
Bahrain[a]	0.15	0.24	0.28	13.30	21.76	31.57	36.55	14.79
Bangladesh[b, c]	0.40	3.50	4.00	58.49	0.30	2.45	2.77	2.47
Bhutan[d]	0.02	0.04	0.05	27.23	2.12	6.15	7.50	5.38
Brunei Darussalam[d]	0.06	0.08	0.09	9.10	15.18	19.14	21.35	6.17
Cambodia[d]	0.03	0.20	0.30	58.49	0.23	1.38	2.04	1.82
China	79.50	210.00	298.00	30.25	6.15	15.87	22.30	16.15
Hong Kong, China	3.21	3.96	4.12	5.12	47.73	57.23	59.10	11.37
India	18.48	46.00	57.00	25.26	1.75	4.03	4.81	3.06
Indonesia[c]	8.08	25.00	28.00	28.22	3.76	11.09	11.95	8.19
Iran, Islamic Republic of	4.30	18.00	21.00	37.33	6.50	25.53	29.08	22.58
Iraq[d]	0.05	0.50	..	77.83	0.20	1.72	..	1.52
Jordan	0.46	1.16	..	26.30	8.79	20.32	..	11.53
Kuwait	0.30	0.90	0.95	25.93	11.78	27.19	32.54	20.76
Lao People's Democratic Republic	0.06	0.25	0.30	37.97	1.00	4.21	5.05	0.97
Lebanon	0.45	0.65	..	9.63	12.86	15.86	..	3.00
Macao, China[b]	0.17	0.32	..	17.38	37.39	60.29	..	22.90
Malaysia	8.69	11.73	13.10	8.55	34.53	43.24	47.24	12.71
Maldives[d]	0.02	0.05	0.06	24.57	6.97	14.76	19.29	12.31
Mongolia[a]	0.10	0.32	..	33.75	4.07	12.17	..	8.10
Myanmar[b]	0.05	0.40	..	68.18	0.11	0.82	..	0.71
Nepal[d]	0.15	0.40	0.50	27.23	0.63	1.51	1.74	1.11
Occupied Palestinian territory[b]	0.15	0.35	..	24.65	4.01	8.71	..	4.70
Oman[d]	0.18	0.32	0.39	17.38	7.48	11.48	14.71	7.24
Pakistan[c]	2.00	17.00	19.00	56.87	1.34	10.37	11.38	10.04
Philippines[d]	4.00	9.20	10.10	20.35	4.93	10.39	11.27	6.33
Qatar[b]	0.14	0.32	..	22.79	22.13	37.65	..	15.51
Republic of Korea	29.22	34.82	35.36	3.89	61.15	71.86	72.73	11.58

Region/Economy	Internet users (millions)			CAGR (%)	Penetration (users per 100 inhabitants)			Change in penetration
	2003	2007	2008	2003 - 2007/2008	2003	2007	2008	2003 - 2007/2008
Saudi Arabia[c]	1.80	6.40	7.80	34.08	8.17	26.67	30.84	22.66
Singapore[c]	1.75	2.53	2.60	8.23	41.73	55.11	53.73	12.00
Sri Lanka[d]	0.23	1.11	1.30	42.02	1.17	5.52	6.70	5.53
Syrian Arab Republic[b, c]	0.50	1.60	1.80	29.20	2.86	8.25	8.80	5.94
Taiwan Province of China	11.70	14.80	15.10	5.23	51.69	64.46	65.55	13.86
Thailand[c]	6.03	13.42	15.50	20.78	9.65	20.42	24.10	14.45
Timor-Leste	0.00	0.01	..	77.83	0.13	0.87	..	0.73
Turkey	5.50	13.34	16.36	24.37	8.05	18.90	22.88	14.83
United Arab Emirates[d]	1.11	1.99	..	15.69	27.48	44.31	..	16.84
Viet Nam	3.10	17.72	20.83	46.40	3.81	20.82	24.18	20.37
Yemen[b, c]	0.10	0.60	0.90	55.18	0.50	2.68	3.90	3.41
Latin America and the Caribbean								
Antigua and Barbuda[d]	0.01	0.03	0.04	26.05	13.99	36.14	41.67	27.67
Argentina	5.70	16.00	20.00	28.54	15.05	40.47	50.32	35.27
Bahamas	0.08	0.16	..	17.48	26.49	48.05	..	21.56
Barbados[d]	0.09	0.16	..	15.20	32.40	56.57	..	24.17
Belize	0.04	0.06	0.06	11.38	12.79	17.68	20.43	7.64
Bolivia, Plurinational State of[d]	0.31	0.83	0.89	23.34	3.44	8.67	9.13	5.69
Brazil[a, c]	19.33	45.00	50.00	20.94	10.98	23.81	25.93	14.94
Chile[c]	4.12	6.56	6.97	11.11	26.09	39.51	41.57	15.48
Colombia	3.08	10.10	17.12	40.88	7.37	22.99	35.46	28.09
Costa Rica[a, b]	0.74	1.10	1.35	12.84	17.73	24.57	29.75	12.02
Cuba	0.09	0.24	0.26	23.64	0.80	2.09	2.31	1.51
Dominica	0.01	0.02	..	9.20	18.80	29.03	..	10.23
Dominican Republic	0.73	1.68	2.56	28.52	8.42	18.34	26.66	18.24
Ecuador	0.57	0.99	1.63	23.37	4.38	7.18	11.67	7.28
El Salvador[d]	0.55	0.74	0.98	12.13	8.44	10.50	13.45	5.01
French Guiana	0.03	..	..	..	16.57	..	..	..
Grenada	0.01	0.03	..	19.26	12.38	24.81	..	12.43
Guatemala[d]	0.50	0.80	0.85	11.20	4.29	5.99	6.21	1.92
Guyana[d]	0.03	0.15	..	49.53	3.38	19.66	..	16.28
Haiti[d]	0.10	0.25	..	25.74	1.20	2.90	..	1.70
Honduras	0.19	0.42	0.66	28.83	2.70	5.63	8.54	5.84
Jamaica[b, c]	0.68	1.00	1.30	14.01	25.52	36.85	47.65	22.13
Martinique	0.08	..	..	..	20.40	..	..	..
Mexico	12.25	20.85	22.34	12.77	12.01	19.66	21.01	9.00
Nicaragua[d]	0.18	0.55	0.60	27.94	3.32	9.89	10.59	7.26
Panama[d]	0.21	0.50	0.63	24.37	6.74	14.97	18.39	11.65
Paraguay[c]	0.14	0.53	0.60	33.78	2.47	8.67	9.62	7.15
Peru	2.85	7.11	7.46	21.21	10.50	25.92	26.42	15.92
Saint Kitts and Nevis[d]	0.02	0.03	..	14.80	39.67	63.46	..	23.80
Saint Lucia[d]	0.02	0.05	..	23.42	12.45	27.10	..	14.65
Saint Vincent and the Grenadines[d]	0.01	0.03	..	22.47	10.08	25.23	..	15.15
Suriname[d]	0.03	0.05	..	18.92	5.15	9.52	..	4.37
Trinidad and Tobago	0.15	0.21	..	9.14	11.70	16.36	..	4.66
Uruguay[a, c]	0.58	0.96	1.00	11.70	16.87	28.97	29.99	13.13
Venezuela, Bolivarian Republic of	1.93	5.72	7.17	29.94	7.53	20.83	25.90	18.37
Oceania								
Fiji[h]	0.00	0.15	..	23.74	7.41	18.12	..	10.71
French Polynesia	0.05	0.07	..	11.68	18.06	26.92	..	8.87
Kiribati	0.00	0.00	..	-4.46	2.70	2.10	..	-0.59
Marshall Islands[d]	0.00	0.00	..	11.96	2.59	3.86	..	1.27
Micronesia, Federated States of	0.01	0.02	..	20.99	5.85	13.50	..	7.64
New Caledonia	0.06	0.10	..	13.62	26.33	41.67	..	15.34
Northern Mariana Islands	0.01	..	..	..	15.32	..	..	..
Papua New Guinea[d]	0.10	0.20	0.25	20.11	1.77	3.16	3.87	2.10
Samoa[d]	0.01	0.01	..	15.83	2.74	4.82	..	2.08
Solomon Islands	0.00	0.01	..	35.12	0.67	2.02	..	1.35
Tonga	0.00	0.01	..	25.74	4.02	9.97	..	5.95
Vanuatu[d]	0.01	0.01	..	7.46	3.61	4.42	..	0.81
Transition economies								
Albania	0.06	0.47	0.54	55.18	1.95	14.88	16.84	14.88
Armenia	0.20	0.40	..	18.92	6.23	12.41	..	6.18

Region/Economy	Internet users (millions)			CAGR (%)	Penetration (users per 100 inhabitants)			Change in penetration
	2003	2007	2008	2003 - 2007/2008	2003	2007	2008	2003 - 2007/2008
Azerbaijan	0.30	0.93	1.00	27.23	3.62	10.84	11.72	8.10
Belarus	1.39	2.65	2.70	14.17	14.10	27.35	28.02	13.92
Bosnia and Herzegovina	0.25	1.06	..	43.33	6.52	27.46	..	20.94
Croatia	0.94	1.30	1.50	9.91	21.05	29.29	33.84	12.80
Georgia[d]	0.15	0.35	0.40	21.67	3.28	7.96	9.17	5.89
Kazakhstan[d]	0.72	1.70	1.90	21.42	4.54	11.24	12.23	7.69
Kyrgyzstan	0.15	0.25	0.28	12.89	2.88	4.76	5.11	2.23
Montenegro	0.08	0.20	..	23.81	13.38	31.15	..	17.77
Republic of Moldova[b, c]	0.29	1.10	1.20	33.03	7.98	30.79	33.64	25.65
Russian Federation	13.00	27.00	29.00	17.41	9.02	18.62	20.45	11.44
Serbia	0.85	1.70	2.00	10.00	11.00	23.03	27.21	15.85
Tajikistan[d]	0.07	0.20	..	30.01	1.07	2.97	..	1.90
The former Yugoslav Republic of Macedonia	0.15	0.47	0.66	34.56	7.20	22.89	32.29	25.10
Turkmenistan	0.01	0.10	..	69.90	0.25	2.01	..	1.77
Ukraine[a]	1.50	4.76	6.72	34.96	3.16	10.27	14.65	11.49
Uzbekistan	0.49	1.20	1.40	23.26	1.92	4.38	5.04	3.12

Source: UNCTAD on the basis of ITU and national sources.
[a] *Estimates for 2003.*
[b] *Estimates for 2007.*
[c] *Estimates for 2008.*
[d] *Estimates for every reported year.*

INFORMATION ECONOMY REPORT 2009

Annex table I.3. Fixed broadband subscribers and penetration, 2003, 2007 and 2008

Region/Economy	Fixed broadband subscribers (millions)			CAGR (%)	Penetration (subscribers per 100 inhabitants)			Change in penetration
	2003	2007	2008	2003-2007/2008	2003	2007	2008	2003-2007/2008
Developed economies								
America								
Bermuda	..	0.02	..	..	..	28.12	..	..
Canada	4.65	8.68	9.21	14.64	14.67	26.31	27.66	12.99
United States of America	28.23	66.21	79.07	22.88	9.66	21.95	26.01	16.35
Asia								
Israel [c]	0.65	1.58	1.70	21.20	9.61	22.01	23.61	14.00
Japan	13.77	28.30	30.11	16.93	10.80	22.15	23.53	12.73
Europe								
Andorra	0.00	0.02	0.02	41.28	4.98	22.28	24.13	19.15
Austria	0.68	1.66	1.72	20.46	8.42	19.87	20.62	12.20
Belgium	1.27	2.71	2.84	17.39	12.28	25.45	26.43	14.15
Bulgaria	0.04	0.58	0.85	81.33	0.58	7.56	11.22	10.64
Cyprus	0.01	0.07	0.14	70.20	1.39	9.10	17.87	16.48
Czech Republic	0.05	1.50	1.86	107.37	0.48	14.54	17.76	17.27
Denmark	0.72	1.98	2.03	23.06	13.30	36.23	36.69	23.39
Estonia	0.08	0.29	0.33	34.05	5.63	21.70	24.58	18.94
Faroe Islands	0.00	0.01	0.01	74.33	1.82	28.26	28.95	27.13
Finland	0.47	1.73	1.92	32.55	9.01	32.71	36.12	27.11
France	3.57	15.55	17.16	36.90	5.96	25.20	27.64	21.68
Germany	4.50	19.60	22.62	38.12	5.45	23.84	27.56	22.11
Greece	0.01	1.02	1.51	172.61	0.09	9.09	13.38	13.29
Hungary	0.19	1.20	1.58	52.37	1.86	11.94	15.72	13.86
Iceland	0.04	0.09	0.10	20.02	13.67	30.39	30.80	17.13
Ireland	0.03	0.89	1.13	101.29	0.85	20.49	24.90	24.06
Italy	2.43	10.12	11.30	36.00	4.23	17.01	18.81	14.59
Latvia	0.02	0.26	0.40	83.56	0.82	11.59	17.51	16.69
Lithuania	0.06	0.41	0.59	55.37	1.88	12.15	17.56	15.68
Luxembourg	0.02	0.12	0.14	54.02	3.53	25.40	28.10	24.57
Malta [a]	0.03	0.06	0.10	27.46	7.52	14.07	24.46	16.94
Monaco	0.01	0.01	..	24.93	15.42	37.43	..	22.01
Netherlands	1.93	5.66	5.70	24.20	11.85	34.50	34.60	22.75
Norway	0.38	1.47	1.59	33.43	8.20	31.09	33.08	24.88
Poland	0.24	3.20	5.01	83.81	0.62	8.39	13.15	12.53
Portugal	0.50	1.63	1.60	26.03	4.82	15.26	15.04	10.23
Romania	0.20	1.95	2.31	63.77	0.90	9.05	10.75	9.84
Slovakia	0.02	0.31	0.59	107.88	0.28	5.81	10.90	10.62
Slovenia	0.06	0.31	0.43	47.81	3.02	15.25	20.75	17.72
Spain	2.12	8.03	9.06	33.69	5.05	17.89	19.76	14.71
Sweden	0.96	3.25	3.35	28.32	10.74	35.43	36.22	25.48
Switzerland	0.84	2.38	2.57	25.12	11.44	31.55	33.47	22.03
United Kingdom	3.20	15.61	16.92	39.53	5.38	25.42	27.47	22.09
Oceania								
Australia	0.70	5.03	5.66	51.96	3.50	23.91	26.49	22.98
New Zealand	0.07	0.83	0.89	65.39	1.80	19.61	20.87	19.08
Developing economies								
Africa								
Algeria	0.02	0.25	0.40	92.84	0.05	0.73	1.16	1.12
Angola	0.00	0.01	..	..	0.00	0.07	..	0.07
Benin	0.00	0.00	..	..	0.00	0.02	..	0.02
Botswana	0.00	0.00	..	..	0.00	0.18	..	0.18
Burkina Faso	0.00	0.00	..	118.20	0.00	0.01	..	0.01
Burundi	0.00	..	..	..	0.00	..	..	..
Cameroon	0.00	0.00	..	..	0.00	0.00	..	0.00
Cape Verde	0.00	0.00	0.01	..	0.00	0.78	1.19	1.19
Central African Republic	0.00	0.00	..	..	0.00	0.00	..	0.00
Chad	0.00	0.00	..	..	0.00	0.00	..	0.00
Comoros	0.00	0.00	0.00	..	0.00	0.00	0.01	0.01
Congo	0.00	0.00	..	..	0.00	0.00	..	0.00
Côte d'Ivoire	0.00	0.02	..	..	0.00	0.11	..	0.11
Democratic Republic of the Congo	0.00	0.00	..	..	0.00	0.00	..	0.00
Djibouti	0.00	0.00	..	..	0.00	0.13	..	0.13
Egypt	0.00	0.43	0.70	170.03	0.01	0.57	0.91	0.90
Equatorial Guinea [d]	0.00	0.00	..	..	0.00	0.04	..	0.04
Eritrea	0.00	0.00	..	..	0.00	0.00	..	0.00

Region/Economy	Fixed broadband subscribers (millions)			CAGR (%)	Penetration (subscribers per 100 inhabitants)			Change in penetration
	2003	2007	2008	2003-2007/2008	2003	2007	2008	2003-2007/2008
Ethiopia	0.00	0.00	0.00	92.23	0.00	0.00	0.00	0.00
Gabon	0.00	0.00	..	185.63	0.00	0.25	..	0.25
Gambia	0.00	0.00	..	..	0.00	0.02	..	0.02
Ghana	0.00	0.01	..	..	0.00	0.06	..	0.06
Guinea	0.00	0.00	..	..	0.00	0.00	..	0.00
Guinea-Bissau	0.00	0.00	..	..	0.00	0.00	..	0.00
Kenya	0.00	0.02	..	..	0.00	0.05	..	0.05
Lesotho	0.00	..	..	..	0.00	..	..	..
Liberia	0.00	..	..	..	0.00	..	..	..
Libyan Arab Jamahiriya	0.00	0.01	..	..	0.00	0.16	..	0.16
Madagascar	0.00	0.00	..	..	0.00	0.01	..	0.01
Malawi	0.00	0.00	..	119.44	0.00	0.01	..	0.01
Mali	0.00	0.00	..		0.00	0.03	..	0.03
Mauritania	0.00	0.00	..		0.00	0.13	..	0.13
Mauritius	0.00	0.04	..	141.18	0.10	3.22	..	3.12
Mayotte	0.00	..	..	..	0.00	..	..	..
Morocco	0.00	0.48	0.48	182.15	0.01	1.53	1.53	1.52
Mozambique	0.00	0.01	..	..	0.00	0.03	..	0.03
Namibia	0.00	0.00	..	..	0.00	0.01	..	0.01
Niger[b]	0.00	0.00	..	..	0.00	0.00	..	0.00
Nigeria	0.00	..	..	..	0.00	..	..	..
Réunion	..	..	0.09	..	..	..	11.61	..
Rwanda	0.00	0.00	..	..	0.00	0.03	..	0.03
Sao Tome and Principe	0.00	0.00	..	..	0.00	0.19	..	0.19
Senegal	0.00	0.04	..	107.67	0.02	0.34	..	0.32
Seychelles[a]	0.00	0.00	..	96.80	0.24	3.53	..	3.29
Sierra Leone	0.00	..	..	..	0.00	..	..	..
Somalia	0.00	..	..	..	0.00	..	..	..
South Africa	0.02	0.80	1.30	129.83	0.04	1.68	2.67	2.62
Sudan	0.00	0.04	..	..	0.00	0.11	..	0.11
Swaziland	0.00	..	..	..	0.00	..	..	..
Togo	0.00	0.01	..	..	0.00	0.08	..	0.08
Tunisia	0.00	0.13	0.23	144.73	0.03	1.26	2.18	2.15
Uganda	0.00	0.00	..	..	0.00	0.01	..	0.01
United Republic of Tanzania	0.00	..	..	..	0.00	..	..	..
Zambia	0.00	0.00	..	..	0.00	0.02	..	0.02
Zimbabwe	0.00	0.02	..	34.69	0.04	0.11	..	0.07
Asia								
Afghanistan[b]	0.00	0.00	..	..	0.00	0.00	..	0.00
Bahrain	0.01	0.07	0.08	53.14	1.41	9.68	10.70	9.29
Bangladesh	0.00	..	..	..	0.00	..	..	..
Bhutan	0.00	0.00	..	..	0.00	0.00	..	0.00
Brunei Darussalam	0.00	0.01	..	30.65	1.06	2.85	..	1.79
Cambodia	0.00	0.01	..	121.67	0.00	0.06	..	0.06
China	13.54	66.46	83.37	43.83	1.05	5.02	6.24	5.19
Hong Kong, China	1.23	1.87	1.95	9.62	18.28	26.98	27.92	9.64
India	0.14	3.13	5.45	107.89	0.01	0.27	0.46	0.45
Indonesia[d]	0.02	0.26	0.59	96.97	0.01	0.11	0.25	0.24
Iran, Islamic Republic of[a]	0.02	..	..	..	0.03	..	..	..
Iraq	0.00	..	..	..	0.00	..	..	..
Jordan	0.00	0.10	..	112.36	0.10	1.78	..	1.68
Kuwait[b]	0.01	0.03	..	17.70	0.31	0.78	..	0.21
Lao People's Democratic Republic	0.00	0.00	..	..	0.00	0.06	..	0.06
Lebanon	0.00	0.20	..	..	0.00	4.88	..	4.88
Macao, China	0.03	0.11	0.12	34.31	6.22	21.40	22.00	15.78
Malaysia	0.11	1.23	1.71	73.16	0.44	4.53	6.18	5.74
Maldives	0.00	0.01	0.01	82.84	0.18	2.44	3.30	3.13
Mongolia	0.00	0.01	..	107.36	0.02	0.28	..	0.27
Myanmar	0.00	0.00	..	..	0.00	0.00	..	0.00
Nepal	0.00	0.01	..	..	0.00	0.05	..	0.05
Occupied Palestinian territory	0.00	0.05	..	..	0.00	1.34	..	1.34
Oman	0.00	0.02	0.03	..	0.00	0.69	1.19	1.19
Pakistan	0.00	0.13	0.17	..	0.00	0.08	0.10	0.10
Philippines[d]	0.03	0.97	1.05	111.01	0.03	1.09	1.17	1.14
Qatar	0.00	0.07	..	123.85	0.44	8.27	..	7.83

Region/Economy	Fixed broadband subscribers (millions)			CAGR (%)	Penetration (subscribers per 100 inhabitants)			Change in penetration
	2003	2007	2008	2003-2007/2008	2003	2007	2008	2003-2007/2008
Republic of Korea	11.18	14.71	15.32	6.51	23.39	30.36	31.51	8.12
Saudi Arabia	0.02	0.62	..	126.19	0.11	2.60	..	2.49
Singapore	0.42	0.86	1.26	24.52	10.05	18.72	26.09	16.04
Sri Lanka	0.00	0.06	..	118.05	0.01	0.31	..	0.30
Syrian Arab Republic [b]	0.00	0.01	..	..	0.00	0.04	..	0.04
Taiwan Province of China	3.00	4.64	4.85	10.05	13.27	20.20	21.05	7.78
Thailand	0.02	0.91	1.26	142.73	0.02	1.39	1.97	1.94
Turkey	0.06	4.50	5.80	152.51	0.08	6.38	8.11	8.03
United Arab Emirates	0.03	0.38	..	88.92	0.74	8.47	..	7.73
Viet Nam	0.01	1.29	2.05	194.94	0.01	1.52	2.38	2.37
Yemen	0.00	..	0.02	..	0.00	..	0.11	0.11
Latin America and the Caribbean								
Antigua and Barbuda [a]	0.00	0.01	..	..	0.00	8.31	..	8.31
Argentina	0.26	2.33	3.01	63.52	0.68	5.90	7.57	6.89
Bahamas [b]	0.03	0.05	..	14.09	9.49	15.32	..	5.82
Barbados [a]	0.00	0.03	..	130.13	0.37	10.24	..	9.87
Belize	0.00	0.01	..	61.53	0.34	2.06	..	1.71
Bolivia, Plurinational State of	0.00	0.03	..	..	0.00	0.36	..	0.36
Brazil	1.20	7.72	10.02	52.89	0.68	4.08	5.19	4.51
Chile	0.36	1.31	1.41	31.63	2.27	7.90	8.43	6.16
Colombia	0.06	0.94	1.78	94.16	0.15	2.15	3.68	3.53
Costa Rica	0.01	0.07	0.10	61.20	0.23	1.55	2.25	2.02
Cuba	0.00	0.00	..	..	0.00	0.02	..	0.02
Dominica	0.00	0.01	..	24.96	3.39	8.98	..	5.59
Dominican Republic	0.00	0.14	0.23	..	0.00	1.57	2.35	2.35
Ecuador	0.00	0.09	0.16	..	0.00	0.62	1.12	1.12
El Salvador	0.02	0.09	0.12	45.91	0.29	1.28	1.70	1.42
French Guiana	..	..	0.02	..	..	..	11.11	..
Grenada [a]	0.00	0.01	..	97.58	0.48	7.19	..	6.71
Guatemala	0.00	0.12	..	..	0.00	0.90	..	0.90
Guyana [b]	0.00	0.02	..	..	0.00	2.62	..	2.62
Haiti	0.00	..	..	..	0.00	..	..	..
Honduras	0.00	..	..	..	0.00	..	..	..
Jamaica [a]	0.01	0.09	..	74.54	0.38	3.42	..	3.04
Martinique	..	..	0.07	..	..	..	16.21	..
Mexico	0.31	4.55	5.70	78.80	0.31	4.29	5.36	5.06
Nicaragua	0.00	0.02	..	44.13	0.08	0.34	..	0.26
Panama	0.01	0.14	..	79.54	0.44	4.31	..	3.86
Paraguay [a]	0.00	0.05	..	168.15	0.02	0.84	..	0.83
Peru	0.09	0.59	..	59.39	0.33	2.13	..	1.80
Saint Kitts and Nevis [a]	0.00	0.01	..	48.74	4.18	18.83	..	14.65
Saint Lucia [a]	0.00	0.01	..	65.10	1.25	8.68	..	7.43
Saint Vincent and the Grenadines	0.00	0.01	..	63.95	0.96	7.74	..	6.78
Suriname [b]	0.00	0.00	..	99.63	0.04	0.51	..	0.48
Trinidad and Tobago	0.00	0.04	0.04	117.47	0.07	2.73	3.21	3.14
Uruguay	0.01	0.16	0.24	85.95	0.32	4.96	7.33	7.01
Venezuela, Bolivarian Republic of	0.12	0.86	1.33	62.60	0.46	3.13	4.80	4.35
Oceania								
Fiji	0.00	0.01	..	..	0.00	1.39	..	1.39
French Polynesia	0.00	0.02	..	125.81	0.36	9.00	..	8.64
Guam	..	0.00	..	..	..	1.56	..	..
New Caledonia	0.00	0.02	..	74.88	0.73	6.50	..	5.77
Samoa [b]	0.00	0.00	..	..	0.00	0.05	..	0.05
Solomon Islands	0.00	0.00	0.00	..	0.00	0.20	0.20	0.20
Tonga [a]	0.00	0.00	..	68.18	0.10	0.80	..	0.70
Vanuatu	0.00	0.00	0.00	131.62	0.01	0.44	0.43	0.42
Transition economies								
Albania	0.00	0.01	..	..	0.00	0.32	..	0.32
Armenia	0.00	0.00	..	..	0.00	0.06	..	0.06
Azerbaijan	0.00	0.01	..	..	0.00	0.07	..	0.07
Belarus	0.00	..	0.25	358.78	0.00	..	2.59	2.59
Bosnia and Herzegovina [a]	0.00	0.08	..	203.36	0.03	2.20	..	2.18
Croatia [b]	0.00	0.35	0.47	189.25	0.05	7.77	10.67	10.62
Georgia	0.00	0.04	0.05	104.15	0.03	0.93	1.15	1.12

Region/Economy	Fixed broadband subscribers (millions)			CAGR (%)	Penetration (subscribers per 100 inhabitants)			Change in penetration
	2003	2007	2008	2003-2007/2008	2003	2007	2008	2003-2007/2008
Kazakhstan	0.00	0.27	..	..	0.00	1.79	..	1.79
Kyrgyzstan	0.00	0.00	..	..	0.00	0.06	..	0.06
Montenegro	0.00	0.01	..	..	0.00	2.30	..	2.30
Republic of Moldova	0.00	0.05	0.08	162.92	0.02	1.32	2.10	2.09
Russian Federation [a]	0.13	4.39	7.01	123.76	0.09	3.02	4.95	4.86
Serbia	..	0.33	..	..	..	4.41	..	..
Tajikistan	0.00	..	..	..	0.00	..	..	..
The former Yugoslav Republic of Macedonia	0.00	0.08	0.17	..	0.00	4.06	8.18	8.18
Turkmenistan	0.00	..	..	..	0.00	..	..	..
Ukraine	0.00	0.00	..	..	0.00	1.72	..	1.72
Uzbekistan [b]	0.00	0.01	..	31.72	0.01	0.03	..	0.02

Source: UNCTAD on the basis of ITU and national sources.
[a] *Estimates for 2003.*
[b] *Estimates for 2007.*
[c] *Estimates for 2008.*
[d] *Estimates for every reported year.*

Annex table II.1 Use of computers by enterprise size (per cent).[a]
Corresponds to the core indicator 'Proportion of businesses using computers' (B1)

Economy/Group	Reference year	"0-9 employees"	"10-49 employees"	"50-249 employees"	"250+ employees"	Total
Developed economies						
Australia[h]	2006	87	97	100	100	89
Austria	2007	..	98	100	100	98
Belgium	2007	..	98	99	100	98
Bermuda[d, g, l]	2006	82	82	82	..	82
Bulgaria	2007	..	82	96	99	85
Cyprus	2007	..	94	100	100	95
Czech Republic[u]	2007	..	97	99	99	97
Denmark[i]	2007	..	99	99	100	99
Estonia[u]	2007	..	94	99	100	95
Finland	2007	..	99	100	100	99
France[i]	2007	..	..	..	..	99
Germany[u]	2007	..	97	100	100	97
Greece	2007	..	97	99	100	97
Hungary[u]	2007	..	90	98	98	91
Iceland	2006	..	100	100	100	100
Ireland[u]	2007	..	96	99	100	97
Italy	2007	..	96	100	100	97
Latvia	2007	..	94	99	99	95
Lithuania[u]	2007	..	89	98	100	91
Luxembourg	2007	..	97	99	99	97
Malta	2007	..	97	99	100	97
Netherlands	2007	..	100	100	100	100
New Zealand[b]	2006	89	96	99	99	94
Norway	2007	..	98	99	98	98
Poland	2007	..	94	100	100	95
Portugal	2007	..	94	99	100	95
Romania	2007	..	80	91	97	82
Slovakia[u]	2007	..	99	99	98	99
Slovenia	2007	..	97	99	100	98
Spain[u]	2007	..	98	100	100	98
Sweden[u]	2007	..	96	99	100	97
Switzerland[e]	2005	95	99	99	100	99
United Kingdom[u]	2007	..	95	99	100	96
Developing economies						
Argentina	2006	100	100	100	100	100
Brazil[b, t, k]	2007	..	93	100	100	94
Chile	2005	..	..	..	..	60
Colombia[l]	2006	69	87	97	98	89
Cuba	2007	86	93	93	96	94
Egypt[d, e, f]	2008	6	40	80	97	40
Hong Kong, China[d]	2007	60	88	99	100	64
India[m]	2005	28	56	74	92	55
Mauritius[b, d]	2006	18	91	100	100	91
Mongolia[d]	2006	..	..	..	..	37
Panama[c]	2006	65	87	98	97	79
Qatar	2005	31	76	99	97	59
Republic of Korea[d]	2006	42	97	100	100	46
Singapore	2007	68	92	100	100	73
Thailand[d, n]	2007	20	84	98	100	22
Turkey	2004	..	80	96	100	88
Uruguay[b, o]	2005	48	79	82	96	68
Transition economies						
Azerbaijan[g]	2007	10	37	50	77	23
Belarus[p]	2005	..	..	..	..	84
Croatia	2007	..	96	100	100	97
Kazakhstan	2007	56	90	96	100	79
Kyrgyzstan[g]	2007	49	93	95	98	80
Russian Federation[g, r]	2006	..	89	98	100	93
Serbia	2007	..	90	98	100	92
The former Yugoslav Republic of Macedonia[b, q]	2007	73	89	97	100	75

Sources: UNCTAD Information Economy Database and Eurostat.
[a] *Data collected through national surveys and censuses conducted between 2004 and 2008. Due to differences in methodology and timeliness of underlying data, comparisons across countries and over time should be made with caution. Different countries report data for different economic activities. Unless otherwise specified, data refer to enterprises which cover ISIC Rev.3.1 activities specified in annex tables II.3 and II.4.*
[b] *Estimates.*

[c] Provisional data.
[d] Data refer to establishments.
[e] Data refer to the sample and have not been extrapolated to the target population.
[f] Due to changes in the sampling frame/methodology, the data for the reference year should not be compared with the data for previous years.
[g] Data include ISIC Rev.3.1.Section L - 'Public administration and defence; compulsory social security'.
[h] Data refer to the year ended 30 June 2006.
[i] Category '50-249' refer to enterprises with 50 or more employees.
[j] Data cover NACE Rev.1 sections D, F, G, H, I, K, O.
[k] Category '10-49' refer to enterprises with 9-49 employees.
[l] Category '0-9' refer to establishments with 1-10 employees.
[m] Data cover only ISIC Rev.3.1 section D -'Manufacturing'.
[n] Categories '0-9', '10-49', '50-249', '250+' refer to establishments with '1-15', '16-50', '50-200' and '200+' employees respectively.
[o] Category '0-9' refer to enterprises with 5-9 employees. Data cover ISIC Rev. 3.1 sections D, E, G, H, I, K71-74, M, N.
[p] Data cover ISIC Rev. 3.1 sections A-K, M-O.
[q] Category '0-9' refer to enterprises with 5-9 employees. Data cover NACE Rev.1 sections D, F, G, I, K, groups 55.1, 55.2, 92.1 and 92.2 .
[r] Small private enterprises not surveyed. Category '10-49' refer to state-owned enterprises with 1-50 employees.
[s] Categories '50-249' and '250+' refer to entreprises with '50-299' and '300 or more' employees respectively.
[t] Data refer to enterprises with 100 or more employees. Categories '50-249' and '250+' refer to enterprises with '100-299' and '300 or more' employees respectively.
[u] Data do not cover enterprises active in 'Electricity, gas and water supply' (NACE Rev.1. section E).

Annex table II.2 Use of Internet by enterprise size (per cent) [a]
Corresponds to the core indicator 'Proportion of businesses using the Internet' (B3)

Economy/Group	Reference Year	0-9 employees	10-49 employees	50-249 employees	250+ employees	Total
Developed economies						
Australia [h]	2006	79	93	98	100	81
Austria	2007	..	97	99	100	97
Belgium	2007	..	96	99	99	97
Bermuda [d, g, i]	2006	71	71	71	..	71
Bulgaria	2007	..	70	92	98	75
Canada [s]	2007	..	94	99	100	95
Cyprus	2007	..	86	99	100	88
Czech Republic	2007	..	94	99	99	95
Denmark [i]	2007	..	97	98	99	98
Estonia	2007	..	93	99	100	94
Finland	2007	..	99	100	100	99
France [i]	2007	..	96	100	100	96
Germany	2007	..	94	99	100	95
Greece	2007	..	92	98	99	93
Hungary	2007	..	85	96	98	86
Iceland	2006	..	99	100	100	99
Ireland	2007	..	94	99	100	95
Italy	2007	..	94	99	99	94
Japan [e, t]	2007	..		98	99	99
Latvia	2007	..	84	97	98	86
Lithuania	2007	..	86	98	100	89
Luxembourg	2007	..	94	97	99	94
Malta	2007	..	94	97	100	95
Netherlands	2007	..	99	99	99	99
New Zealand [b]	2006	85	94	98	98	91
Norway	2007	..	95	99	98	96
Poland	2007	..	90	99	100	92
Portugal	2007	..	88	98	100	90
Romania	2007	..	63	80	95	67
Slovakia	2007	..	98	99	98	98
Slovenia	2007	..	96	99	100	96
Spain	2007	..	94	99	100	94
Sweden	2007	..	94	99	99	95
Switzerland [e]	2005	93	97	99	100	98
United Kingdom	2007	..	92	99	100	94
Developing economies						
Argentina	2006	67	90	98	100	95
Brazil [b, f, k]	2007	..	90	98	99	91
Chile	2005	..	..	..	..	49
Colombia [l]	2006	58	83	96	97	86
Cuba	2007	86	80	65	71	70
Egypt [d, e, f]	2008	2	20	53	83	24
Hong Kong, China [d]	2007	56	83	92	100	60
Mauritius [b, d]	2006	18	82	95	100	84
Panama [c]	2006	52	75	95	97	68
Qatar	2005	19	58	99	81	45
Republic of Korea [d]	2006	40	96	100	100	44
Singapore	2007	62	88	100	100	67
Thailand [d, n]	2007	11	64	87	95	13
Turkey	2004		78	92	99	80
Uruguay [b, o]	2005	31	66	79	94	54
Transition economies						
Azerbaijan [g]	2007	4	17	25	58	11
Belarus [p]	2005	..	..	..	..	38
Croatia	2007	..	92	98	100	93
Kazakhstan	2007	37	70	78	92	62
Kyrgyzstan [g]	2007	27	27	34	50	30
Russian Federation [g, r]	2006	..	46	74	92	61
Serbia	2007	..	86	86	94	87
The former Yugoslav Republic of Macedonia [b, q]	2007	46	70	82	97	48

Sources: UNCTAD Information Economy Database and Eurostat.
Notes: see notes for annex table II.1.

Annex table II.3. Use of computers by economic activity (per cent) [a]
Corresponds to the core indicator 'Proportion of businesses using computers' (B1)

Economy/Group	Reference Year	A Agriculture, hunting and forestry	B Fishing	C Mining and quarrying	D Manufacturing	E Electricity, gas and water supply	F Construction	G Wholesale and retail trade; repair of motor vehicles, motorcycles, etc.	G50 Sale, maintenance and repair of motor vehicles and motorcycles, etc.	G51 Wholesale trade and commission trade, except of motor vehicles and motorcycles	G52 Retail trade, except of motor vehicles and motorcycles, etc.	H Hotels and restaurants	I Transport, storage and communications	I60 Land transport; transport via pipelines	I61 Water transport	I62 Air transport	I63 Supporting and auxiliary transport activities; activities of travel agencies	I64 Post and telecommunications	J Financial intermediation	K Real estate, renting and business activities	K70 Real estate activities	K71 Renting of machinery and equipment	K72 Computer and related activities	K73 Research and development	K74 Other business activities	M Education	N Health and social work	O Other community, social and personal service activities
Developed economies																												
Australia [f]	2006	..	..	89	89	96	88	..	..	97	83	76	..	79	..	..	..	83	94	94	..	..	..	..	..	..	97	..
Austria [n]	2007	..	..	..	97	..	98	98	96	100	97	99	98	..	..	..	..	..	..	99	..	..	..	..	..	..	..	100
Belgium [n]	2007	..	..	..	99	..	98	99	..	100	..	100	94	..	..	..	..	..	..	99	..	..	..	..	..	..	..	98
Bermuda [d,g]	2006	82	..	..	82	83	82	82	92	94	78	82	82	..	..	..	..	..	83	82	..	..	..	..	..	83	82	82
Bulgaria [n]	2007	..	..	..	80	100	88	88	..	..	..	93	83	..	..	..	..	..	..	89	..	..	..	..	..	..	..	..
Czech Republic [n]	2007	..	..	..	98	100	97	98	100	100	98	100	97	..	..	..	..	..	..	95	..	..	..	..	..	..	..	100
Denmark [n]	2007	..	..	..	..	..	99	99	100	100	..	..	..	..	..	..	..	..	..	..	..	..	..	..	..	..	..	100
Estonia [n]	2007	..	..	..	96	100	94	96	..	..	..	90	97	..	..	..	..	..	..	95	..	..	..	..	..	..	..	93
Finland [n]	2007	..	..	..	99	..	98	100	100	100	..	100	96	..	..	..	..	..	..	100	..	..	..	..	..	..	..	100
France [n]	2007	..	..	..	97	..	100	99	100	100	..	..	..	..	..	..	..	..	..	..	..	..	..	..	..	..	..	..
Germany [n]	2007	..	..	..	96	100	98	98	..	..	98	98	94	..	..	..	..	..	..	99	..	..	..	..	..	..	..	99
Greece [n]	2007	..	..	..	98	100	93	98	100	99	..	99	95	..	..	..	..	..	..	95	..	..	..	..	..	..	..	100
Hungary [n]	2007	..	..	..	92	100	92	91	..	..	..	91	92	..	..	..	..	..	..	89	..	..	..	..	..	..	..	95
Iceland [n]	2006	..	..	..	100	100	100	100	..	..	..	100	100	..	..	..	..	..	100	100	..	..	..	..	..	..	..	100
Ireland [n]	2007	..	..	..	98	100	98	96	..	..	..	94	96	..	..	..	..	..	..	97	..	..	..	..	..	..	..	100
Italy [n]	2007	..	..	..	97	100	95	97	99	99	94	100	96	..	..	..	..	..	..	98	..	..	..	..	..	..	..	98
Latvia [n]	2007	..	..	..	94	..	98	94	99	98	89	100	94	..	..	..	..	..	..	95	..	..	..	..	..	..	..	100
Lithuania [n]	2007	..	..	..	87	100	91	94	..	..	..	96	91	..	..	..	..	..	..	94	..	..	..	..	..	..	..	100
Luxembourg [n]	2007	..	..	..	95	..	99	97	..	..	..	92	94	..	..	..	..	..	..	99	..	..	..	..	..	..	..	100
Malta [n]	2007	..	..	..	99	..	90	98	96	98	97	100	98	..	..	..	..	..	..	96	..	..	..	..	..	..	..	100
Netherlands [n]	2007	..	..	..	100	100	100	100	..	98	97	98	100	96	100	100	100	94	100	100	..	..	..	..	..	..	..	100
New Zealand [b]	2006	82	93	83	97	100	95	95	99	100	89	78	97	96	..	100	100	100	100	98	96	95	99	100	93	97	99	94
Norway [n]	2007	..	..	..	98	..	98	98	..	..	..	99	95	..	..	..	..	..	..	98	..	..	..	..	..	..	..	100
Poland [n]	2007	..	..	..	95	..	96	95	..	..	..	98	91	..	..	..	..	..	..	97	..	..	..	..	..	..	..	100
Portugal [n]	2007	..	..	..	97	..	88	99	..	..	..	99	77	..	..	..	..	..	..	97	..	..	..	..	..	..	..	100
Romania [n]	2007	..	..	..	81	..	85	82	91	89	76	86	..	..	..	..	..	..	..	86	..	..	..	..	..	..	..	95
Slovakia [n]	2007	..	..	..	99	100	100	99	..	..	..	100	100	..	..	..	..	..	..	100	..	..	..	..	..	..	..	100
Slovenia [n]	2007	..	..	..	100	100	89	100	..	..	..	100	100	..	..	..	..	..	..	99	..	..	..	..	..	..	..	100
Spain [n]	2007	..	..	..	98	100	96	99	..	..	..	99	98	..	..	..	..	..	..	99	..	..	..	..	..	..	..	98
Sweden [n]	2007	..	..	..	97	99	93	98	..	..	99	96	93	..	..	..	..	..	..	99	..	..	..	..	..	..	..	97
Switzerland [e]	2005	..	..	..	99	100	99	98	..	97	99	95	99	..	..	..	..	..	100	99	..	..	..	..	..	..	..	..
United Kingdom [n]	2007	..	..	..	96	91	97	94	..	..	..	..	92	..	..	..	..	..	..	97	..	..	..	..	..	..	..	100
Developing economies																												
Argentina	2006	..	..	..	100	..	..	..	..	..	..	..	..	..	..	..	..	..	..	..	..	..	..	..	..	..	..	..

Economy/Group	Reference Year	A — Agriculture, hunting and forestry	B — Fishing	C — Mining and quarrying	D — Manufacturing	E — Electricity, gas and water supply	F — Construction	G — Wholesale and retail trade; repair of motor vehicles, motorcycles, etc.	G50 — Sale, maintenance and repair of motor vehicles and motorcycles, etc.	G51 — Wholesale trade and commission trade, except of motor vehicles and motorcycles	G52 — Retail trade, except of motor vehicles and motorcycles, etc.	H — Hotels and restaurants	I — Transport, storage and communications	I60 — Land transport; transport via pipelines	I61 — Water transport	I62 — Air transport	I63 — Supporting and auxiliary transport activities; activities of travel agencies	I64 — Post and telecommunications	J — Financial intermediation	K — Real estate, renting and business activities	K70 — Real estate activities	K71 — Renting of machinery and equipment	K72 — Computer and related activities	K73 — Research and development	K74 — Other business activities	M — Education	N — Health and social work	O — Other community, social and personal service activities
Brazil [b,h]	2007	:	:	:	100	:	100	100	80	92	47	62	100	:	:	:	:	:	:	100	:	:	:	:	93	:	:	100
Chile	2005	:	:	:	:	:	:	:	:	:	:	:	:	:	:	:	:	:	:	:	73	85	98	:	:	:	:	76
Colombia [l]	2006	89	96	100	83	100	99	97	96	98	95	94	90	96	100	100	100	100	100	98	100	100	100	100	99	99	98	65
Cuba	2007	60	:	50	98	0	86	100	96	99	81	45	:	50	97	100	35	60	96	99	67	:	100	100	100	99	98	18
Egypt [d,e]	2008	:	:	:	33	76	48	66	67	56	27	:	:	:	:	:	:	:	86	:	:	:	:	:	:	:	:	48
Hong Kong, China [d,i]	2007	:	:	:	61	:	:	:	:	:	:	:	43	:	:	:	:	:	:	:	:	:	:	:	:	:	:	:
India	2005	18	:	39	56	100	97	95	100	98	90	92	95	83	100	100	100	100	99	99	100	100	96	100	99	95	100	96
Mauritius [b,d,k]	2006	69	0	50	91	100	53	23	27	26	18	34	51	42	50	91	51	64	32	50	31	32	71	75	54	74	42	43
Mongolia [d]	2006	14	:	50	39	53	92	81	89	77	87	55	85	65	90	96	93	97	100	87	67	91	100	100	94	88	90	87
Panama [c]	2006	78	:	100	74	92	92	:	51	87	59	42	:	79	100	100	94	100	100	:	94	67	100	100	92	92	95	28
Qatar	2005	:	:	98	42	100	93	:	:	68	39	17	18	:	:	:	:	:	:	90	:	:	:	:	:	:	:	:
Republic of Korea [d,l]	2006	58	:	:	59	:	72	75	23	47	19	49	66	19	:	:	:	:	96	:	56	41	91	:	91	59	72	53
Singapore	2007	:	:	:	77	:	72	:	:	:	:	12	93	:	:	:	75	:	62	90	:	:	91	86	75	83	:	:
Thailand [d]	2007	:	:	:	20	:	57	91	:	:	:	98	:	:	:	:	:	:	:	95	35	41	91*	:	75	:	:	96
Turkey [n]	2004	:	:	:	85	:	80	:	:	:	:	:	:	:	:	:	:	:	:	:	:	:	:	86	:	:	:	:
Transition economies																												
Azerbaijan	2007	:	:	24	33	62	31	21	15	28	15	15	41	22	78	70	38	82	69	23	4	100	25	37	25	59	24	8
Croatia [n]	2007	:	:	:	95	100	96	97	100	98	95	94	99	98	100	100	100	:	98	98	92	:	100	100	98	:	:	100
Kazakhstan	2007	86	:	85	78	80	95	:	72	52	63	89	73	76	100	56	56	77	65	65	52	75	71	70	65	91	95	78
Kyrgyzstan	2007	76	:	60	70	88	64	56	52	93	86	88	94	92	98	100	93	83	92	91	88	78	69	94	91	93	98	80
Russian Federation [m]	2006	96	86	96	94	90	96	89	93	93	90	96	100	100	100	:	:	99	95	100	100	:	99	97	100	98	100	100
Serbia [n]	2007	:	:	:	94	90	90	85	94	82	90	:	:	:	:	:	:	100	100	100	:	:	100	:	:	:	:	100

Sources: UNCTAD Information Economy Database and Eurostat.

a Data collected through national surveys and censuses conducted between 2004 and 2008. Due to differences in methodology and timeliness of underlying data, comparisons across countries and over time should be made with caution.

b Estimates

c Provisional data

d Data refer to establishments.

e Data refer to the sample and have not been extrapolated to the target population.

f Data refer to the year ended 30 June 2006. Data under I60 represent the overall proportion for divisions 60-63.

g Section A represents the overall proportion for sections A and B. Section K refers to divisions 70, 71, 74 and international businesses.

h Section O represents the overall proportion for section H, divisions 92 ('Recreational, cultural and sporting activities') and 93 ('Other service activities').

i Section K represents the overall proportion for sections H, K, division 63, division 93 ('Other service activities'), group 851 ('Human health activities'); group 921 ('Cinema, radio, television and other enter-tainment activities') and group 803 ('Higher education services').

j Industry breakdown is given according to the national classification HKSIC: section D includes manufacturing, electricity and gas; section G includes wholesale, retail, import/export trade, restaurants and hotels; section I includes transport, storage and communications; section J includes financing, insurance, real estate and business services; section O includes community, social and personal services.

k Section M includes technical and vocational institutions providing training courses in IT.

l Section A represents the overall proportion for sections A, B and C. Section M represents the overall proportion for sections E, L ('Public administration and defence, compulsory social security'), M, N, divi-sions 92 ('Recreational, cultural and sporting activities') and 93 ('Other service activities').

m Section A refers to division 02 ('Forestry, logging and related service activities'); section M refers to group 803 ('Higher education'); section O refers to division 92 ('Recreational, cultural and sporting activities'). Breakdown is given according to NACE Rev. 1. Section H refers to groups 55.1 and 55.2 - 'Hotels and 'Camping sites and other provision of short stay accomodation'; section O refers to groups 92.1 and 92.2 - 'Motion picture and Video activities' and 'Radio and television activities'.

n Section A refers to division 92 ('Recreational, cultural and sporting activities') and 93 ('Other service activities').

Annex table II.4. Use of Internet by economic activity (per cent) [a]
Corresponds to the core indicator 'Proportion of businesses using the Internet' (B3)

Economy/Group	Reference Year	A	B	C	D	E	F	G	G50	G51	G52	H	I	I60	I61	I62	I63	I64	J	K	K70	K71	K72	K73	K74	M	N	O
Developed economies																												
Australia [f]	2006	..		81	80	89	80	..	..	91	72	67	..	66	..	..	..	68	93	90	..	..	..	..	..	..	92	
Austria [n]	2007	..		..	96	..	97	98	96	99	96	97	94					..	93	99						..	..	100
Belgium [n]	2007	..		..	98	..	97	96				98	94							98								98
Bermuda [d,g]	2006	71		..	71	72	71	71	80	77	63	71	71					71	71	71						71	71	71
Bulgaria [n]	2007				73		78	72		77		84	76						71		85								100
Canada	2007				99	100	65	95		99	94	82	92							100	93								
Czech Republic [n]	2007				96	100	97	99	98	99	..	98	96								94								100
Denmark [n]	2007				95	100	92	95	100	99	98	90	95																
Estonia [n]	2007				95	100	98	95	..	..	..	100	94								94								100
Finland [n]	2007				99		97	99		99	92	97	94							100	100								97
France [n]	2007				95	100	96	95	99	99		96	94							99	99								99
Germany [n]	2007				93	100	92	94	100	95	90	97	95							98								99
Greece [n]	2007				91		92	87				91	88							91								99
Hungary [n]	2007				86	92	86	87			95	100	88						87									100
Iceland [n]	2006				99		100	98				100	100						100	100								100
Ireland [n]	2007				97		97	92				94	96							97								100
Italy [n]	2007				94		92	95	98	98	90	100	95						97	96								96
Japan [e]	2007				100		99	99					97						97	98								100
Latvia [n]	2007				82		91	84	95	92	76	100	84							89								100
Lithuania [n]	2007				85	100	89	91				89	89							93								100
Luxembourg [n]	2007				93		94	93				95	91							99								100
Malta [n]	2007				92		88	96	96	97	95	98	98							95								100
Netherlands [n]	2007				99		100	98				98	99							99								100
New Zealand [b]	2006	77	67	73	93		92	92	98	97	84	82	94	89	100	95	100	94	100	96	95	90	100	100	96	93	93	94
Norway [n]	2007				97		96	93				98	95							97								100
Poland [n]	2007				91		94	90				98	89							96								100
Portugal [n]	2007				89		81	95				97	91							97								100
Romania [n]	2007				66		74	63	75	74	54	74	71							75								95
Slovakia [n]	2007				98	99	99	98				93	100							99								100
Slovenia [n]	2007				100		87	98				100	100							97								100
Spain [n]	2007				93	100	92	97				99	94							97								98
Sweden [n]	2007				96	97	93	96				99	88							96								98
Switzerland [e]	2005				98	100	98	97		97	97	90	96							100	98								97

Economy/ Group	Reference Year	Agriculture, hunting and forestry A	Fishing B	Mining and quarrying C	Manufacturing D	Electricity, gas and water supply E	Construction F	Wholesale and retail trade; repair of motor vehicles, motorcycles, etc. G	Sale, maintenance and repair of motor vehicles and motorcycles, etc. G50	Wholesale trade and commission trade, except of motor vehicles and motorcycles G51	Retail trade, except of motor vehicles and motorcycles, etc. G52	Hotels and restaurants H	Transport, storage and communications I	Land transport; transport via pipelines I60	Water transport I61	Air transport I62	Supporting and auxiliary transport activities; activities of travel agencies I63	Post and telecommunications I64	Financial intermediation J	Real estate, renting and business activities K	Real estate activities K70	Renting of machinery and equipment K71	Computer and related activities K72	Research and development K73	Other business activities K74	Education M	Health and social work N	Other community, social and personal service activities O
United Kingdom [n]	2007	..	..	..	95	95	93	91	..	..	..	92	88	..	..	..	..	..	..	96	..	..	..	..	..	..	..	100
Developing economies																												
Argentina	2006	..	..	..	95	..	..	..	..								..	..	..	..	..	..	..	..	..	..	..	..
Brazil [b,h]	2007	..	..	..	97	..	98	97	..	..	..	..	99	..	..	..	..	..	..	99	..	..	..	..	..	..	..	91
Chile	2005	..	..	..	..	..	..	..	70	84	34	47	..	..	..	..	..	..	..	70	70	97	..	88	..	..	..	63
Colombia [i]	2006	..	..	..	78	..	..	93	92	96	89	..	..	..	..	..	..	..	..	97	..	..	..	..	..	..	..	..
Cuba	2007	45	82	86	80	97	80	90	76	81	21	38	68	56	100	100	88	100	96	92	88	100	100	100	93	62	83	29
Egypt [d,e]	2008	20		50	17	0	67	..	67	34	12	25	..	28	97	100	18	16	74	..	67	..	83	..	..	..	..	12
Hong Kong, China [d,j]	2007	..	..	..	59	..	46	62	..	..	..	..	38	..	..	..	..	..	84	..	..	..	..	..	..	..	..	41
Mauritius [b,d,k]	2006	57	[illegible]	50	86	100	88	87	81	93	82	83	89	63	100	100	96	100	97	95	100	67	100	100	95	87	77	89
Panama [c]	2006	56	..	87	62	92	76	71	83	62	85	39	78	52	75	92	90	94	..	81	53	91	100	100	91	72	67	76
Qatar	2005		..	97	31	100	65	..	41	71	47	34	..	40	100	100	87	100	87		41	51	100	..	70	65	59	16
Republic of Korea [d,l]	2006	56	..	..	57	..	72	..	..	66	37	15	18	..	..	..	..	..	95	87	..	..	..	..	..	57	..	..
Singapore	2007	..	..	..	71	..	64	70	..		..	41	59	..	..	..	..	..	57	..	48	..	90	..	87	78	63	46
Thailand [d]	2007	..	..	..	13	..	44	..	14	33	11	5		14			72	..	..	..	12	17	78	86	42	..	..	..
Turkey [n]	2004	..	..	..	78	..	70	83	..	..	..	84	87	..	..	..	..	..	..	91	..	..	..	..	..	..	..	96
Transition economies																												
Azerbaijan	2007	..	..	15	18	25	8	13	8	19	8	10	25	7	67	57	30	53	47	16	2	..	18	24	17	22	8	4
Croatia [n]	2007	..	..		90	100	94	93	98	94	89	90	96	93	100	100	100	100	..	96	85	100	100	100	96	..	..	100
Kazakhstan	2007	39		67	61	53	87	..	..	..	..	..	..	..	..	..	..	65	..	..	..	..	60	58		84	..	..
Kyrgyzstan	2007	5	0	33	41	40	23	47	63	47	45	39	46	19	50	50	43	60	50	36	20	25	67	44	36	25	16	33
Russian Federation [m]	2006	67	51	80	77	58	70	63	79	77	55	47	67	51	85	95	67	95	84	63	47	50	90	88	66	94	64	43
Serbia [n]	2007	..	..	..	89	..	79	82	87	81	83	80	93	92	..	..	..	100	..	94	93	..	100	..	..	..	..	100

Sources: UNCTAD Information Economy Database and Eurostat.
Notes: see notes for annex table II.3.

Annex table II.5. Internet applications by enterprises (per cent). Enterprises with 10 or more employees. [a] Corresponds to the core indicators B5, B7, B8, B12

Economy/Group	Reference year	Proportion of enterprises: With a website B5	Receiving orders over the Internet B7	Placing orders over the Internet B8	Proportion of enterprises using the Internet for: Sending and receiving e-mail B12.a	Information about goods or services B12.b.i	Information from public authorities B12.b.ii	Information searches or research B12.b.iii	Internet banking or financial services B12.c	Interacting with general government organizations B12.d	Providing customer services B12.e	Delivering products online B12.f
Developed economies												
Australia [h]	2006	55	27	49	..	51	..	..	88	74	..	..
Austria [k]	2007	78	20	56	..	45	60	..	85	81	..	..
Belgium [k]	2007	72	18	53	..	55	..	..	87	51	..	..
Bermuda [d, g]	2006	43	6	24	..	..	..	..	..	..	..	..
Bulgaria [k]	2007	31	2	5	..	23	40	..	44	45	..	..
Canada	2007	70	13	65	..	..	..	..	..	..	..	..
Cyprus [k]	2007	47	6	22	..	57	..	..	54	54	..	..
Czech Republic [k, x]	2007	71	10	32	..	73	..	..	88	..	..	..
Denmark [j, k]	2007	84	33	59	..	53	83	..	93	..	..	..
Estonia [k, x]	2007	62	6	20	..	51	..	..	93	..	..	..
Finland [k]	2007	81	13	55	..	68	..	..	90	94	..	..
France [j, k]	2007	57			..	25	61	..	76	69	..	..
Germany [k, x]	2007	78	25	60	..	69	..	..	76	56	..	..
Greece [k]	2007	60	8	15	..	64	71	..	72	82	..	..
Hungary [k, x]	2007	47	6	19	..	36	..	..	66	55	..	..
Iceland [i]	2006	77	31	58	..	..	85	..	90	99	..	..
Ireland [k, x]	2007	64	22	53	..	42	..	..	81	89	..	..
Italy [k]	2007	57	4	29	..	55	74	..	85	84	..	..
Japan [e, t]	2007	84	20	35	..	..	..	..	..	..	..	..
Latvia [k]	2007	39	4	14	..	49	42	..	79	45	..	..
Lithuania [k, x]	2007	48	15	21	..	58	..	..	83	76	..	..
Luxembourg [k]	2007	63	11	34	..	48	..	..	75	85	..	..
Malta [k]	2007	61	14	36	..	48	74	..	78	77	..	..
Netherlands [k]	2007	80	28	41	..	34	..	..	85	81	..	..
New Zealand [b, l]	2006	59	35	57	..	..	64	..	82	73	28	..
Norway [k]	2007	72	31	67	..	86	..	..	85	71	..	..
Poland [k]	2007	53	9	22	..	45	..	..	74	64	..	..
Portugal [k]	2007	42	7	20	..	38	..	..	73	72	..	..
Romania [k]	2007	28	3	9	..	44	39	..	42	42	..	..
Slovakia [k, x]	2007	70	7	19	..	74	..	..	88	85	..	..
Slovenia	2007	67	10	24	..	74	..	..	91	83	..	..
Spain [k, x]	2007	49	8	18	..	31	..	..	81	58	..	..
Sweden [k, x]	2007	85	26	71	..	70	..	..	90	79	..	..
Switzerland [e, m]	2005	90	23	57	..	96	..	58	83	56	21	22
United Kingdom [k, x]	2007	75	17	59	..	45	..	..	74	54	..	..
Developing economies												
Argentina	2006	72	43	46	93	85	72	..	81	55	41	7
Brazil [b, f, n]	2007	44	42	59	90	87	61	82	71	82	45	12
Colombia [o]	2006	44	39	37	86	61	49	54	74	51	45	10
Cuba [p]	2007	26	2	3	70	70	70	70	10		39	2
Egypt	2006	18	4	4	24	20	12	9	8	4	11	8
Hong Kong, China [d, q]	2007	45	4	22	83	82	64		38		20	60
Mauritius [b, d]	2006	39	29	31	..	..	..	..	..	..	..	..
Panama [c]	2006	..	31	35	78	65	54	49	56	29	31	..
Qatar	2005	68	35	28	..	..	..	..	..	..	..	..
Republic of Korea [d]	2006	58	7	34	88	55	46	72	64	38	35	10
Singapore	2007	63	36	37	89	86	80	86	57	83		37
Thailand [k, r]	2007	36	8	11	51	41	..	68	8	..	18	13
Turkey [s]	2004	48	..	..	..	55	45		61	46	41	3
Uruguay [b, u]	2005	27	25	25	66	52	45	25	35	23	35	3
Transition economies												
Azerbaijan [g]	2007	4	..	2	..	..	9	..	7	6	..	..
Croatia	2007	52	12	20	..	..	46	..	81	51	..	..
Kazakhstan	2007	18	22	23	71	48	39	67	38	33	35	4
Kyrgyzstan [g]	2007	9	..	..	27	..	3	..	..	..	..	2
Russian Federation [g, w]	2006	21	13	21	58	35	29	55	11	33	..	3

		Proportion of enterprises:			Proportion of enterprises using the Internet for:							
Economy/Group	Refer- ence year	With a website B5	Receiving orders over the Internet B7	Placing orders over the Internet B8	Sending and receiving e-mail B12.a	Information about goods or services B12.b.i	Information from public authorities B12.b.ii	Information searches or research B12.b.iii	Internet banking or financial services B12.c	Interacting with general government organizations B12.d	Providing customer services B12.e	Delivering products online B12.f
Serbia [k]	2007	53	15	17	..	47	44	..	56	52	..	..
The former Yugoslav Republic of Macedonia [b, v]	2007	39	4	8	..	39	50	..	46	52	..	..

Sources: UNCTAD Information Economy Database and Eurostat.

[a] Data collected through national surveys and censuses conducted between 2004 and 2008. Due to differences in methodology and timeliness of underlying data, comparisons across countries and over time should be made with caution. Different countries report data for different economic activities. Unless otherwise specified, data refer to enterprises which cover ISIC Rev.3.1 activities specified in annex table II.4.

[b] Estimates

[c] Provisional data

[d] Data refer to establishments.

[e] Data refer to the sample and have not been extrapolated to the target population.

[f] Due to changes in the sampling frame/methodology, the data for the reference year should not be compared with the data for previous years.

[g] Data include ISIC Rev.3.1.section L - 'Public administration and defence; compulsory social security'.

[h] Data refer to the year ended 30 June 2006. B12.b.i refers to enterprises gathering information or researching for assessing or development of businesses' range of products, services, processes or methods; monitoring competitors and identifying future market trends. B12.d refers to enterprises making electronic lodgements with government organizations.

[i] B12.c excludes enterprises of ISIC-Rev.3.1.section J 'Financial intermediation'.

[j] Data cover NACE Rev.1 sections D, F, G, H, I, K, O.

[k] B12.b.i. refers to enterprises using the Internet for market monitoring (e.g. prices).

[l] B12.e refers to enterprises providing customer services (B12.e) and delivering products online (B12.f).

[m] B12.e refers to enterprises providing after-sales services. B12.f refers to enterprises delivering and/or offering products/services on firm homepage.

[n] Data refer to national projection for enterprises with more than 9 employees.

[o] Data refer to enterprises with 11 or more employees.

[p] Estimates for indicators B12.a-f.

[q] B12.b.i includes also other information searches and research (B12.b.iii). B12.b.ii includes transactions with government organizations/public authorities (B12.d).

[r] Data refer to establishments with 16 or more employees. B12.e refers to establishments using the Internet for advertising own goods and services.

[s] B12.d includes enterprises using the Internet for e-procurement to government organizations.

[t] Data refer to enterprises with 100 or more employees.

[u] Data cover ISIC Rev. 3.1 sections D, E, G, H, I, K71-74, M, N.

[v] Data under B7, B8, B12.b.ii, B12.d refer to 2006. Data cover NACE Rev.1 sections D, F, G, I, K, groups 55.1, 55.2, 92.1 and 92.2 .

[w] Small private enterprises not surveyed. B12.c refers to enterprises using the Internet for payment of delivered products. B12.d refers to enterprises using the Internet for lodging statistical forms and fiscal declarations.

[x] Data do not cover enterprises active in 'Electricity, gas and water supply' (NACE Rev.1. section E).

Annex table III.1. Exports of ICT goods, 1998, 2003 and 2007 (millions of dollars) [c]

Economy/Group	1998	2003	2007	Compound annual growth rate (CAGR) (%) 2003 - 2006/2007
World	813,289.6	1,130,721.0	1,730,482.8	
Developed economies	502,903.9	574,814.9	734,326.9	
America	149,680.6	148,647.4	183,087.7	
Canada	14,572.7	12,015.4	18,463.9	11.3
United States of America	135,107.6	136,630.6	164,622.9	4.8
Asia	98,672.8	111,765.8	115,454.3	
Israel	5,060.6	5,111.0	3,255.6	-10.7
Japan	93,612.2	106,654.9	112,198.7	1.3
Europe	252,378.4	312,088.6	432,762.1	
Andorra [a]	1.4	12.3	..	11.8
Austria	4,073.7	6,627.5	9,602.5	9.7
Belgium	9,562.9	12,487.6	12,814.8	0.6
Bulgaria	31.2	160.3	442.0	28.9
Cyprus	14.4	17.8	94.7	52.0
Czech Republic	1,513.0	5,922.4	17,945.7	31.9
Denmark	3,861.9	5,136.3	6,271.0	5.1
Estonia	461.6	881.3	826.6	-1.6
Finland	8,656.4	11,085.0	15,409.2	8.6
France	32,256.6	28,211.1	32,790.3	3.8
Germany	47,516.7	70,348.5	104,715.7	10.5
Greece	257.3	455.3	699.7	11.3
Hungary	4,760.6	11,966.5	23,194.0	18.0
Iceland	3.6	16.8	17.1	0.5
Ireland	18,637.3	22,565.0	23,531.7	1.1
Italy	11,890.0	12,547.0	15,767.6	5.9
Latvia	44.7	54.4	311.6	54.7
Lithuania	158.0	348.0	700.3	19.1
Luxembourg	..	1,102.8	1,143.1	0.9
Malta	1,004.0	1,286.7	1,491.6	3.8
Netherlands	31,583.7	45,504.9	70,620.8	11.6
Norway	1,513.1	1,471.4	2,687.9	16.3
Poland	1,295.1	2,651.8	8,587.4	34.1
Portugal	1,465.0	2,716.0	4,299.5	12.2
Romania	61.6	665.6	1,265.5	17.4
Slovakia	386.4	1,032.2	8,779.0	70.8
Slovenia	351.5	535.6	761.3	9.2
Spain	5,682.8	7,615.5	8,193.8	1.8
Sweden	13,224.5	11,374.4	16,044.0	9.0
Switzerland	4,090.1	4,236.6	6,194.1	10.0
United Kingdom	48,019.2	43,052.2	37,559.6	-3.4
Oceania	2,172.1	2,313.1	3,022.8	
Australia	1,873.2	1,948.2	2,453.7	5.9
New Zealand	298.9	364.9	569.1	11.8
Developing economies	309,269.2	553,764.3	992,587.2	
Africa	1,162.7	1,758.1	2,985.9	14.2
Algeria	1.8	2.1	2.8	7.3
Benin	0.2	0.1	..	..
Botswana	..	4.5	9.8	21.5
Burkina Faso	1.2	1.1	..	..
Burundi	0.0	0.5	0.8	11.0
Cameroon [a]	..	2.2	..	-24.0
Cape Verde	0.8	..	1.3	..
Central African Republic	0.2	0.0	..	..
Comoros [a]	0.0	0.0	..	-56.7
Côte d'Ivoire	7.3	18.6	34.5	16.6
Egypt	2.5	4.3	6.3	10.5
Eritrea	..	0.0	..	..
Ethiopia	..	0.0	3.3	238.9
Gabon [a]	6.5	3.6	..	2.5
Gambia	0.1	0.0	0.0	-9.9
Ghana	0.6	0.6	0.7	4.1
Guinea	0.1	..	..	..
Kenya	0.7	8.2	39.6	48.2
Lesotho	..	9.5	..	..

Economy/Group	1998	2003	2007	Compound annual growth rate (CAGR) (%) 2003 - 2006/2007
Madagascar	0.7	2.8	8.9	33.8
Malawi	0.3	0.0	3.1	193.9
Mali	0.3	1.2	2.4	19.5
Mauritius	13.4	52.3	96.6	16.6
Mayotte	..	0.1	0.9	66.4
Morocco	442.8	693.5	836.6	4.8
Mozambique	..	2.8	3.8	8.3
Namibia	..	30.0	22.9	-6.5
Niger	0.6	0.5	1.8	40.4
Nigeria[a]	0.1	0.4	..	52.7
Rwanda	0.0	1.3	1.5	5.3
Sao Tome and Principe	..	..	0.0	..
Senegal	2.6	3.1	8.2	27.7
Seychelles	0.6	0.4	0.2	-14.8
South Africa	466.6	615.0	1142.4	16.7
Sudan	3.9	..	..	..
Swaziland	..	6.8	0.0	-71.0
Togo	1.0	0.2	0.3	3.4
Tunisia	198.2	289.0	640.3	22.0
Uganda	0.5	2.7	92.4	140.9
United Republic of Tanzania	4.4	0.5	7.9	104.1
Zambia	4.5	0.2	5.2	136.9
Zimbabwe	..	..	11.2	..
Asia	280,821.7	511,839.1	929,866.5	
Bahrain	..	9.8	16.5	13.9
Bangladesh[a]	0.1	5.2	..	33.0
Bhutan	0.0	..	..	..
Brunei Darussalam[a]	22.2	15.6	..	-2.5
Cambodia	..	2.4	..	..
China	27,419.4	123,303.4	355,568.4	30.3
Hong Kong, China	39,837.5	78,056.5	148,083.9	17.4
India	317.4	1,261.9	1,876.8	10.4
Indonesia[b]	2,575.0	6,280.2	5,997.9	-1.1
Iran, Islamic Republic of[a]	1.7	25.6	..	36.8
Jordan	10.0	84.6	495.8	55.6
Kuwait	..	24.6	..	..
Lebanon	13.0	14.9	..	..
Macao, China[a]	49.6	69.8	..	17.1
Malaysia	37,459.7	53,134.0	73,187.1	8.3
Mongolia	1.0	0.2	1.2	65.0
Nepal	0.8	0.6	..	..
Occupied Palestinian territory	..	..	3.0	..
Oman	82.6	44.3	448.1	78.3
Pakistan	..	16.8	91.2	52.7
Philippines	19,404.4	24,157.9	14,673.5	-11.7
Qatar	..	15.2	25.2	13.5
Republic of Korea	33,905.7	66,545.3	97,370.6	10.0
Saudi Arabia	103.5	144.6	910.6	58.4
Singapore	60,587.0	77,930.2	108,324.7	8.6
Sri Lanka	..	110.0	..	..
Syrian Arab Republic	..	1.2	64.3	169.6
Taiwan Province of China	42,517.2	56,706.9	85,342.2	10.8
Thailand	15,471.4	20,845.1	34,150.5	13.1
Turkey	1,042.6	2,124.8	3,227.7	11.0
Viet Nam[a]	..	907.4	..	31.2
Yemen	..	..	7.4	..
Latin America and the Caribbean	27,264.0	40,156.7	59,724.7	
Anguilla	..	0.2	0.3	14.9
Antigua and Barbuda	..	..	9.5	..
Argentina	143.3	130.0	307.1	24.0
Bahamas	5.4	2.5	2.2	-3.5
Barbados	25.3	16.5	16.8	0.4
Belize	0.2	0.5	0.1	-28.7
Bolivia, Plurinational State of	12.3	11.7	0.2	-64.2
Brazil	1,189.8	2,331.9	3,171.8	8.0
Chile	22.7	36.9	94.1	26.4
Colombia	13.2	36.4	63.2	14.8
Costa Rica	1,114.9	1,540.7	2,531.1	13.2

Economy/Group	1998	2003	2007	Compound annual growth rate (CAGR) (%) 2003 - 2006/2007
Cuba[a]	..	34.8	..	17.6
Dominica	..	0.1	0.1	12.0
Ecuador	2.1	7.4	46.6	58.4
El Salvador	1.6	7.6	14.9	18.6
Grenada[a]	6.0	0.8	..	-7.9
Guatemala	2.1	13.2	28.9	21.6
Guyana	0.3	0.5	8.8	107.4
Honduras	11.9	0.9	5.5	59.0
Jamaica	2.8	3.9	5.1	6.6
Mexico	24,678.2	35,905.8	53,342.6	10.4
Montserrat	..	0.2	0.1	-18.0
Nicaragua	0.7	1.2	2.3	17.2
Panama	0.0	0.8	0.0	-81.2
Paraguay	2.4	1.9	5.0	26.6
Peru	7.2	12.6	14.3	3.2
Saint Kitts and Nevis	..	0.2	13.2	189.2
Saint Lucia[a]	2.9	8.1	..	1.2
Saint Vincent and the Grenadines	0.3	0.8	6.9	71.9
Trinidad and Tobago	6.7	10.9	26.0	24.1
Turks and Caicos Islands	..	0.1	..	..
Uruguay	3.4	3.0	8.0	27.5
Venezuela, Bolivarian Republic of[a]	8.3	34.7	..	-8.5
Oceania	20.8	10.3	10.1	
Fiji	..	0.4	5.6	88.3
French Polynesia	8.5	1.7	1.1	-9.0
New Caledonia	..	1.6	2.8	13.8
Papua New Guinea	12.3	6.5	..	..
Samoa	..	0.1	0.5	59.5
Tuvalu	..	0.0	..	..
Vanuatu	..	..	0.1	..
Transition economies	1,116.5	2,141.9	3,568.6	
Albania	3.0	4.1	11.0	27.7
Armenia		5.0	19.0	39.6
Azerbaijan	11.2	1.9	11.3	55.4
Belarus	158.2	162.9	182.2	2.8
Bosnia and Herzegovina	..	5.0	20.0	41.4
Croatia	161.7	412.2	675.9	13.2
Georgia	1.4	2.1	4.4	20.7
Kazakhstan	13.6	34.8	31.0	-2.8
Kyrgyzstan	..	1.1	8.9	69.8
Republic of Moldova	7.5	7.6	34.3	45.7
Russian Federation	609.0	896.1	1,679.8	17.0
Serbia	..	..	131.7	..
The former Yugoslav Republic of Macedonia	2.2	8.1	13.8	14.3
Ukraine	148.9	601.0	745.3	5.5
Least developed countries (LDCs)	21.6	34.9	147.7	

Source: UNCTAD on the basis of United Nations Comtrade data.

[a] CAGR 2003-2006.

[b] Data for 1998 include East Timor.

[c] Information used in this report on trade in ICT goods is based on COMTRADE data extracted in April–May 2009. The data are based on the Harmonized System (HS) classification. ICT goods are defined here following the OECD HS-96 definition (2003). Depending on economies and years, trade flows have been reported to COMTRADE either under the HS-96, HS-02 or HS-07 definition. However, in the cases listed below, data were available only in HS-92. UNCTAD has devised a mechanism to allow for an approximate conversion of the trade data on ICT goods from the HS-92 to the HS-96 nomenclature. This enables more complete geographical and time coverage. For data reported under HS-02 and HS-07, COMTRADE proposes an automatic conversion to HS-96.

In the following cases, HS-92 was the basis for the data: Anguilla (2000–2007); Azerbaijan (1998); Bahrain (2000–2001); Bangladesh (1998, 2000–2001); Barbados (1998–1999); Bhutan (1998); Brunei Darussalam (1998, 2001); Burkina Faso (1998–2000); Burundi (1998–2002); Cameroon (1998, 1999 only for imports); Central African Republic (2004–2005); Comoros (1998–2007); Côte d'Ivoire (1998–2000, 2002–2003); Egypt (1998–2007); Ethiopia (1998–2000); Ghana (1998–2002); Grenada (1998–1999); Kazakhstan (1999); Kiribati (1998–1999); Kuwait (2000–2004); Lesotho (2000–2004); Malawi (1998, exports only); Montserrat (2000); Morocco (1998–2000); Nigeria (1998); Oman (1998–1999); Papua New Guinea (1998, 2000); Philippines (1998–1999); Republic of Moldova (1998–1999); Rwanda (1998–1999); Saint Lucia (1998–1999); Saudi Arabia (1998); Seychelles (2003–2004, 2007); Sierra Leone (2002); Sudan (1998); Suriname (1999–2001); Taiwan, Province of China (1998–1999); Thailand (1998); Tonga (2000–2007); Trinidad and Tobago (1998); Tunisia (1998–1999); Tuvalu (2001–2006); Ukraine (1998–2000); Vanuatu (2000).

Annex table III.2. Economies with the largest increases and declines in their market share of ICT goods exports, 1998-2007 [a]

Economy	Share of the world market of ICT goods exports (per cent)		Change in market share
	1998	2007	1998-2007
Largest increases in market share			
China	3.37	20.55	17.18
Hong Kong, China	4.90	8.56	3.66
Republic of Korea	4.17	5.63	1.46
Czech Republic	0.19	1.04	0.85
Hungary	0.59	1.34	0.75
Slovakia	0.05	0.51	0.46
Poland	0.16	0.50	0.34
Germany	5.84	6.05	0.21
Netherlands	3.88	4.08	0.20
Thailand	1.90	1.97	0.07
India	0.04	0.11	0.07
Portugal	0.18	0.25	0.07
Romania	0.01	0.07	0.07
Turkey	0.13	0.19	0.06
Austria	0.50	0.55	0.05
Largest declines in market share			
United States of America	16.61	9.51	-7.10
Japan	11.51	6.48	-5.03
United Kingdom	5.90	2.17	-3.73
France	3.97	1.89	-2.07
Philippines	2.39	0.85	-1.54
Singapore	7.45	6.26	-1.19
Ireland	2.29	1.36	-0.93
Canada	1.79	1.07	-0.72
Sweden	1.63	0.93	-0.70
Italy	1.46	0.91	-0.55
Belgium	1.18	0.74	-0.44
Israel	0.62	0.19	-0.43
Malaysia	4.61	4.23	-0.38
Taiwan Province of China	5.23	4.93	-0.30
Spain	0.70	0.47	-0.23

Source: UNCTAD on the basis of United Nations Comtrade data.
[a] See notes to annex table III.1.

Annex table III.3. Imports of ICT goods, 1998, 2003 and 2007 (millions of dollars) [c]

Economy/Group	1998	2003	2007	CAGR (%) 2003-2006/2007
World	818,888.5	1,156,810.3	1,811,599.9	
Developed economies	544,297.1	665,630.8	952,421.7	
America	195,491.6	225,381.9	309,300.2	
Canada	26,566.8	25,503.4	35,907.3	8.9
United States of America	168,899.2	199,853.6	273,360.3	8.1
Asia	44,481.3	64,917.5	81,421.8	
Israel	3,566.2	3,697.2	5,625.1	11.1
Japan	40,915.1	61,220.3	75,796.7	5.5
Europe	294,267.8	362,180.1	540,526.6	
Andorra	87.4	187.4	..	..
Austria	6,797.9	8,590.3	11,721.0	8.1
Belgium	11,104.8	14,326.4	17,682.6	5.4
Bulgaria	248.4	738.7	1,795.8	24.9
Cyprus	227.1	307.0	480.2	11.8
Czech Republic	2,966.1	7,120.6	18,473.4	26.9
Denmark	5,080.5	6,873.4	9,422.7	8.2
Estonia	650.1	1,070.0	1,193.0	2.8
Faroe Islands [a]	26.0	33.2	..	15.5
Finland	5,106.6	5,867.2	10,950.5	16.9
France	34,561.5	35,836.7	48,828.9	8.0
Germany	55,646.8	73,803.8	105,501.9	9.3
Greece	2,245.2	2,833.0	4,786.7	14.0
Hungary	4,722.5	10,424.6	19,541.0	17.0
Iceland	217.3	228.8	432.8	17.3
Ireland	13,559.2	14,049.7	17,610.1	5.8
Italy	20,171.3	24,015.5	31,448.8	7.0
Latvia	252.7	365.2	985.6	28.2
Lithuania	359.7	592.4	1,517.1	26.5
Luxemburg	..	1,241.0	1,496.5	4.8
Malta	922.6	1,129.3	1,223.1	2.0
Netherlands	32,910.6	44,028.6	65,822.5	10.6
Norway	3,633.1	3,939.6	7,017.7	15.5
Poland	4,382.1	5,930.5	14,000.6	24.0
Portugal	3,238.1	4,452.1	6,778.1	11.1
Romania	1,054.1	2,087.6	5,125.9	25.2
Slovakia	1,138.4	1,932.0	8,133.7	43.2
Slovenia	608.9	830.5	1,424.5	14.4
Spain	11,678.7	16,345.4	30,850.4	17.2
Sweden	10,812.6	10,223.7	16,651.0	13.0
Switzerland	7,796.0	8,307.2	10,907.4	7.0
United Kingdom	52,061.6	54,468.6	68,722.8	6.0
Oceania	10,056.4	13,151.2	21,173.1	
Australia	8,666.9	11,263.3	18,357.8	13.0
New Zealand	1,389.4	1,887.9	2,815.3	10.5
Developing economies	270,179.0	483,490.5	830,296.8	
Africa	8,390.4	10,358.5	19,850.1	
Algeria	559.7	1,104.4	1,598.8	9.7
Benin	27.7	32.7	..	..
Botswana	..	283.1	220.6	-6.0
Burkina Faso	27.7	33.6	..	..
Burundi	7.2	6.8	10.8	12.2
Cameroon	30.9	78.5	..	..
Cape Verde	15.6	13.0	27.6	20.7
Central African Republic	2.2	2.7	..	..
Comoros	2.1	3.2	5.6	14.8
Côte d'Ivoire	104.9	114.1	283.0	25.5
Egypt	830.6	475.8	1,299.5	28.6
Eritrea	..	22.5	..	..
Ethiopia	81.4	182.3	411.6	22.6
Gabon [a]	58.1	60.1	..	24.0
Gambia	11.9	7.3	14.9	19.5
Ghana	87.2	148.8	450.9	31.9
Guinea	25.3	..	..	..
Kenya	158.9	164.0	502.8	32.3

Economy/Group	1998	2003	2007	CAGR (%) 2003-2006/2007
Lesotho	..	22.4	..	..
Madagascar	30.5	56.1	131.0	23.6
Malawi	..	32.3	51.7	12.5
Mali	19.3	51.9	91.7	15.3
Mauritania[a]	..	8.9	..	35.6
Mauritius	85.6	153.6	238.3	11.6
Mayotte		13.6	29.0	20.9
Morocco	826.5	944.4	2,130.2	22.5
Mozambique	..	89.3	118.7	7.4
Namibia	..	92.8	232.2	25.8
Niger	8.8	33.0	42.3	6.5
Nigeria[a]	228.1	768.0	..	27.2
Rwanda	8.3	21.4	55.8	27.1
Sao Tome and Principe	..	1.9	2.9	10.4
Senegal	70.9	77.2	194.3	26.0
Seychelles	19.2	12.6	28.5	22.6
South Africa	4,237.2	3,938.8	7,707.1	18.3
Sudan	70.3	211.3	1,821.9	71.4
Swaziland	..	37.4	43.7	4.0
Togo	27.8	11.3	33.1	30.8
Tunisia	471.1	743.3	1,124.8	10.9
Uganda	59.9	92.8	350.5	39.4
United Republic of Tanzania	111.8	130.8	369.1	29.6
Zambia	83.6	80.6	155.5	17.9
Zimbabwe	..	..	71.7	..
Asia	219,183.3	421,586.5	732,015.4	
Bahrain	..	229.7	264.3	3.6
Bangladesh[a]	189.4	318.1	..	52.6
Bhutan	6.4	..	..	..
Brunei Darussalam[a]	123.4	110.4	..	0.2
Cambodia	..	33.1	..	..
China	25,513.6	110,530.2	255,195.1	23.3
Hong Kong, China	46,383.7	82,686.4	154,416.2	16.9
India	2,122.1	6,867.9	18,091.2	27.4
Indonesia[b]	1,041.4	1,332.0	3,993.3	31.6
Iran, Islamic Republic of[a]	1,119.5	1,676.3	..	-22.6
Jordan	160.9	346.6	1,140.8	34.7
Kuwait	..	559.5	..	..
Lebanon	360.0	299.0	..	..
Macao, China[a]	94.7	308.9	..	17.4
Malaysia	24,646.4	37,662.9	52,899.8	8.9
Maldives	22.7	33.2	74.5	22.4
Mongolia	30.8	43.6	107.4	25.2
Nepal	50.2	97.6	..	..
Occupied Palestinian territory	..	..	86.8	..
Oman	254.1	143.5	650.9	45.9
Pakistan	..	651.2	2,357.4	37.9
Philippines	13,150.8	21,277.3	11,931.7	-13.5
Qatar	..	292.2	1,554.4	51.9
Republic of Korea	19,313.1	37,543.5	54,089.9	9.6
Saudi Arabia	1,495.4	2,313.4	7,186.3	32.8
Singapore	42,028.3	56,243.9	80,070.0	9.4
Sri Lanka	..	311.4	..	..
Syrian Arab Republic	..	131.2	296.1	22.6
Taiwan Province of China	27,585.0	36,402.4	49,824.0	8.2
Thailand	9,627.1	16,707.1	27,043.9	12.8
Turkey	3,864.3	4,883.5	9,830.5	19.1
Viet Nam[a]	..	1,550.6	..	30.0
Yemen	..	..	307.1	..
Latin America and the Caribbean	42,481.9	51,239.8	78,151.6	
Anguilla	..	3.8	6.9	15.7
Antigua and Barbuda	..	..	47.1	..
Argentina	3,638.6	1,146.8	4,981.3	44.4
Bahamas	83.0	72.5	99.7	8.3
Barbados	86.8	116.4	142.3	5.2
Belize	16.4	19.6	18.7	-1.2

Economy/Group	1998	2003	2007	CAGR (%) 2003-2006/2007
Bolivia	159.5	70.3	169.4	24.6
Brazil	7,676.0	6,173.2	8,389.6	8.0
Chile	1,823.2	1,454.3	3,341.1	23.1
Colombia	2,009.8	1,660.8	3,961.7	24.3
Costa Rica	1,085.5	1,821.9	2,442.0	7.6
Cuba [a]	..	284.3	..	1.5
Dominica		11.2	13.2	4.2
Ecuador	369.5	743.3	1,038.6	8.7
El Salvador	159.8	283.5	636.6	22.4
Grenada [a]	10.6	25.2	..	-9.8
Guatemala	296.6	478.0	903.8	17.3
Guyana	20.3	15.7	67.9	44.3
Honduras	112.5	179.7	416.2	23.4
Jamaica	152.7	301.5	241.3	-5.4
Mexico	21,552.2	33,986.5	41,928.0	5.4
Montserrat	..	1.4	1.5	2.3
Nicaragua	55.1	139.6	220.6	12.1
Panama	337.8	270.1	461.2	14.3
Paraguay	275.9	175.3	1,531.8	71.9
Peru	796.0	809.4	1,629.8	19.1
Saint Kitts and Nevis	..	16.2	22.4	8.5
Saint Lucia	18.1	50.8	29.2	-13.0
Saint Vincent and the Grenadines	9.5	21.8	20.9	-1.0
Suriname	..	28.9	57.9	19.0
Trinidad and Tobago	151.6	164.8	264.6	12.6
Turks and Caicos Islands	..	7.6	..	..
Uruguay	285.6	100.5	363.7	37.9
Venezuela, Bolivarian Republic of	1,299.3	605.1	4,702.8	67.0
Oceania	123.4	305.7	279.7	
Cook Islands	..	4.1	..	..
Fiji	..	55.6	63.0	3.2
French Polynesia	56.8	87.1	97.2	2.8
Kiribati	1.1	..	..	..
New Caledonia	..	80.3	96.8	4.8
Papua New Guinea	65.0	67.7	..	..
Samoa	..	7.8	10.7	8.3
Tonga	..	3.2	5.5	15.1
Tuvalu	0.5	..	..	..
Vanuatu	..	..	6.4	..
Transition economies	4,412.5	7,689.1	28,881.4	
Albania	17.0	74.5	146.1	18.3
Armenia	..	62.1	196.0	33.3
Azerbaijan	112.3	115.5	300.3	34.7
Belarus	288.0	410.4	860.0	20.3
Bosnia and Herzegovina	..	151.8	365.3	24.5
Croatia	457.4	1,207.6	1,781.3	10.2
Georgia	65.1	54.6	369.4	61.3
Kazakhstan	292.9	555.8	1,699.1	32.2
Kyrgyzstan	..	27.7	124.1	45.5
Republic of Moldova	72.1	53.5	158.8	31.3
Russian Federation	2,589.9	1,022.6	19,303.1	48.0
Serbia	..	..	1,255.5	..
The former Yugoslav Republic of Macedonia	64.4	143.5	272.6	17.4
Ukraine	457.7	808.3	1,969.8	24.9
Least developed countries (LDCs)	947.0	1,701.9	4,260.1	

Source: UNCTAD on the basis of UN Comtrade data.
[a] *CAGR 2003-2006.*
[b] *Data for 1998 include East Timor.*
[c] *See notes to annex table III.1.*

Annex table III.4. Exports of IT and ICT-enabled services, 2000, 2006 and 2007 (millions of dollars)

Economy/Group	2000	2006	2007	CAGR (%) 2003-2006/2007
World	648,762.0	1,354,319.9	1,635,063.0	
Developed economies	521,955.7	1,062,065.7	1,280,068.9	
America	147,970.1	260,481.5	304,053.6	
Canada	20,736.0	32,382.2	34,238.1	7.4
United States of America [a]	127,234.1	228,099.3	269,815.6	11.3
Asia	42,027.0	72,264.4	78,250.4	
Israel	8,544.4	12,223.6	12,878.1	6.0
Japan	33,482.6	60,040.8	65,372.3	10.0
Europe	325,320.9	719,804.9	886,506.6	
Austria	8,172.0	17,905.2	23,090.7	16.0
Belgium/Luxembourg	29,520.5			
Belgium	..	29,006.0	40,045.6	..
Bulgaria	372.5	916.8	1,170.1	17.8
Cyprus	1,090.0	2,534.4	3,295.1	17.1
Czech Republic	2,221.3	4,351.1	5,154.8	12.8
Denmark	9,260.5	12,145.4	14,260.1	6.4
Estonia	201.2	922.8	1,306.7	30.6
Faroe Islands	10.2	..	..	..
Finland	4,147.4	11,925.9	14,286.5	19.3
France [b]	27,927.3	45,388.7	51,768.5	9.2
Germany	35,936.1	94,736.6	110,883.0	17.5
Greece	1,805.4	2,976.5	3,774.4	11.1
Hungary	1,485.9	6,291.2	8,289.3	27.8
Iceland	189.6	503.9	668.7	19.7
Ireland	14330.8	60,161.7	74,868.5	26.6
Italy	17,867.5	40,664.4	46,799.4	14.7
Latvia	215.7	694.6	1,067.6	25.7
Lithuania	155.2	568.2	412.1	15.0
Luxembourg	..	43,728.1	56,217.9	..
Malta	187.2	1,470.5	2,024.3	40.5
Netherlands	21,796.0	44,153.2	50,829.6	12.9
Norway [c]	5,804.6	13,098.6	16,713.9	16.3
Poland	1,977.0	5,066.0	7,231.0	20.4
Portugal	2,045.1	4,704.4	6,039.0	16.7
Romania	699.0	3,549.9	6,112.0	36.3
Slovakia	722.6	1,882.3	2,619.6	20.2
Slovenia	363.2	1,080.9	1,486.7	22.3
Spain	13,291.3	34,229.1	44,664.8	18.9
Sweden	10,913.0	30,304.4	38,896.3	19.9
Switzerland [d]	18,256.4	38,576.7	47,298.5	14.6
United Kingdom [e]	77,317.0	166,267.8	205,232.1	15.0
Oceania	6,637.7	9,514.9	11,258.4	
Australia	5,781.3	8,128.2	9,973.1	8.1
New Zealand	856.4	1,386.6	1,285.2	6.0
Developing economies	122,656.5	276,810.8	333,676.4	
Africa	8,378.2	13,218.7	15,059.7	
Angola	251.2	49.6	69.0	-16.9
Benin	31.3	50.9	..	8.5
Botswana	30.8	144.5	280.3	37.1
Burkina Faso	5.1	..	..	..
Burundi	0.4	3.5	3.8	37.7
Cameroon	373.7	214.9	112.6	-15.7
Cape Verde	14.7	29.0	42.1	16.2
Congo	84.2	193.3	236.2	15.9
Côte d'Ivoire	270.6	389.2	457.4	7.8
Djibouti	8.3	13.5	..	8.4
Egypt	2,604.0	2,323.7	2,423.2	-1.0
Eritrea	9.5	..	..	..
Ethiopia	104.4	132.8	256.4	13.7
Gabon	55.5	..	..	..
Gambia	..	9.8	11.3	..
Ghana	56.8	191.7	392.9	31.8
Guinea	5.1	..	24.2	24.9
Kenya	33.1	301.8	142.4	23.2
Lesotho	11.2	23.0	24.4	11.7

Economy/Group	2000	2006	2007	CAGR (%) 2003-2006/2007
Liberia	..	3.8	4.3	..
Libyan Arab Jamahiriya	28.0	67.0	..	15.7
Madagascar	120.9	..	..	..
Mali	17.3	73.9	..	27.4
Mauritius	291.7	277.7	452.0	6.5
Morocco	329.5	1,796.4	2,491.1	33.5
Mozambique	153.5	85.0	93.9	-6.8
Namibia	12.8	22.6	25.5	10.3
Niger	4.3	38.1	..	44.0
Nigeria	1,511.6	..	..	..
Rwanda	3.4	12.8	24.7	32.7
Sao Tome and Principe	2.8	1.3	0.6	-19.1
Senegal	133.5	302.3	..	14.6
Seychelles	10.3	20.4	21.6	11.2
Sierra Leone	10.7	5.9	4.8	-10.9
South Africa	1,028.9	2,308.5	2,943.3	16.2
Sudan	3.2	33.6	65.8	54.0
Swaziland	231.4	186.7	406.2	8.4
Togo	27.1	81.5	..	20.2
Tunisia	352.4	500.1	572.4	7.2
Uganda	8.1	117.1	112.6	45.6
United Republic of Tanzania	141.9	173.1	305.5	11.6
Zambia	5.2	39.8	44.6	36.1
Asia	97,510.0	238,586.3	287,347.1	
Bahrain	79.2	1,537.2	1,670.0	54.6
Bangladesh	141.2	411.2	499.2	19.8
Brunei Darussalam	..	139.5	..	..
Cambodia	47.3	111.1	162.6	19.3
China	9,641.7	33,703.6	47,720.1	25.7
Hong Kong, China [f]	21,346.4	38,346.6	45,785.8	11.5
India [f,g]	10,089.5	58,091.3	69,000.8	31.6
Indonesia	..	4,084.7	4,053.3	..
Iran, Islamic Republic of	185.0	..	..	..
Jordan	579.4	262.2	349.9	-7.0
Kuwait	90.0	4,112.3	5,424.8	79.6
Lebanon	..	6,106.9	6,943.1	..
Macao, China	..	252.1	326.6	..
Malaysia	5,684.2	6,026.1	6,863.7	2.7
Maldives	4.5	10.6	7.3	7.2
Mongolia	7.9	43.0	..	32.6
Myanmar	220.7	79.9	..	-15.6
Nepal	190.8	88.7	102.6	-8.5
Occupied Palestinian territory	76.0	..	..	..
Oman	35.7	75.4	132.6	20.6
Pakistan	363.0	847.0	808.0	12.1
Philippines	660.0	1,723.0	2,087.0	17.9
Republic of Korea	9,195.5	16,653.4	21,837.0	13.2
Saudi Arabia	4,778.9	7,297.1	7,901.3	7.4
Singapore	11,129.1	32,145.4	37,059.9	18.8
Sri Lanka	267.6	413.5	433.6	7.1
Syrian Arab Republic	153.0	407.0	..	17.7
Taiwan Province of China	11,912.0	17,313.0	18,773.0	6.7
Thailand	3,922.2	5,529.7	6,569.9	12.8
Turkey	7,643.0	2,514.0	2,729.0	10.7
Yemen	80.2	255.8	106.1	4.1
Latin America and the Caribbean	16,385.6	24,597.8	30,910.0	
Anguilla	5.3	12.5	14.7	15.6
Antigua and Barbuda	49.4	58.6	65.4	4.1
Argentina	719.4	3,111.9	4,147.1	28.4
Aruba	96.7	174.3	163.8	7.8
Bahamas	153.4	289.4	321.7	11.2
Barbados	304.9	..	..	..
Belize	13.4	46.8	50.4	20.8
Bolivia, Plurinational State of	88.7	105.8	133.2	6.0
Brazil	5,514.2	10,168.5	13,526.2	13.7
Chile	987.5	1,823.0	2,126.3	11.6

Economy/Group	2000	2006	2007	CAGR (%) 2003-2006/2007
Colombia	365.9	848.6	785.9	11.5
Costa Rica	351.0	918.1	1,227.3	19.6
Dominica	32.1	23.2	24.1	-4.0
Dominican Republic	211.0	282.0	306.5	5.5
Ecuador	101.3	116.7	116.2	2.0
El Salvador	193.6	197.0	217.7	1.7
Grenada	48.0	23.6	24.3	-9.3
Guatemala	137.1	319.3	356.7	14.6
Guyana	87.0	113.1	113.7	3.9
Haiti	30.0	13.6	12.5	-11.7
Honduras	170.4	142.8	134.2	-3.4
Jamaica	326.9	284.5	312.4	-0.6
Mexico	3,903.0	2,282.9	2,816.7	-4.6
Montserrat	5.9	5.2	5.4	-1.3
Netherlands Antilles	636.7	749.2	754.5	2.5
Nicaragua	28.3	32.9	34.6	2.9
Panama	351.0	717.8	1,060.8	17.1
Paraguay	430.8	547.8	544.1	3.4
Peru	365.2	418.1	638.4	8.3
Saint Kitts and Nevis	24.5	27.7	29.1	2.5
Saint Lucia	28.8	26.1	27.5	-0.7
Saint Vincent and the Grenadines	47.6	44.0	46.8	-0.3
Suriname	32.3	91.2	123.1	21.0
Trinidad and Tobago	122.8	..	..	..
Uruguay	161.4	289.8	318.1	10.2
Venezuela, Bolivarian Republic of	260.0	292.0	331.0	3.5
Oceania	382.6	408.1	359.7	
Fiji	86.6	57.7	..	-6.6
French Polynesia	..	172.9	205.1	..
New Caledonia	..	79.1	96.6	..
Papua New Guinea	223.6	..	..	..
Samoa	..	35.3	23.8	..
Solomon Islands	39.7	34.5	..	-2.3
Tonga	..	4.6	7.7	..
Vanuatu	32.7	24.0	26.4	-3.0
Transition economies	4,149.9	15,443.4	21,317.6	
Albania	22.2	303.4	276.5	43.4
Armenia	28.6	92.1	121.8	23.0
Azerbaijan	47.0	271.1	343.7	32.9
Belarus	269.9	337.7	484.8	8.7
Bosnia and Herzegovina	115.8	218.5	244.0	11.2
Croatia	542.6	1,465.1	1,668.1	17.4
Georgia	7.2	77.6	78.2	40.6
Kazakhstan	87.5	284.6	487.6	27.8
Kyrgyzstan	23.5	108.1	151.9	30.6
Republic of Moldova	31.5	124.6	159.9	26.1
Russian Federation	2,409.9	10,106.1	14,233.0	28.9
Tajikistan	..	39.9	47.9	..
The former Yugoslav Republic of Macedonia	116.2	217.6	225.3	9.9
Ukraine	448.0	1,797.0	2,795.0	29.9
Least developed countries (LDCs)	1,845.1	2,310.0	1,986.6	

Source: UNCTAD on the basis of IMF balance-of-payments data.
a   *Including Puerto Rico and United States Virgin Islands.*
b   *Including French Guiana, Guadeloupe, Martinique, Monaco and Réunion.*
c   *Including Svalbard and Jan Mayen Islands, excluding Bouvet Island.*
d   *Including Liechtenstein.*
e   *Including Channel Islands and Isle of Man.*
f   *Export value for 2007 was estimated based on the growth rate for "other services" between 2006 and 2007.*
g   *Including Sikkim.*

Annex table III.5. Economies with the largest increases and declines in their market share of IT and ICT-enabled services exports, 2000-2007

Economy	Share of the world market of IT and ICT-enabled services export (per cent)		Change in market share
	2000	2007	2000-2007
Largest increases in market share			
India [f, g]	1.56	4.22	2.66
Ireland	2.21	4.58	2.37
China	1.49	2.92	1.43
Germany	5.54	6.78	1.24
Sweden	1.68	2.38	0.70
Spain	2.05	2.73	0.68
Unitod Kingdom [e]	11.92	12.55	0.63
Singapore	1.72	2.27	0.55
Russian Federation	0.37	0.87	0.50
Kuwait	0.01	0.33	0.32
Hungary	0.46	0.51	0.28
Romania	0.26	0.37	0.27
Finland	0.88	0.87	0.23
Austria	1.32	1.41	0.15
Argentina	0.23	0.25	0.14
Largest declines in market share			
United States of America [a]	19.61	16.50	-3.11
Japan	5.16	4.00	-1.16
France [b]	4.30	3.17	-1.14
Canada	3.20	2.09	-1.10
Turkey	1.18	0.17	-1.01
Taiwan Province of China	1.84	1.15	-0.69
Denmark	1.43	0.87	-0.56
Israel	1.32	0.79	0.53
Hong Kong, China [f]	3.29	2.80	-0.49
Malaysia	0.88	0.42	-0.46
Mexico	0.17	0.17	-0.43
Australia	0.60	0.61	-0.28
Saudi Arabia	0.54	0.48	-0.25
Egypt	0.17	0.15	-0.25
Netherlands	3.26	3.11	-0.25

Source: UNCTAD on the basis of IMF balance-of-payments data.
Notes: see notes to annex table III.4.

Annex table III.6. Imports of IT and ICT-enabled services, 2000, 2006 and 2007 (millions of dollars)

Economy/Group	2000	2006	2007	CAGR (%) 2000-2006/2007
World	589,561.4	1,128,592.2	1,337,690.0	
Developed economies	438,881.0	822,377.2	973,631.0	
America	96,341.7	177,143.2	199,202.2	
Canada	21,706.1	34,160.2	36,008.4	7.5
United States of America[a]	74,635.6	142,983.0	163,193.8	11.8
Asia	49,386.2	64,854.3	73,710.7	
Israel	4,681.6	6,867.8	8,512.2	8.9
Japan	44,704.6	57,986.5	65,198.5	5.5
Europe	285,728.6	569,285.8	686,652.0	
Austria	6,091.2	12,806.4	15,177.7	13.9
Belgium	..	22,833.4	33,906.5	..
Belgium/Luxembourg	22,267.1	..		
Bulgaria	367.7	1,246.2	1,335.7	20.2
Cyprus	268.8	784.6	918.7	19.2
Czech Republic	3,226.4	6,113.6	6,853.4	11.4
Denmark	7,048.9	12,676.9	14,670.9	11.0
Estonia	229.2	626.9	988.6	23.2
Faroe Islands	22.7	..		
Finland	3,853.6	10,043.8	12,184.7	17.9
France[b]	22,480.7	45,304.6	52,933.7	13.0
Germany	49,103.3	89,825.3	104,077.1	11.3
Greece	1,855.9	3,977.9	5,540.6	16.9
Hungary	2,289.2	6,805.8	8,784.7	21.2
Iceland	246.4	673.4	700.1	16.1
Ireland	26,042.3	68,975.9	76,496.4	16.6
Italy	24,663.9	49,692.8	59,984.1	13.5
Latvia	190.3	577.3	808.9	23.0
Lithuania	171.8	422.2	485.4	16.0
Luxembourg	11,287.9	25,212.5	31,491.0	15.8
Malta	215.8	1,077.2	1,482.0	31.7
Netherlands	23,886.6	37,612.3	42,470.5	8.6
Norway[c]	5,062.4	9,697.2	11,683.7	12.7
Poland	3,699.0	7,229.0	9,372.0	14.2
Portugal	2,568.1	4,411.9	5,183.9	10.6
Romania	868.0	2,955.0	4,729.0	27.4
Slovakia	973.0	2,127.0	2,769.4	16.1
Slovenia	506.5	1,404.6	1,854.4	20.4
Spain	16,580.1	39,422.9	52,111.9	17.8
Sweden	11,357.6	20,769.5	25,391.0	12.2
Switzerland[d]	3,888.0	12,806.8	15,876.4	22.3
United Kingdom[e]	34,416.6	71,172.9	86,389.7	14.1
Oceania	7,424.5	11,093.9	14,066.1	
Australia	5,875.5	8,575.7	11,223.3	9.7
New Zealand	1,548.9	2,518.2	2,842.9	9.1
Developing economies	142,501.8	282,122.4	332,115.0	
Africa	13,812.5	24,144.0	31,030.1	
Angola	1,823.0	3,609.8	6,259.7	19.3
Benin	35.4	80.7	..	14.7
Botswana	112.7	218.3	283.0	14.1
Burkina Faso	26.8	..		..
Burundi	3.1	14.2	10.4	19.2
Cameroon	501.4	540.2	381.5	-3.8
Cape Verde	16.0	29.2	39.2	13.6
Congo	596.1	1,928.5	2,826.0	24.9
Côte d'Ivoire	432.7	568.5	552.9	3.6
Djibouti	18.6	20.4	..	1.5
Egypt	3,877.0	3,813.2	4,367.9	1.7
Eritrea	5.4	..	..	..
Ethiopia	108.8	244.7	245.6	12.3
Gabon	494.2	..	..	..
Gambia	..	53.6	32.7	..
Ghana	142.1	357.7	394.5	15.7
Guinea	57.3		76.4	4.2
Kenya	192.3	386.5	196.2	0.3
Lesotho	0.0	1.5	2.7	122.9

Economy/Group	2000	2006	2007	CAGR (%) 2000-2006/2007
Libyan Arab Jamahiriya	18.0	314.0	199.2	41.0
Madagascar	52.3	..	..	..
Malawi	29.1	..	..	..
Mali	43.9	129.8	..	19.8
Mauritius	305.3	446.9	590.8	9.9
Morocco	475.2	1,115.4	1,435.6	17.1
Mozambique	137.5	182.2	283.3	10.9
Namibia	116.5	128.2	122.9	0.8
Niger	14.3	71.5	..	30.8
Nigeria	1,929.3	..	6,019.8	17.7
Rwanda	8.7	68.0	101.1	41.9
Sao Tome and Principe	2.8	1.9	1.5	-8.3
Senegal	109.3	248.4	..	14.7
Seychelles	55.9	78.3	70.8	3.4
Sierra Leone	32.3	21.1	23.5	-4.4
South Africa	1,130.8	3,930.8	4,706.6	22.6
Sudan	21.3	69.9	82.5	21.3
Swaziland	234.1	266.7	367.7	6.7
Togo	29.8	57.6	..	11.6
Tunisia	197.0	466.4	496.8	14.1
Uganda	309.6	372.1	423.1	4.6
United Republic of Tanzania	75.2	127.6	229.6	17.3
Zambia	41.7	95.0	136.0	18.4
Asia	99,743.0	214,708.1	252,496.8	
Bahrain	99.5	460.7	523.8	26.8
Bangladesh	218.5	362.8	415.1	9.6
Brunei Darussalam	..	257.3	..	..
Cambodia	80.0	139.7	173.5	11.7
China	11,353.6	39,586.3	53,288.0	24.7
Hong Kong, China	5,430.3	11,005.9	..	12.5
India [1]	7,375.1	29,597.8	..	26.1
Indonesia	..	7,993.0	8,896.0	..
Iran	230.0	..	..	..
Iraq	..	1,723.9	..	..
Jordan	419.5	481.1	639.6	6.2
Kuwait	57.7	223.7	283.6	25.5
Lebanon	..	4,213.2	5,137.2	..
Macao, China	..	1,190.0	1,912.1	..
Malaysia	7,547.1	8,581.9	9,858.5	3.9
Maldives	8.2	32.6	35.5	23.4
Mongolia	21.1	70.3	..	22.2
Myanmar	31.0	255.9	..	42.2
Nepal	55.2	116.7	155.2	15.9
Occupied Palestinian territory	107.7	..	..	..
Oman	640.5	1,875.8	2,528.9	21.7
Pakistan	342.0	3,464.5	3,520.0	39.5
Philippines	1,357.0	1,512.0	1,796.0	4.1
Republic of Korea	14,760.7	26,036.4	31,742.0	11.6
Saudi Arabia	8,683.5	14,092.7	21,883.6	14.1
Singapore	12,199.1	30,261.8	35,208.0	16.3
Sri Lanka	371.3	517.4	556.2	5.9
Syrian Arab Republic	101.0	612.9	..	36.1
Taiwan Province of China	10,714.0	14,527.0	14,561.0	4.5
Thailand	5,691.9	11,352.5	14,213.1	14.0
Turkey	3,383.0	3,338.0	4,283.0	3.4
Yemen	296.5	795.5	887.0	16.9
Latin America and the Caribbean	28,249.4	42,275.7	47,919.1	
Anguilla	16.5	29.8	35.3	11.5
Antigua and Barbuda	57.0	91.0	102.2	8.7
Argentina	2,122.2	2,873.7	3,572.1	7.7
Aruba	172.8	285.0	278.6	7.1
Bahamas	357.4	551.4	575.0	7.0
Barbados	200.4	..	..	..
Belize	38.3	45.7	59.4	6.5
Bolivia, Plurinational State of	103.6	251.8	257.0	13.9
Brazil	7,374.4	14,816.5	17,980.6	13.6

Economy/Group	2000	2006	2007	CAGR (%) 2000-2006/2007
Chile	1,853.0	2,430.0	2,681.7	5.4
Colombia	875.3	1,843.4	2,009.1	12.6
Costa Rica	358.9	501.6	544.4	6.1
Dominica	16.4	15.3	16.4	0.0
Dominican Republic	202.7	238.9	257.1	3.5
Ecuador	487.5	627.4	650.0	4.2
El Salvador	333.3	357.9	365.9	1.3
Grenada	41.4	29.5	31.7	-3.7
Guatemala	177.4	321.4	361.7	10.7
Guyana	81.0	126.1	129.5	6.9
Haiti	7.0	15.8	21.3	17.2
Honduras	113.5	108.5	90.9	-3.1
Jamaica	586.4	805.8	929.9	6.8
Mexico	9,235.6	11,537.4	11,864.0	3.6
Montserrat	5.1	6.5	7.1	4.7
Netherlands Antilles	346.6	349.2	338.7	-0.3
Nicaragua	103.4	104.0	119.0	2.0
Panama	300.1	448.5	532.2	8.5
Paraguay	72.5	63.6	71.9	-0.1
Peru	886.4	1,047.7	1,236.5	4.9
Saint Kitts and Nevis	26.8	37.9	40.7	6.2
Saint Lucia	39.7	45.5	47.5	2.6
Saint Vincent and the Grenadines	17.6	26.8	29.6	7.7
Suriname	65.2	168.7	204.6	17.7
Trinidad and Tobago	42.9	..	..	..
Uruguay	161.3	274.7	347.8	11.6
Venezuela, Bolivarian Republic of	1,370.0	1,799.0	2,130.0	6.5
Oceania	696.9	994.6	669.0	
Fiji	84.0	114.9	..	5.4
French Polynesia	..	199.4	118.0	..
New Caledonia		612.5	512.4	..
Papua New Guinea	559.1	..	..	..
Samoa	..	14.2	20.1	..
Solomon Islands	24.9	32.3	..	4.5
Tonga	..	7.4	4.2	
Vanuatu	28.9	13.9	14.2	-9.6
Transition economies	8,178.6	24,092.6	31,944.1	
Albania	47.0	335.5	270.1	28.4
Armenia	21.3	79.0	112.6	26.9
Azerbaijan	108.8	773.0	1,042.2	38.1
Belarus	187.7	351.4	449.3	13.3
Bosnia and Herzegovina	51.2	92.7	102.2	10.4
Croatia	773.3	2,041.3	1,990.5	14.5
Georgia	16.8	128.4	182.6	40.6
Kazakhstan	554.6	3,049.7	3,857.3	31.9
Kyrgyzstan	72.8	183.1	138.4	9.6
Republic of Moldova	44.5	91.5	127.9	16.3
Russian Federation	4,645.5	14,242.1	19,749.5	23.0
Tajikistan	..	68.1	210.7	..
The former Yugoslav Republic of Macedonia	96.2	212.7	220.0	13.2
Ukraine	1,559.0	2,414.0	3,482.0	12.2
LDCs	3,736.1	7,334.6	9,700.6	

Source: UNCTAD on the basis of IMF balance-of-payments data.
a   *Including Puerto Rico and the United States Virgin Islands.*
b   *Including French Guiana, Guadeloupe, Martinique, Monaco and Réunion.*
c   *Including Svalbard and Jan Mayen Islands, excluding Bouvet Island.*
d   *Including Liechtenstein.*
e   *Including Channel Islands and Isle of Man.*
f   *Including Sikkim.*

SELECTED UNCTAD PUBLICATIONS IN THE AREA OF SCIENCE, TECHNOLOGY AND ICT FOR DEVELOPMENT

A. Flagship reports

Information Economy Report 2009: Trends and Outlook in Turbulent Times (October 2009). United Nations publication. New York and Geneva.

Information Economy Report 2007–2008: Science and Technology for Development – the New Paradigm of ICT. United Nations publication. Sales No. E.07.II.D.13. New York and Geneva.

Information Economy Report 2006: the Development Perspective. United Nations publication. Sales No. E.06. II.D.8. New York and Geneva.

Information Economy Report 2005: E-commerce and Development. United Nations publication. Sales No. E.05. II.D.19. New York and Geneva.

E-Commerce and Development Report 2004. United Nations publication. New York and Geneva.

E-Commerce and Development Report 2003. United Nations publication. Sales No. E.03.II.D.30. New York and Geneva.

E-Commerce and Development Report 2002. United Nations publication. New York and Geneva.

E-Commerce and Development Report 2001. United Nations publication. Sales No. E.01.II.D.30. New York and Geneva.

B. Science, Technology and Innovation Policy Reviews

Science, Technology and Innovation Policy Review of Angola. United Nations publication. UNCTAD/SDTE/ STICT/2008/1. New York and Geneva.

Science, Technology and Innovation Policy Review: the Islamic Republic of Iran. United Nations publication. UNCTAD/ITE/IPC/2005/7. New York and Geneva.

Investment and Innovation Policy Review of Ethiopia. United Nations publication. UNCTAD/ITE/IPC/Misc.4. New York and Geneva.

Science, Technology and Innovation Policy Review: Colombia. United Nations publication. Sales No. E.99. II.D.13. New York and Geneva.

Science, Technology and Innovation Policy Review: Jamaica. United Nations publication. Sales No. E.98.II.D.7. New York and Geneva.

C. Other publications

Manual for the Production of Statistics on the Information Economy 2009 Revised Edition. United Nations publication. New York and Geneva.

Estudio sobre las perspectivas de la armonización de la ciberlegislación en América Latina. UNCTAD publication. UNCTAD/DTL/STICT/2009/1. Geneva. (In Spanish only).

WSIS Follow-up Report 2008. United Nations publication. New York and Geneva.

Measuring the Impact of ICT Use in Business: the Case of Manufacturing in Thailand. United Nations publication. Sales No. E.08.II.D.13. New York and Geneva.

World Information Society Report 2007: Beyond WSIS. Joint United Nations and ITU publication. Geneva.

Manual for the Production of Statistics on the Information Economy. United Nations publication. UNCTAD/SDTE/ ECB/2007/2. New York and Geneva.

World Information Society Report 2006. Joint United Nations and ITU publication. Geneva.

The Digital Divide: ICT Diffusion Index 2005. United Nations publication. New York and Geneva.

The Digital Divide: ICT Development Indices 2004. United Nations publication. New York and Geneva.

Africa's Technology Gap: Case Studies on Kenya, Ghana, Tanzania and Uganda. United Nations publication. UNCTAD/ITE/IPC/Misc.13. New York and Geneva.

The Biotechnology Promise: Capacity-Building for Participation of Developing Countries in the Bioeconomy. United Nations publication. UNCTAD/ITE/IPC/2004/2. New York and Geneva.

Information and Communication Technology Development Indices. United Nations publication. Sales No. E.03. II.D.14. New York and Geneva.

Investment and Technology Policies for Competitiveness: Review of Successful Country Experiences. United Nations publication. UNCTAD/ITE/IPC/2003/2. New York and Geneva.

Investment and Technology Policies for Competitiveness: Review of Successful Country Experiences. United Nations publication. UNCTAD/ITE/IPC/2003/2. New York and Geneva.

Electronic Commerce and Music Business Development in Jamaica: a Portal to the New Economy? United Nations publication. Sales No. E.02.II.D.17. New York and Geneva.

Changing Dynamics of Global Computer Software and Services Industry: Implications for Developing Countries. United Nations publication. Sales No. E.02.II.D.3. New York and Geneva.

Partnerships and Networking in Science and Technology for Development. United Nations publication. Sales No. E.02.II.D.5. New York and Geneva.

Transfer of Technology for Successful Integration into the Global Economy: a Case Study of Embraer in Brazil. United Nations publication. UNCTAD/ITE/IPC/Misc.20. New York and Geneva.

Transfer of Technology for Successful Integration into the Global Economy: a Case Study of the South African Automotive Industry. United Nations publication. UNCTAD/ITE/IPC/Misc.21. New York and Geneva.

Transfer of Technology for the Successful Integration into the Global Economy: a Case Study of the Pharmaceutical Industry in India. United Nations publication. UNCTAD/ITE/IPC/Misc.22. New York and Geneva.

Coalition of Resources for Information and Communication Technologies. United Nations publication. UNCTAD/ITE/TEB/13. New York and Geneva.

Key Issues in Biotechnology. United Nations publication. UNCTAD/ITE/TEB/10. New York and Geneva.

An Assault on Poverty: Basic Human Needs, Science and Technology. Joint publication with IDRC. ISBN 0-88936-800-7.

Compendium of International Arrangements on Transfer of Technology: Selected Instruments. United Nations publication. Sales No. E.01.II.D.28. New York and Geneva.

D. Publications by the Partnership on Measuring ICT for Development

The Global Information Society: a Statistical View 2008. United Nations publication. Santiago.

Measuring ICT: the Global Status of ICT Indicators Partnership on Measuring ICT for Development. United Nations ICT Task Force. New York.

Core ICT Indicators. UNESCWA. Beirut.

E. Issues in Brief

Measuring the Information Economy: How ICT Contributes to Development. Issues in Brief No. 7. UNCTAD/IAOS/MISC/2005/13.

E-Tourism in Developing Countries: More Links, Fewer Leaks. Issues in Brief No. 6. UNCTAD/IAOS/MISC/2005/11.

ICT and E-Commerce: an Opportunity for Developing Countries. Issues in brief No. 1. UNCTAD/ISS/MISC/2003/6.

READERSHIP SURVEY

Information Economy Report 2009: Trends and Outlook in Turbulent Times

In order to improve the quality of this report and other publications of the Science, Technology and ICT Branch of UNCTAD, we welcome the views of our readers on this publication. It would be greatly appreciated if you would complete the following questionnaire and return it to:

ICT Analysis Section, office E-7075
Science, Technology and ICT Branch
Division of Technology and Logistics
United Nations
Palais des Nations,
CH-1211, Geneva, Switzerland
Fax: 41 22 917 00 52
ICT4D@unctad.org

1. Name and address of respondent (optional)

....

....

....

2. Which of the following best describes your area of work?

Government ministry (please specify)	☐	Not-for-profit organization	☐
National statistics office	☐	Public enterprise	☐
Telecommunication regulatory authority	☐	Academic or research institution	☐
Private enterprise	☐	Media	☐
International organization	☐	Other (please specify)	☐

3. In which country do you work? ....

4. What is your assessment of the contents of this publication?

Excellent ☐
Good ☐
Adequate ☐
Poor ☐

5. How useful is this publication to your work?

Very useful	☐
Somewhat useful	☐
Irrelevant	☐
Poor	☐

6. Please indicate the three things you liked best about this publication.

a) ....

b) ....

c) ....

7. Please indicate the three things you liked least about this publication.

a) ....

b) ....

c) ....

8. What additional aspects would you like future editions of this report to cover:

....

....

....

9. Other comments:

....

....

....